THE SATSUMA
REBELLION

ILLUSTRATED JAPANESE HISTORY
—THE LAST STAND OF THE SAMURAI

SEAN MICHAEL WILSON

ILLUSTRATIONS BY
AKIKO SHIMOJIMA

North Atlantic Books
Berkeley, California

Published by
North Atlantic Books
Berkeley, California

Cover design by Jasmine Hromjak
Interior design and artwork by Akiko Shimojima
Printed in the Canada

Thanks to Davide Calzetti for his support with Japanese historical information.

The Satsuma Rebellion: Illustrated Japanese History—The Last Stand of the Samurai is sponsored and published by the Society for the Study of Native Arts and Sciences (dba North At-lantic Books), an educational nonprofit based in Berkeley, California, that collaborates with partners to develop cross-cultural perspectives, nurture holistic views of art, science, the humanities, and healing, and seed personal and global transformation by publishing work on the relationship of body, spirit, and nature.

North Atlantic Books' publications are available through most bookstores. For further information, visit our website at www.northatlanticbooks.com or call 800-733-3000.

Library of Congress Cataloguing-in-Publication data

Names: Wilson, Sean Michael, author. | Shimojima, Akiko, illustrator.
Title: The Satsuma Rebellion : the last stand of the samurai / Sean Michael
    Wilson ; illustrations by Akiko Shimojima.
Description: Berkeley, California : North Atlantic Books, 2018. | Series:
    Illustrated Japanese history
Identifiers: LCCN 2017054225 | ISBN 9781623171674 (pbk.)
Subjects: LCSH: Satsuma Rebellion, 1877.
Classification: LCC DS882.5 .W53 2018 | DDC 952.03/1—dc23
LC record available at https://lccn.loc.gov/2017054225

1 2 3 4 5 6 7 8 9 Marquis 23 22 21 20 19 18

Printed on recycled paper

North Atlantic Books is committed to the protection of
our environment. We partner with FSC-certified printers using
soy-based inks and print on recycled paper whenever possible.

AUTHOR'S PREFACE

The Satsuma Rebellion is the second in the Illustrated Japanese History series. It follows the first book, *Black Ships*, both in terms of basic chronology and in the social and military consequences of the dramatic events of the 1850s that played themselves out in the 1860s–1870s. In *Black Ships* Akiko Shimojima and I focused on Commodore Perry and some key Japanese figures of the time, while also looking at the wider historical and cultural situation.

We take the same twofold approach here, considering the background context but focusing on the figure of Saigo Takamori, one of the most well-known figures in all of Japanese history. And, as always, we try to avoiding falling into the clichéd trap of Hollywood movies by exaggerating the violence that occurred or conjuring up some love-interest that did not actually exist. Instead, we make an effort to research the period, the clothes, the manners, the buildings, and the realistic drama of the events and characters.

By coincidence, in 2018 the Japanese historical drama series *Segodon*, broadcast by NHK as part of its annual Taiga Drama program, will be centered around Saigo Takamori, including the Satsuma Rebellion. So, we can anticipate growing interest in the Satsuma Rebellion.

There is also—as with several of our Japanese history/martial arts books—a connection to Kumamoto, the city in Japan where I now live. The rebels carried out a long siege of the castle here in spring 1877, and a major battle took place over an eight-day period just outside the city, at Tabaruzaka, with more than 4,000 people killed or wounded on both sides.

An editor in Japan said to me, "I would like to know why the Satsuma Rebellion caught your attention and you determined that it would appeal to the American and British audiences. After all, it's a losers' battle with a sad ending." I think, at root, I'm interested in all history, of any country. But since I am in Japan it makes sense to focus here. In truth the first time the Satsuma Rebellion caught my eye was because of the orange fruit called satsuma that I used to eat as a child in Scotland. I remember one day when I was about twelve years old thinking, "Hmm, that's a strange word … sat-su-ma … what does it mean?," and my mother telling me it was a place in Japan. Later, I checked it in a history book and read about a conflict with the name The Satsuma Rebellion. As a child who grew up on Luke Skywalker's rebellion against the imperial forces in *Star Wars,* that title immediately caught my attention.

So, it is with a pleasing feeling of bringing a childhood interest to fruition that we present you with our comic book version of the story. It may be the story of losers, with a sad ending, but they were very interesting losers, with dignity and fiery passion—even if it was for a troubled and contentious cause.

—Sean Michael Wilson, Kumamoto, Japan

CHAPTER 1

A HOUSE IN TURMOIL

THERE ARE THREE DISTINCT JAPANS IN EXISTENCE SIDE BY SIDE TODAY—THE OLD, WHICH HAS NOT WHOLLY DIED OUT; THE NEW, HARDLY YET BORN EXCEPT IN SPIRIT; AND THE TRANSITION, PASSING NOW THROUGH ITS MOST CRITICAL THROES.

—JAMES STAFFORD RANSOME, 1899

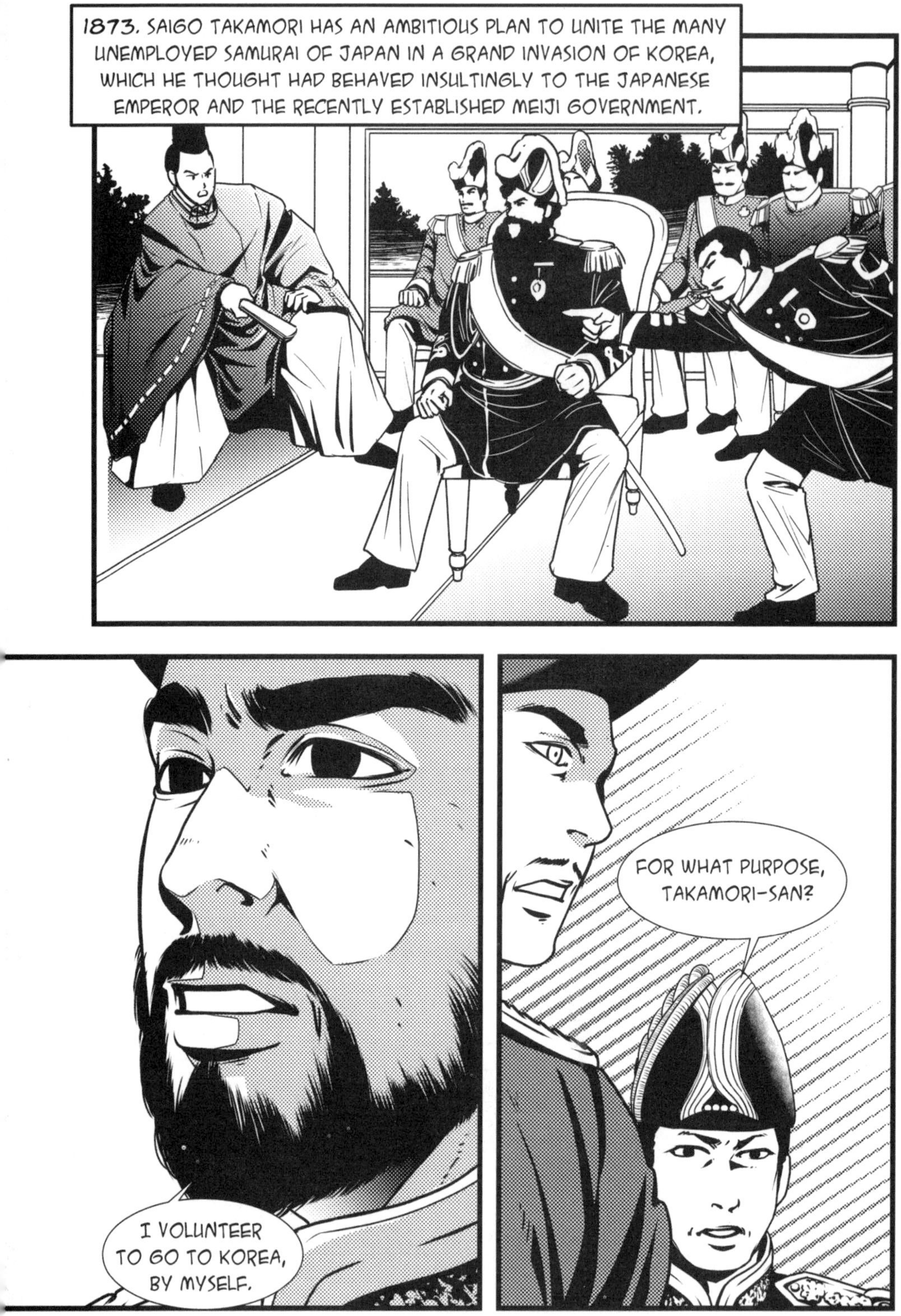
1873. SAIGO TAKAMORI HAS AN AMBITIOUS PLAN TO UNITE THE MANY UNEMPLOYED SAMURAI OF JAPAN IN A GRAND INVASION OF KOREA, WHICH HE THOUGHT HAD BEHAVED INSULTINGLY TO THE JAPANESE EMPEROR AND THE RECENTLY ESTABLISHED MEIJI GOVERNMENT.
I VOLUNTEER TO GO TO KOREA, BY MYSELF.
FOR WHAT PURPOSE, TAKAMORI-SAN?

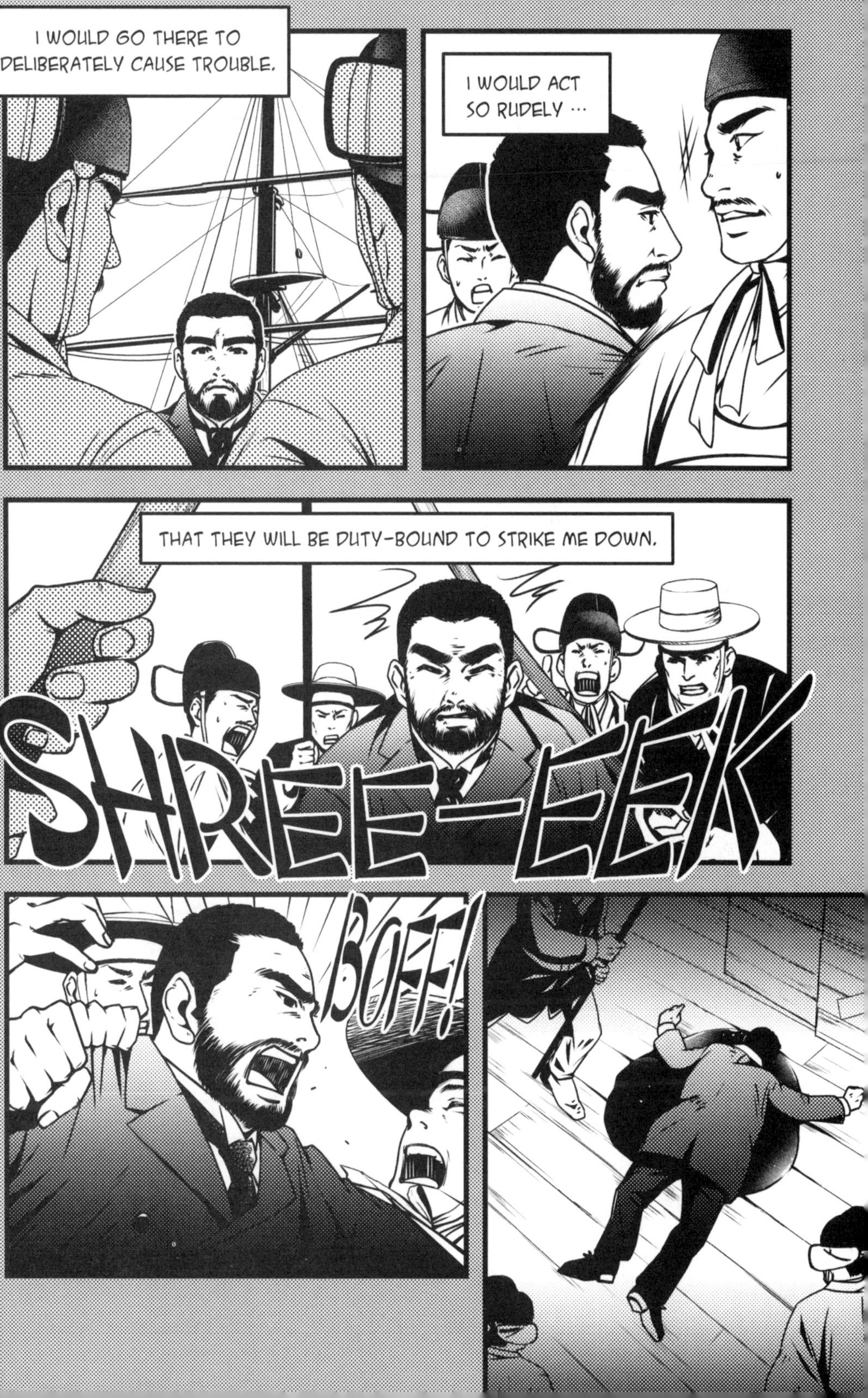
I WOULD GO THERE TO DELIBERATELY CAUSE TROUBLE.
I WOULD ACT SO RUDELY ...
THAT THEY WILL BE DUTY-BOUND TO STRIKE ME DOWN.
SHREE-EEK
BOFF!

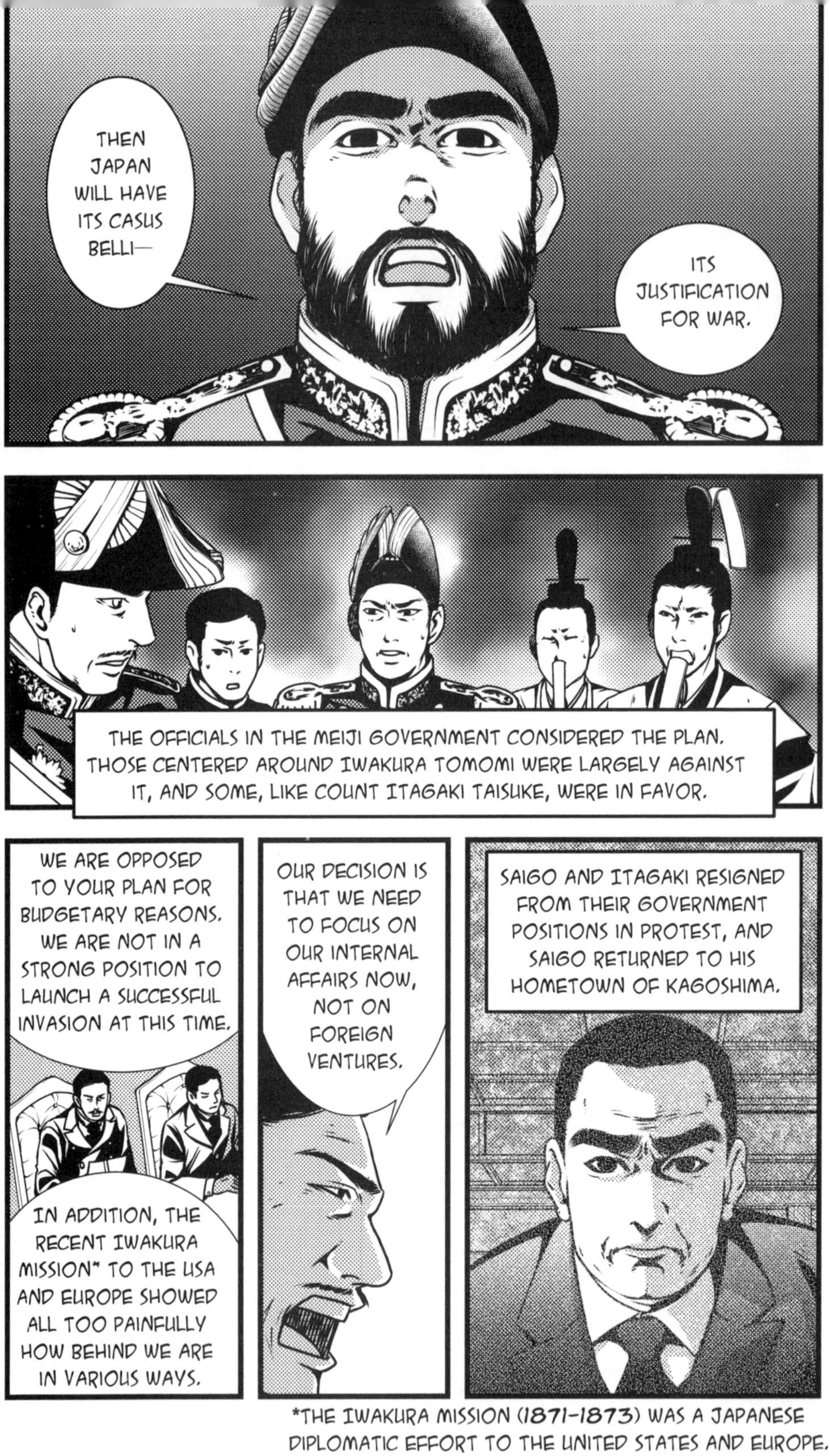
THEN JAPAN WILL HAVE ITS CASUS BELLI—
ITS JUSTIFICATION FOR WAR.
THE OFFICIALS IN THE MEIJI GOVERNMENT CONSIDERED THE PLAN. THOSE CENTERED AROUND IWAKURA TOMOMI WERE LARGELY AGAINST IT, AND SOME, LIKE COUNT ITAGAKI TAISUKE, WERE IN FAVOR.
WE ARE OPPOSED TO YOUR PLAN FOR BUDGETARY REASONS. WE ARE NOT IN A STRONG POSITION TO LAUNCH A SUCCESSFUL INVASION AT THIS TIME.
IN ADDITION, THE RECENT IWAKURA MISSION* TO THE USA AND EUROPE SHOWED ALL TOO PAINFULLY HOW BEHIND WE ARE IN VARIOUS WAYS.
OUR DECISION IS THAT WE NEED TO FOCUS ON OUR INTERNAL AFFAIRS NOW, NOT ON FOREIGN VENTURES.
SAIGO AND ITAGAKI RESIGNED FROM THEIR GOVERNMENT POSITIONS IN PROTEST, AND SAIGO RETURNED TO HIS HOMETOWN OF KAGOSHIMA.

*THE IWAKURA MISSION (1871–1873) WAS A JAPANESE DIPLOMATIC EFFORT TO THE UNITED STATES AND EUROPE.

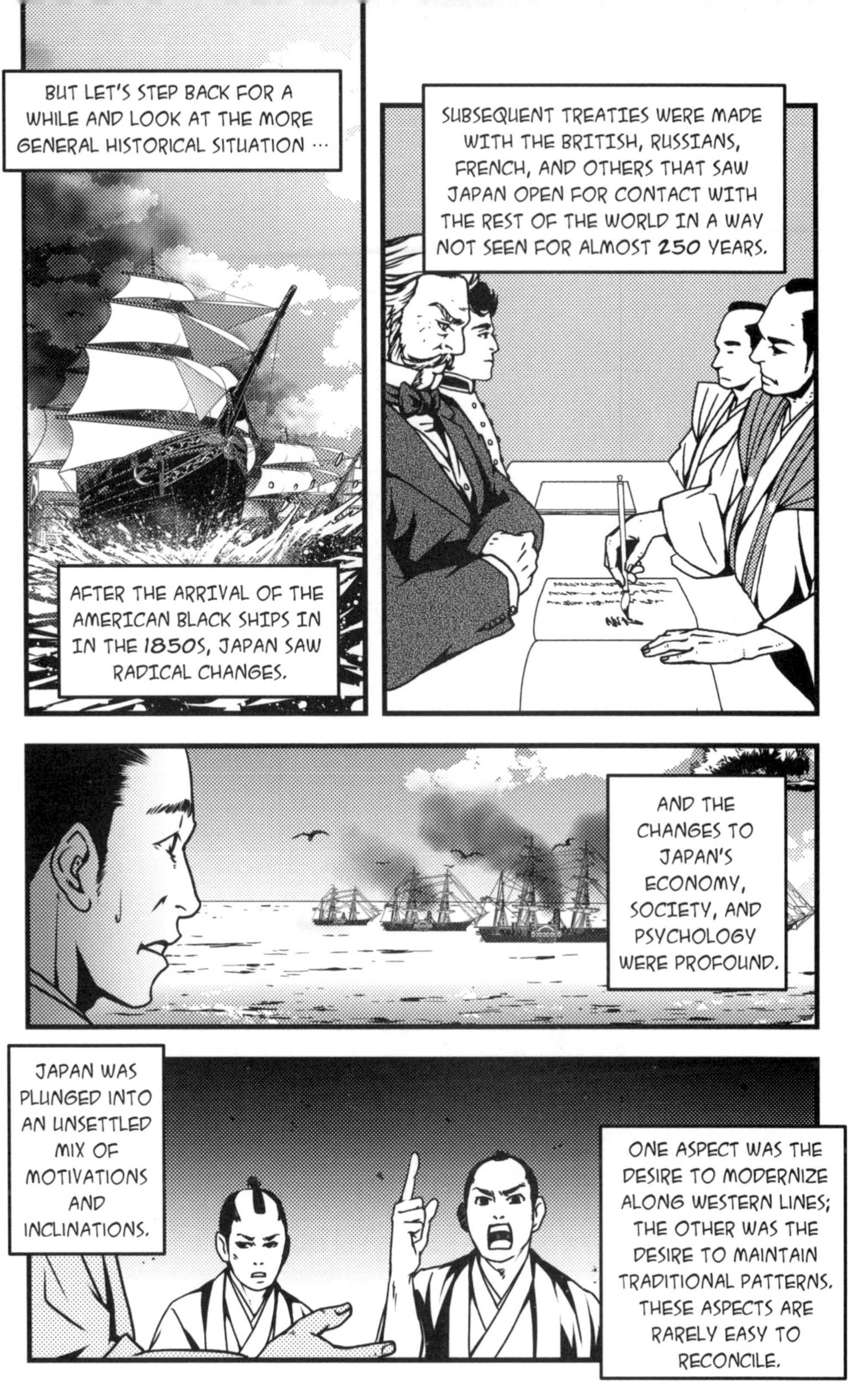
BUT LET'S STEP BACK FOR A WHILE AND LOOK AT THE MORE GENERAL HISTORICAL SITUATION …
AFTER THE ARRIVAL OF THE AMERICAN BLACK SHIPS IN IN THE 1850S, JAPAN SAW RADICAL CHANGES.
SUBSEQUENT TREATIES WERE MADE WITH THE BRITISH, RUSSIANS, FRENCH, AND OTHERS THAT SAW JAPAN OPEN FOR CONTACT WITH THE REST OF THE WORLD IN A WAY NOT SEEN FOR ALMOST 250 YEARS.
AND THE CHANGES TO JAPAN'S ECONOMY, SOCIETY, AND PSYCHOLOGY WERE PROFOUND.
JAPAN WAS PLUNGED INTO AN UNSETTLED MIX OF MOTIVATIONS AND INCLINATIONS.
ONE ASPECT WAS THE DESIRE TO MODERNIZE ALONG WESTERN LINES; THE OTHER WAS THE DESIRE TO MAINTAIN TRADITIONAL PATTERNS. THESE ASPECTS ARE RARELY EASY TO RECONCILE.

THE WEAKNESS SHOWN IN THE 1850S AND 1860S LED TO THE END OF THE TOKUGAWA SHOGUNATE THAT HAD CONTROLLED JAPAN SINCE 1603.

ITS END CAME ABOUT VERY QUICKLY—IT CAME CRASHING DOWN JUST 14 YEARS AFTER THE ARRIVAL OF THE BLACK SHIPS.

DURING THAT PERIOD, JAPAN SAW CONFLICT BETWEEN FORCES LOYAL TO THE TOKUGAWA AND THOSE OF THE NATIONALISTS, THE ISHIN SHISHI. THESE INCLUDED SOME OF THE CLANS WHO HAD BEEN SIDELINED AFTER THE BATTLE OF SEKIGAHARA (1600), SUCH AS THE CLANS OF THE SOUTHWEST, THE CHOSHU, AND SATSUMA, SYMBOLIZED IN THE PHRASE SONNO JOI, "REVERE THE EMPEROR, EXPEL THE BARBARIANS."

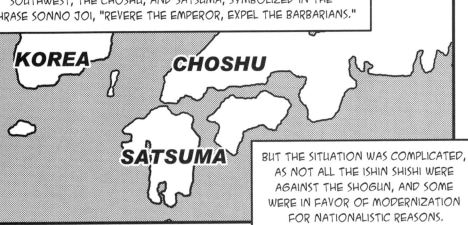

KOREA

CHOSHU

SATSUMA

BUT THE SITUATION WAS COMPLICATED, AS NOT ALL THE ISHIN SHISHI WERE AGAINST THE SHOGUN, AND SOME WERE IN FAVOR OF MODERNIZATION FOR NATIONALISTIC REASONS.

THE BAKUMATSU, THE GOVERNMENT IN THE FINAL YEARS OF THE SHOGUNATE, WAS CHALLENGED BY SEVERAL OUTBURSTS OF VIOLENCE FROM BOTH EXTERNAL AND INTERNAL ENEMIES. IT WAS ALSO SHAKEN WITH SOCIAL AND ECONOMIC DISRUPTION.

SINCE 1854 AND COMMODORE PERRY'S FORCED OPENING OF JAPAN, THERE HAD BEEN AN INFLUX OF FOREIGN DIPLOMATS, BUSINESSPEOPLE, AND MILITARY FORCES. PERHAPS UNDERSTANDABLY, SOME JAPANESE TOOK GREAT OFFENSE TO THIS. THEREFORE, VARIOUS VIOLENT ATTACKS ON FOREIGNERS OCCURRED, AND ALSO AGAINST JAPANESE WHO COLLABORATED WITH THEM.

IN AUGUST 1859, A RUSSIAN SAILOR WAS SLICED IN THE STREETS OF YOKOHAMA, AND IN EARLY 1860, TWO DUTCH CAPTAINS WERE ALSO ATTACKED THERE. A SERVANT OF A FRENCH MINISTER WAS ATTACKED LATER IN 1860. AND IN JULY 1861, A GROUP OF SAMURAI ATTACKED THE BRITISH LEGATION, WHICH RESULTED IN TWO DEATHS.

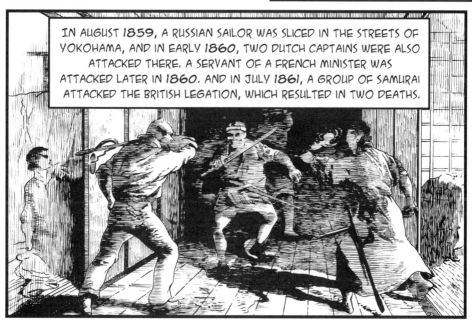

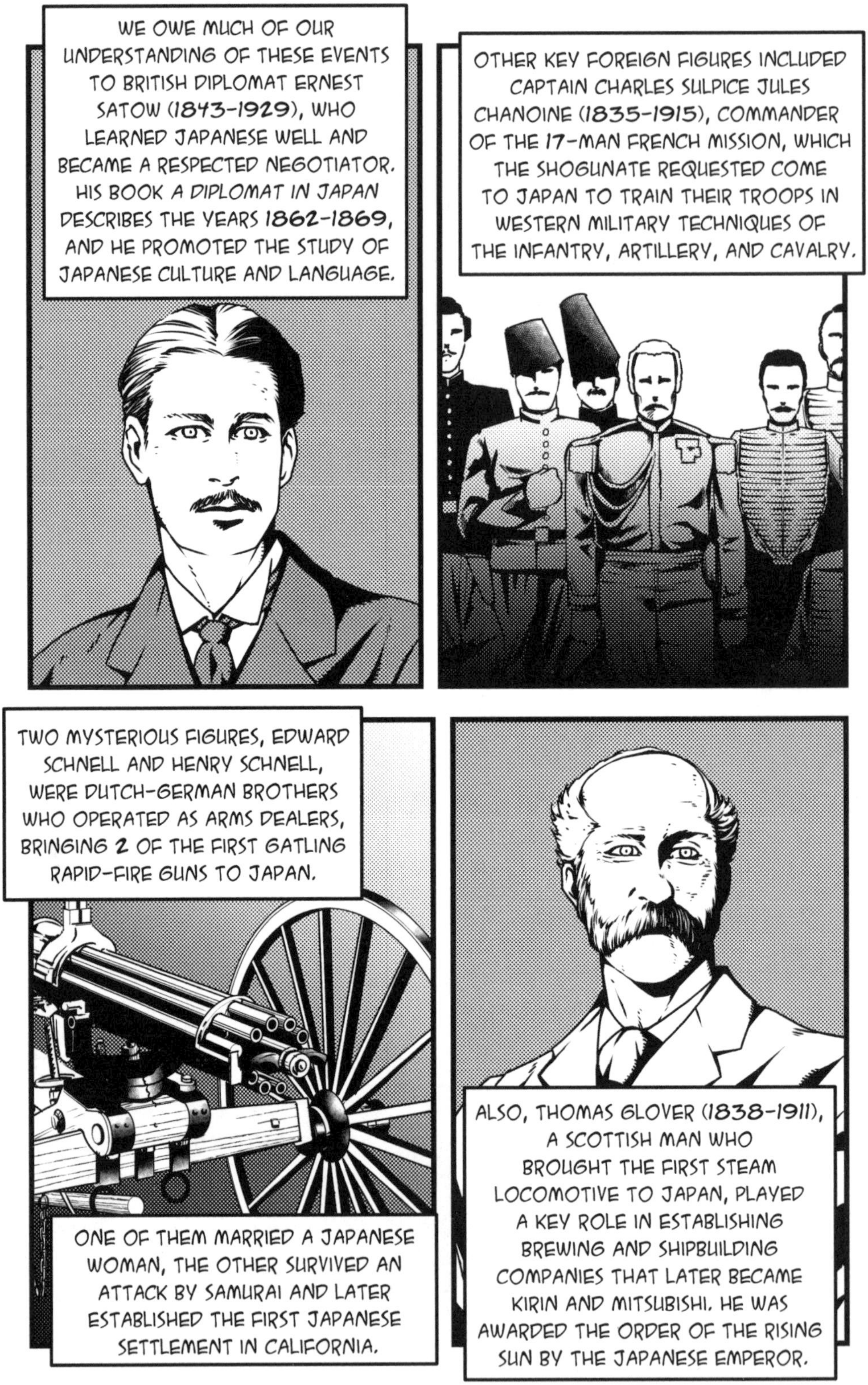
WE OWE MUCH OF OUR UNDERSTANDING OF THESE EVENTS TO BRITISH DIPLOMAT ERNEST SATOW (1843-1929), WHO LEARNED JAPANESE WELL AND BECAME A RESPECTED NEGOTIATOR. HIS BOOK A DIPLOMAT IN JAPAN DESCRIBES THE YEARS 1862-1869, AND HE PROMOTED THE STUDY OF JAPANESE CULTURE AND LANGUAGE.
OTHER KEY FOREIGN FIGURES INCLUDED CAPTAIN CHARLES SULPICE JULES CHANOINE (1835-1915), COMMANDER OF THE 17-MAN FRENCH MISSION, WHICH THE SHOGUNATE REQUESTED COME TO JAPAN TO TRAIN THEIR TROOPS IN WESTERN MILITARY TECHNIQUES OF THE INFANTRY, ARTILLERY, AND CAVALRY.
TWO MYSTERIOUS FIGURES, EDWARD SCHNELL AND HENRY SCHNELL, WERE DUTCH-GERMAN BROTHERS WHO OPERATED AS ARMS DEALERS, BRINGING 2 OF THE FIRST GATLING RAPID-FIRE GUNS TO JAPAN.
ONE OF THEM MARRIED A JAPANESE WOMAN, THE OTHER SURVIVED AN ATTACK BY SAMURAI AND LATER ESTABLISHED THE FIRST JAPANESE SETTLEMENT IN CALIFORNIA.
ALSO, THOMAS GLOVER (1838-1911), A SCOTTISH MAN WHO BROUGHT THE FIRST STEAM LOCOMOTIVE TO JAPAN, PLAYED A KEY ROLE IN ESTABLISHING BREWING AND SHIPBUILDING COMPANIES THAT LATER BECAME KIRIN AND MITSUBISHI. HE WAS AWARDED THE ORDER OF THE RISING SUN BY THE JAPANESE EMPEROR.

THOUGH SUCH FOREIGNERS BECAME RESPECTED FIGURES AMONG THE JAPANESE, OTHERS WERE NOT SO FORTUNATE, SUCH AS HENDRICK C. J. HEUSKEN (1832-1861), A DUTCH-AMERICAN INTERPRETER IN THE FIRST AMERICAN CONSULATE IN SHIMODA. IN 1861 HE WAS ATTACKED AND MURDERED.

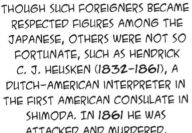

COUNT FRIEDRICH ALBRECHT ZU EULENBURG WAS IN JAPAN TRYING TO NEGOTIATE A COMMERCIAL TREATY FOR PRUSSIA, AND REQUESTED THAT THE AMERICANS LOAN HEUSKEN TO SERVE AS INTERPRETER.

AFTER HAVING DINNER WITH COUNT EULENBURG ON THE NIGHT OF JANUARY 14, 1861, HEUSKEN WAS RETURNING TO HIS TOKYO QUARTERS WITH 3 MOUNTED OFFICERS AND 4 FOOTMEN BEARING LANTERNS, WHEN SUDDENLY ...

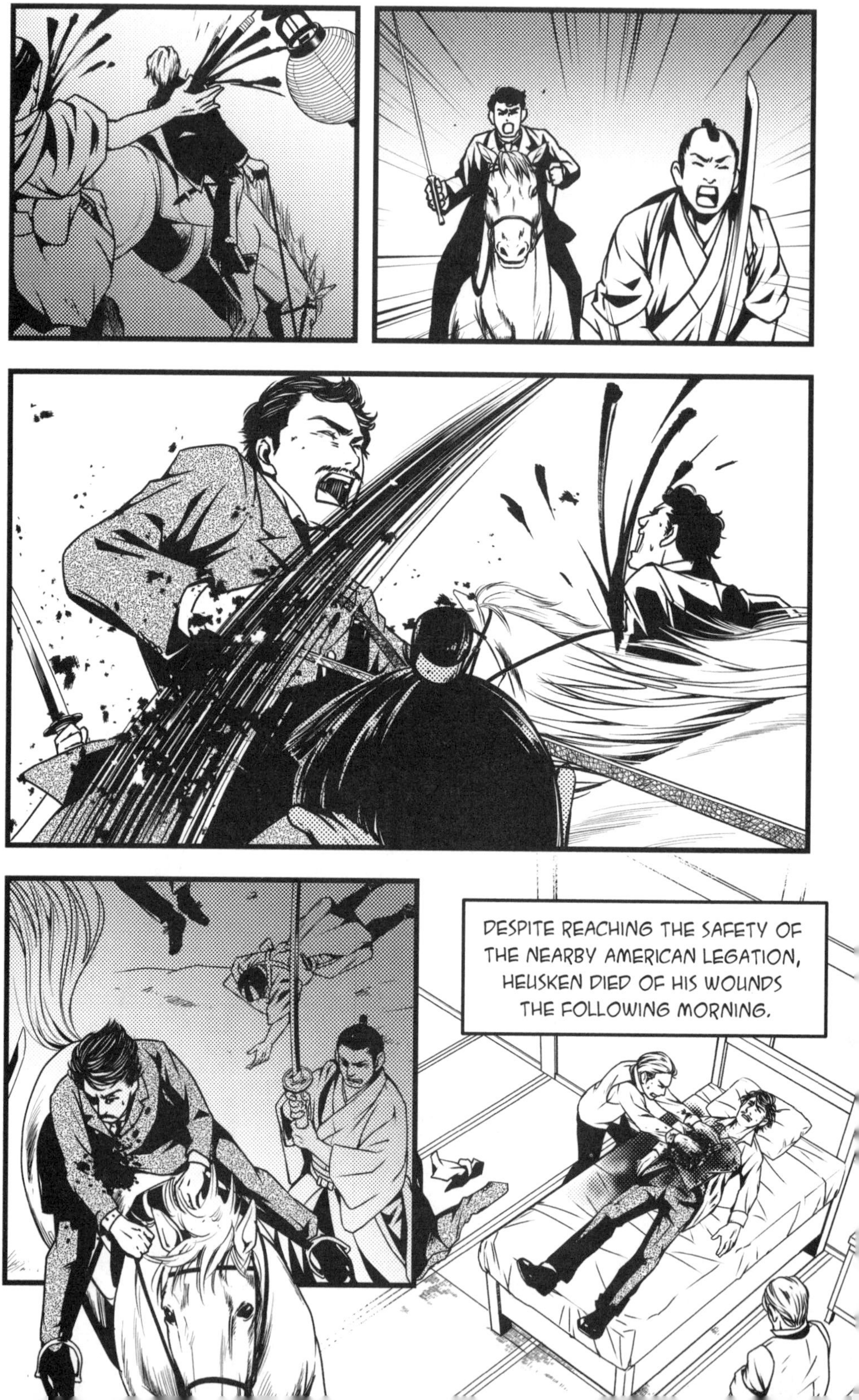
DESPITE REACHING THE SAFETY OF THE NEARBY AMERICAN LEGATION, HEUSKEN DIED OF HIS WOUNDS THE FOLLOWING MORNING.

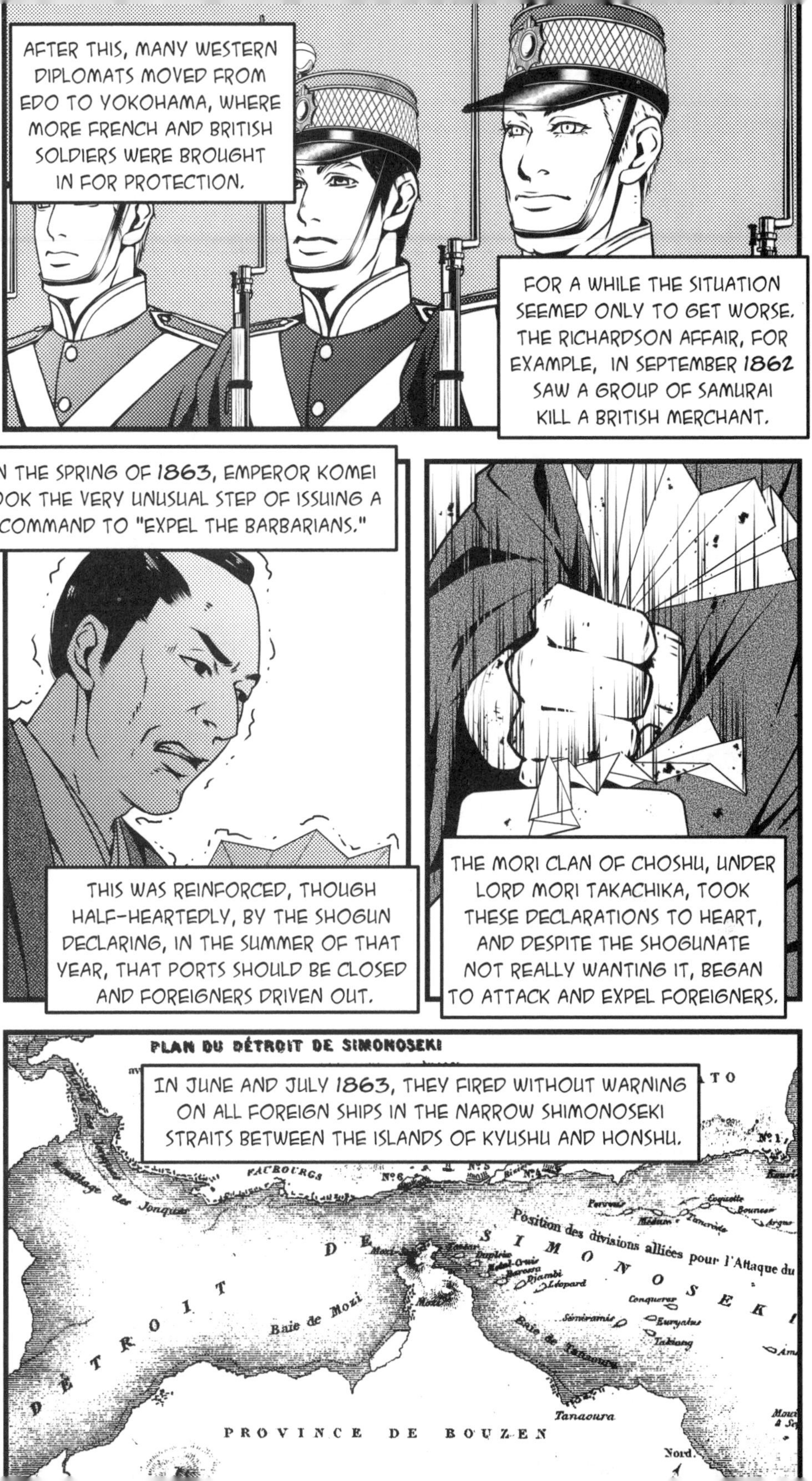
AFTER THIS, MANY WESTERN DIPLOMATS MOVED FROM EDO TO YOKOHAMA, WHERE MORE FRENCH AND BRITISH SOLDIERS WERE BROUGHT IN FOR PROTECTION.
FOR A WHILE THE SITUATION SEEMED ONLY TO GET WORSE. THE RICHARDSON AFFAIR, FOR EXAMPLE, IN SEPTEMBER 1862 SAW A GROUP OF SAMURAI KILL A BRITISH MERCHANT.
IN THE SPRING OF 1863, EMPEROR KOMEI TOOK THE VERY UNUSUAL STEP OF ISSUING A COMMAND TO "EXPEL THE BARBARIANS."
THIS WAS REINFORCED, THOUGH HALF-HEARTEDLY, BY THE SHOGUN DECLARING, IN THE SUMMER OF THAT YEAR, THAT PORTS SHOULD BE CLOSED AND FOREIGNERS DRIVEN OUT.
THE MORI CLAN OF CHOSHU, UNDER LORD MORI TAKACHIKA, TOOK THESE DECLARATIONS TO HEART, AND DESPITE THE SHOGUNATE NOT REALLY WANTING IT, BEGAN TO ATTACK AND EXPEL FOREIGNERS.
PLAN DU DÉTROIT DE SIMONOSEKI
IN JUNE AND JULY 1863, THEY FIRED WITHOUT WARNING ON ALL FOREIGN SHIPS IN THE NARROW SHIMONOSEKI STRAITS BETWEEN THE ISLANDS OF KYUSHU AND HONSHU.
FAUBOURGS
Position des divisions alliées pour l'Attaque du
DÉTROIT DE SIMONOSEKI
Baie de Mozi
Tanaoura
PROVINCE DE BOUZEN
Nord.

IRONICALLY, THEY USED 5 GUNS THAT HAD BEEN PRESENTED TO THEM BY THE USA!

BUR-R-R

R-R-RG!

KREESH!!

WHAT THE HELL?!

THEY'RE FIRING FROM SHORE, CAPTAIN!

BUR-R-RG!!

KR EE EEG

AS WELL AS THIS ATTACK, FIGURES OF THE SHOGUNATE WHO WERE SEEN TO BE IN FAVOR OF FOREIGN INFLUENCE WERE ATTACKED BY THE MASTERLESS SAMURAI, THE RONIN.

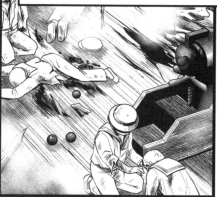

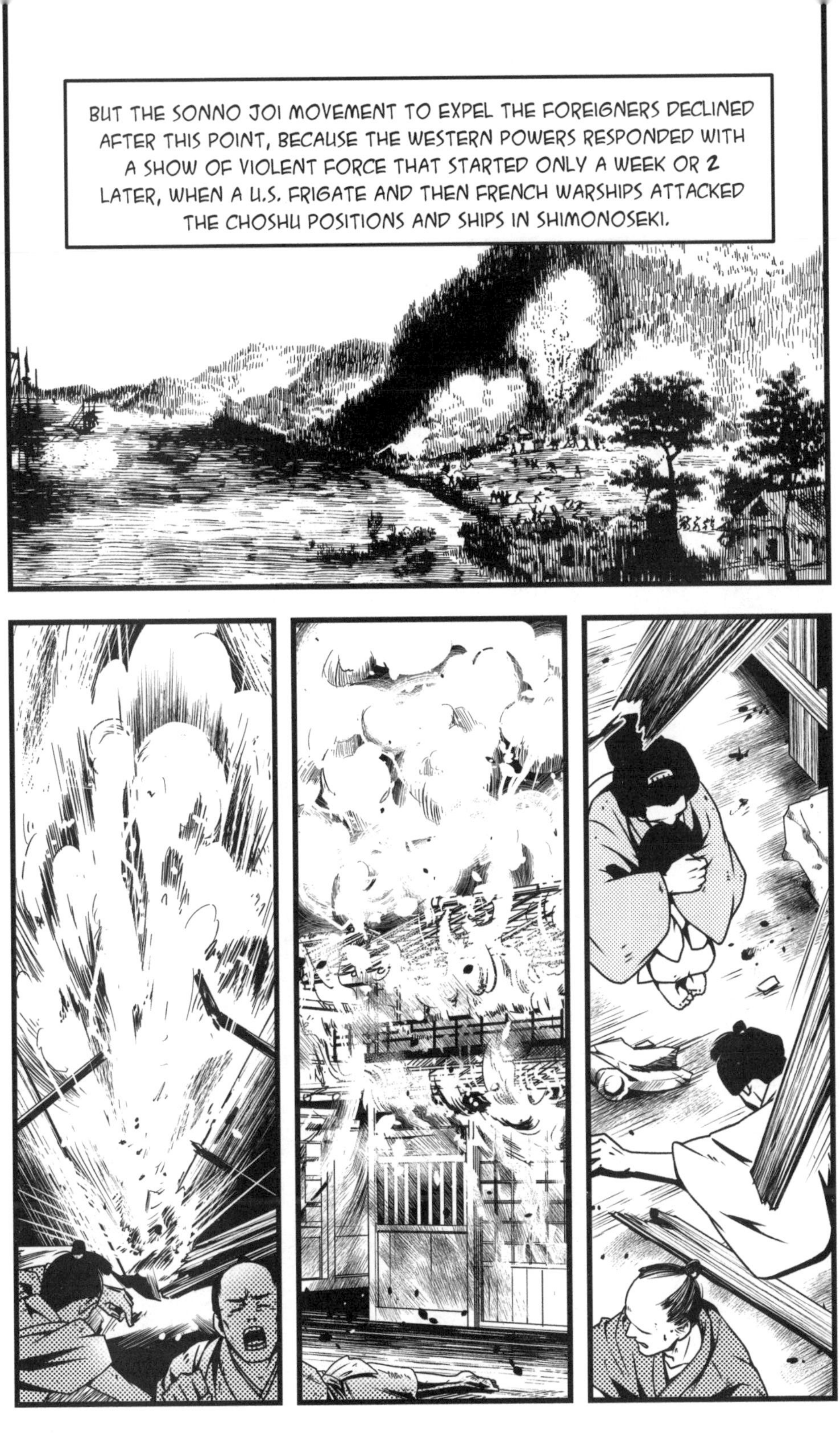
BUT THE SONNO JOI MOVEMENT TO EXPEL THE FOREIGNERS DECLINED AFTER THIS POINT, BECAUSE THE WESTERN POWERS RESPONDED WITH A SHOW OF VIOLENT FORCE THAT STARTED ONLY A WEEK OR 2 LATER, WHEN A U.S. FRIGATE AND THEN FRENCH WARSHIPS ATTACKED THE CHOSHU POSITIONS AND SHIPS IN SHIMONOSEKI.

A PERIOD OF CRISIS FOLLOWED THAT MIXED FRANTIC DIPLOMATIC EFFORTS TO RESOLVE THE SITUATION WITH WIDESPREAD DESTRUCTION OF HOMES, CHURCHES, AND SHIPPING BY THE MORE WARLIKE JAPANESE, INCLUDING THE U.S. LEGATION IN TOKYO.

AT THIS TIME, THE EARLY AMERICAN INFLUENCE WAS DECREASING DUE TO THE DISRUPTION OF THEIR CIVIL WAR (1861-1865), SO THE BRITISH, DUTCH, FRENCH, AND LATER GERMAN INFLUENCE OVER JAPAN GREW INSTEAD.

SO, A COMBINED-OPERATION COALITION WAS FORMED OF 9 SHIPS FROM BRITAIN, 4 FROM THE NETHERLANDS, 3 FROM FRANCE, AND JUST 1 FROM THE USA.

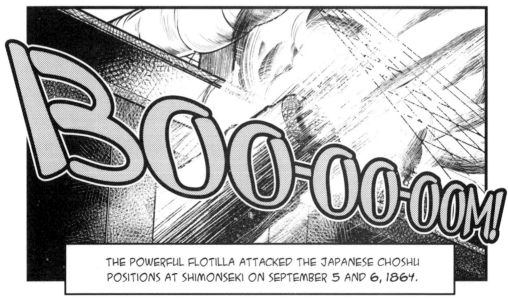

BOO-OO-OOM!

THE POWERFUL FLOTILLA ATTACKED THE JAPANESE CHOSHU POSITIONS AT SHIMONSEKI ON SEPTEMBER 5 AND 6, 1864.

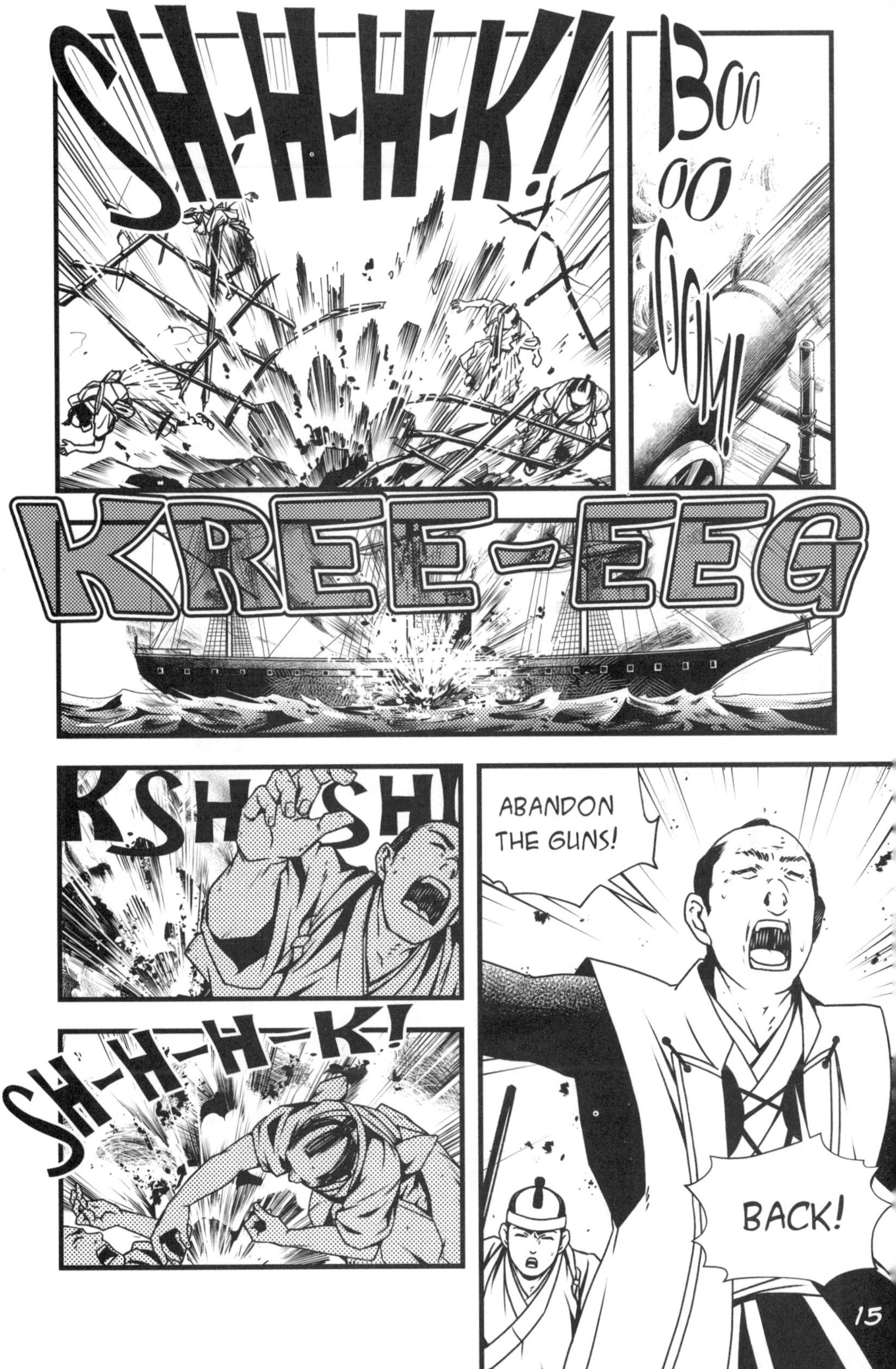
SH-H-H-K!
BOOOOOOM!
KREE-EEG
KSH-SH!
ABANDON THE GUNS!
SH-H-H-K!
BACK!

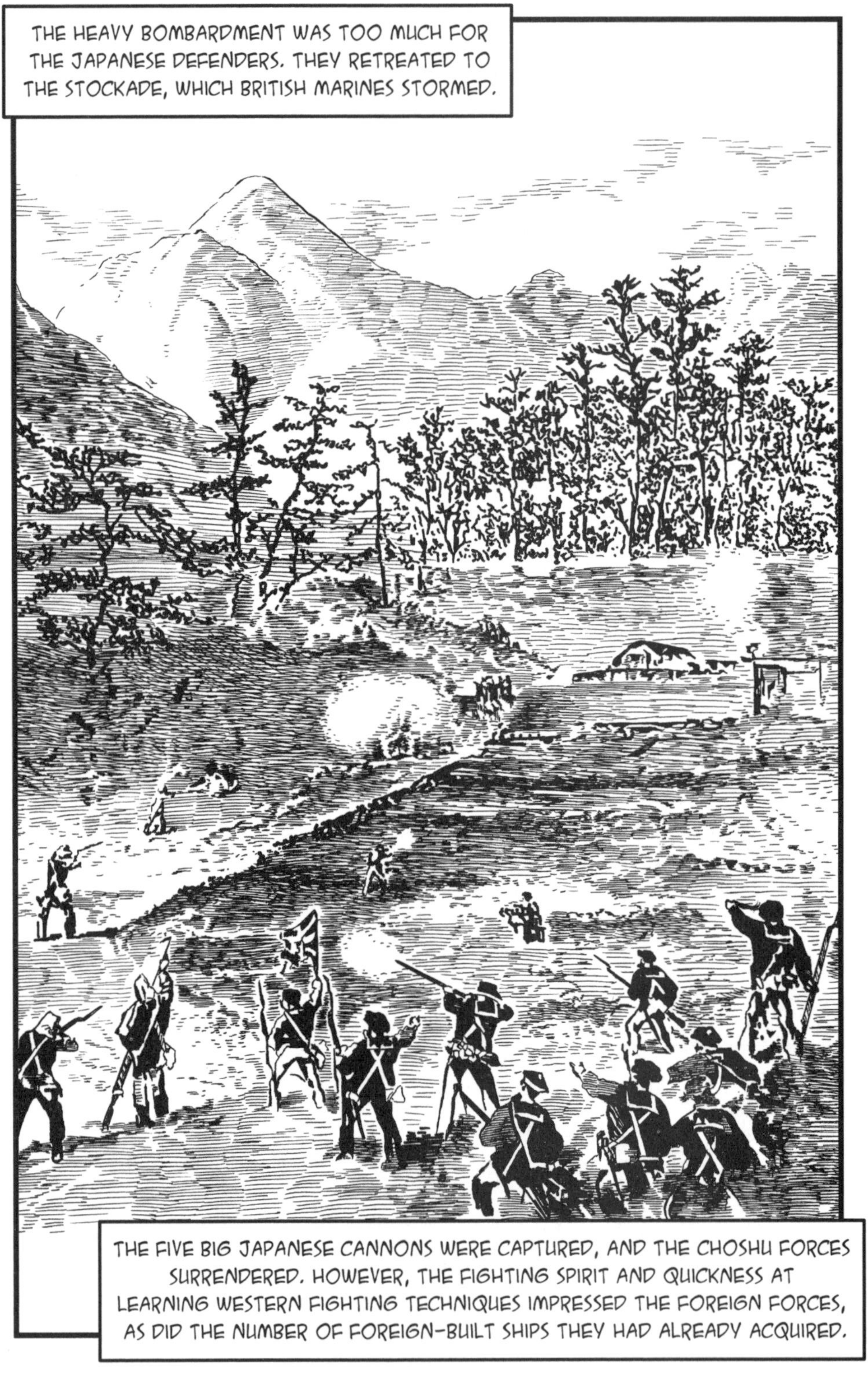
THE HEAVY BOMBARDMENT WAS TOO MUCH FOR THE JAPANESE DEFENDERS. THEY RETREATED TO THE STOCKADE, WHICH BRITISH MARINES STORMED.
THE FIVE BIG JAPANESE CANNONS WERE CAPTURED, AND THE CHOSHU FORCES SURRENDERED. HOWEVER, THE FIGHTING SPIRIT AND QUICKNESS AT LEARNING WESTERN FIGHTING TECHNIQUES IMPRESSED THE FOREIGN FORCES, AS DID THE NUMBER OF FOREIGN-BUILT SHIPS THEY HAD ALREADY ACQUIRED.

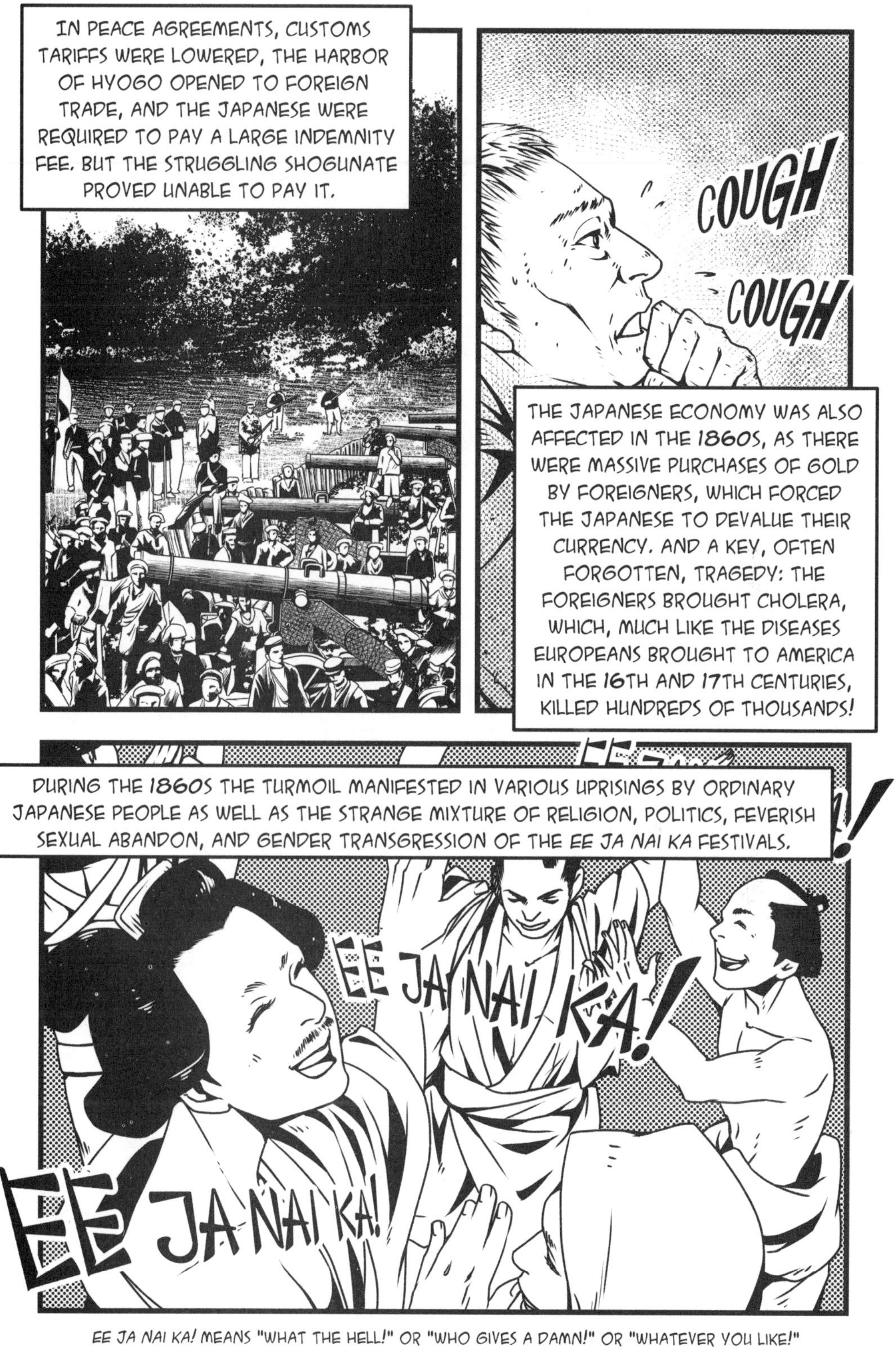

IN PEACE AGREEMENTS, CUSTOMS TARIFFS WERE LOWERED, THE HARBOR OF HYOGO OPENED TO FOREIGN TRADE, AND THE JAPANESE WERE REQUIRED TO PAY A LARGE INDEMNITY FEE. BUT THE STRUGGLING SHOGUNATE PROVED UNABLE TO PAY IT.
COUGH
COUGH
THE JAPANESE ECONOMY WAS ALSO AFFECTED IN THE 1860S, AS THERE WERE MASSIVE PURCHASES OF GOLD BY FOREIGNERS, WHICH FORCED THE JAPANESE TO DEVALUE THEIR CURRENCY. AND A KEY, OFTEN FORGOTTEN, TRAGEDY: THE FOREIGNERS BROUGHT CHOLERA, WHICH, MUCH LIKE THE DISEASES EUROPEANS BROUGHT TO AMERICA IN THE 16TH AND 17TH CENTURIES, KILLED HUNDREDS OF THOUSANDS!
DURING THE 1860S THE TURMOIL MANIFESTED IN VARIOUS UPRISINGS BY ORDINARY JAPANESE PEOPLE AS WELL AS THE STRANGE MIXTURE OF RELIGION, POLITICS, FEVERISH SEXUAL ABANDON, AND GENDER TRANSGRESSION OF THE EE JA NAI KA FESTIVALS.
EE JA NAI KA!
EE JA NAI KA!

EE JA NAI KA! MEANS "WHAT THE HELL!" OR "WHO GIVES A DAMN!" OR "WHATEVER YOU LIKE!"

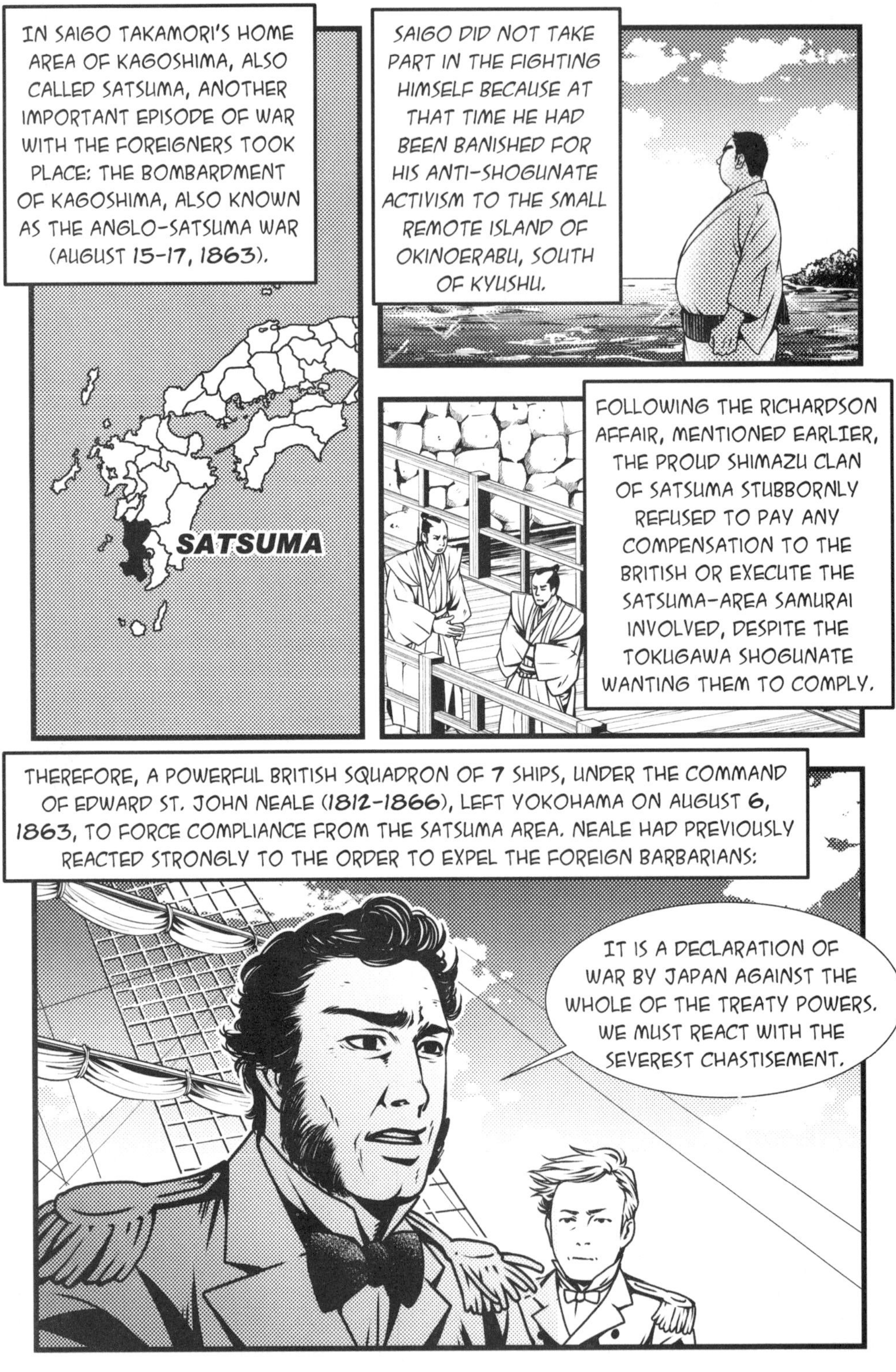
IN SAIGO TAKAMORI'S HOME AREA OF KAGOSHIMA, ALSO CALLED SATSUMA, ANOTHER IMPORTANT EPISODE OF WAR WITH THE FOREIGNERS TOOK PLACE: THE BOMBARDMENT OF KAGOSHIMA, ALSO KNOWN AS THE ANGLO-SATSUMA WAR (AUGUST 15-17, 1863).
SATSUMA
SAIGO DID NOT TAKE PART IN THE FIGHTING HIMSELF BECAUSE AT THAT TIME HE HAD BEEN BANISHED FOR HIS ANTI-SHOGUNATE ACTIVISM TO THE SMALL REMOTE ISLAND OF OKINOERABU, SOUTH OF KYUSHU.
FOLLOWING THE RICHARDSON AFFAIR, MENTIONED EARLIER, THE PROUD SHIMAZU CLAN OF SATSUMA STUBBORNLY REFUSED TO PAY ANY COMPENSATION TO THE BRITISH OR EXECUTE THE SATSUMA-AREA SAMURAI INVOLVED, DESPITE THE TOKUGAWA SHOGUNATE WANTING THEM TO COMPLY.
THEREFORE, A POWERFUL BRITISH SQUADRON OF 7 SHIPS, UNDER THE COMMAND OF EDWARD ST. JOHN NEALE (1812-1866), LEFT YOKOHAMA ON AUGUST 6, 1863, TO FORCE COMPLIANCE FROM THE SATSUMA AREA. NEALE HAD PREVIOUSLY REACTED STRONGLY TO THE ORDER TO EXPEL THE FOREIGN BARBARIANS:
IT IS A DECLARATION OF WAR BY JAPAN AGAINST THE WHOLE OF THE TREATY POWERS. WE MUST REACT WITH THE SEVEREST CHASTISEMENT.

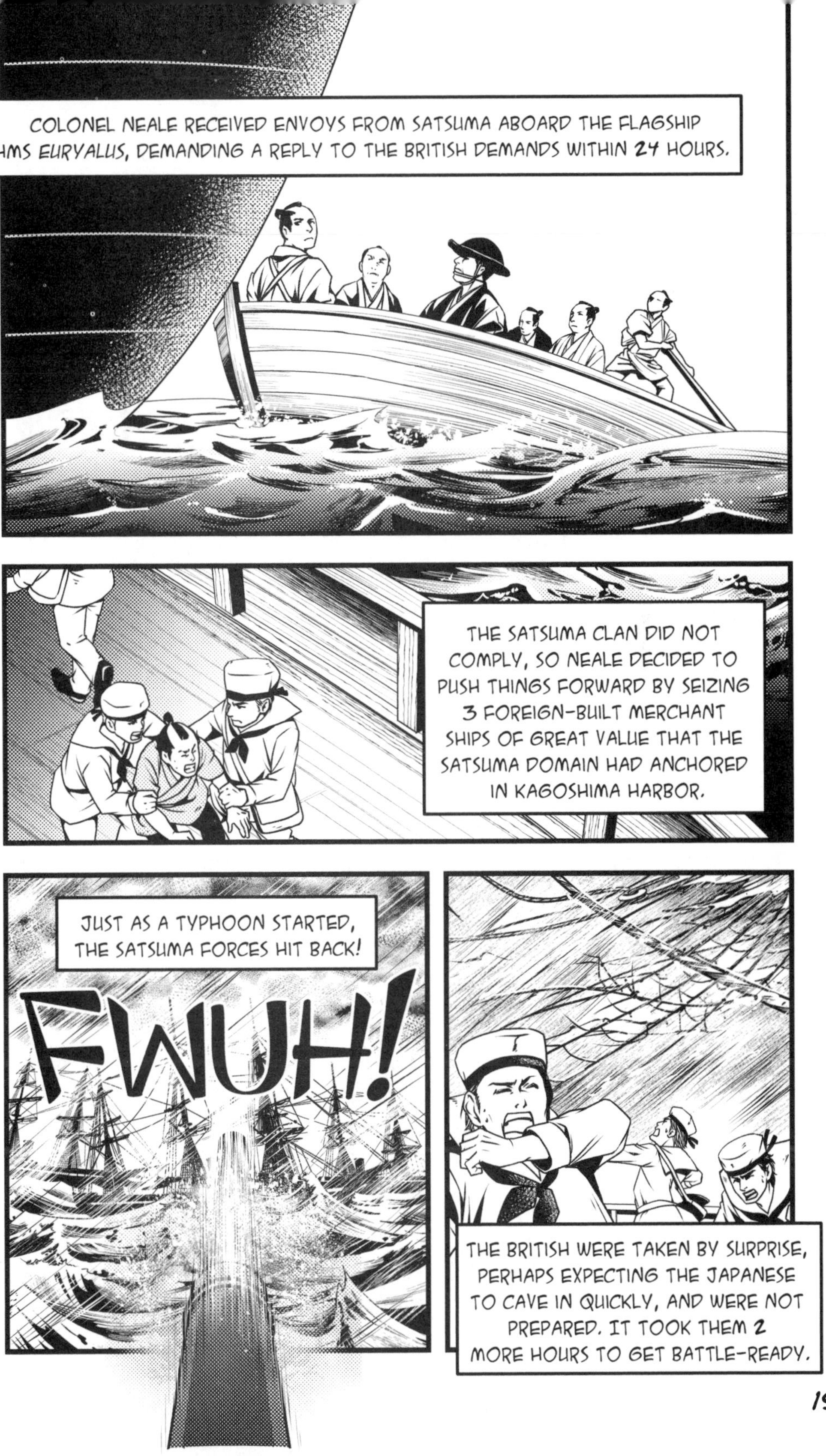
COLONEL NEALE RECEIVED ENVOYS FROM SATSUMA ABOARD THE FLAGSHIP HMS *EURYALUS*, DEMANDING A REPLY TO THE BRITISH DEMANDS WITHIN 24 HOURS.
THE SATSUMA CLAN DID NOT COMPLY, SO NEALE DECIDED TO PUSH THINGS FORWARD BY SEIZING 3 FOREIGN-BUILT MERCHANT SHIPS OF GREAT VALUE THAT THE SATSUMA DOMAIN HAD ANCHORED IN KAGOSHIMA HARBOR.
JUST AS A TYPHOON STARTED, THE SATSUMA FORCES HIT BACK!
FWUH!
THE BRITISH WERE TAKEN BY SURPRISE, PERHAPS EXPECTING THE JAPANESE TO CAVE IN QUICKLY, AND WERE NOT PREPARED. IT TOOK THEM 2 MORE HOURS TO GET BATTLE-READY.

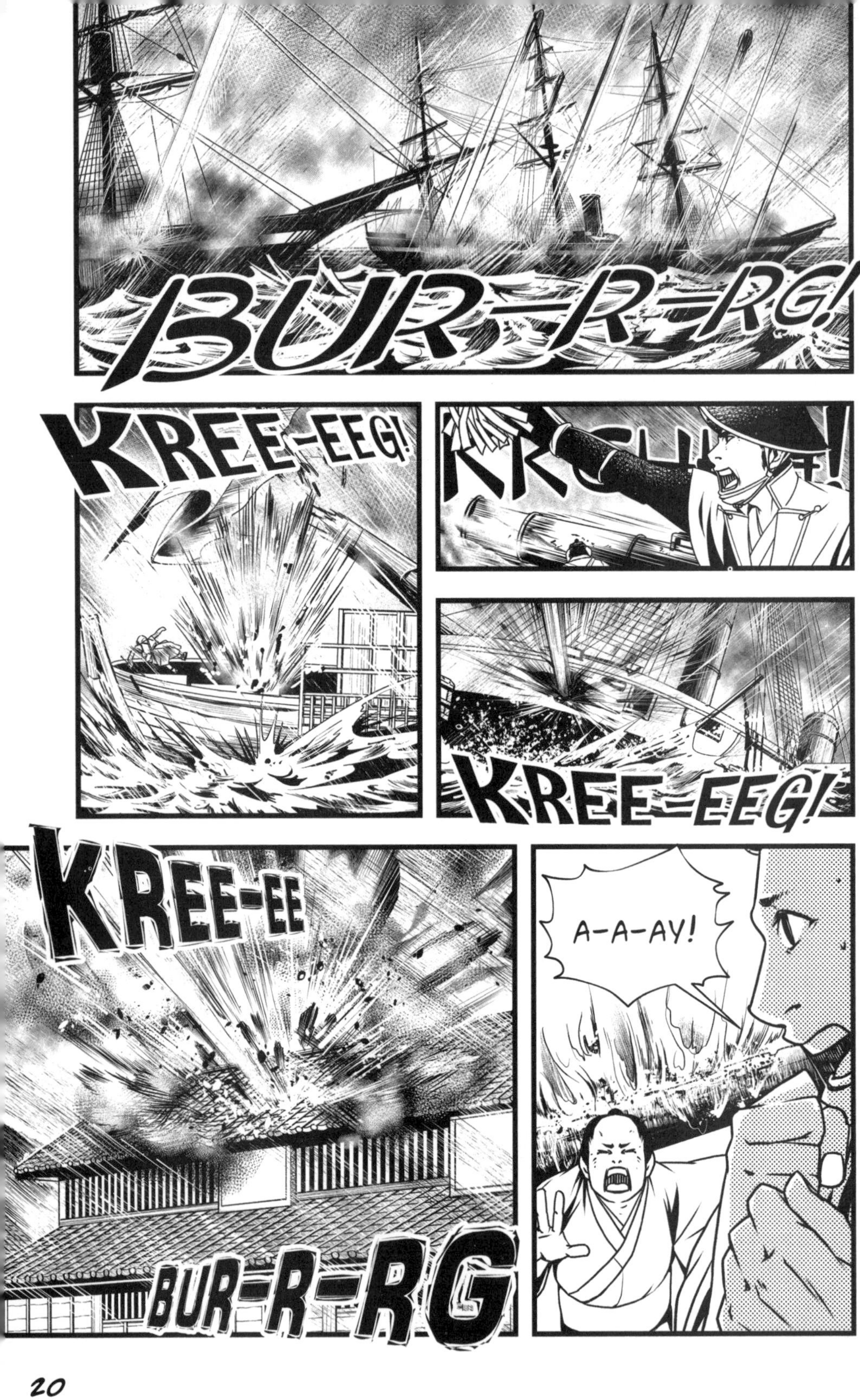
BUR-R-RG!
KREE-EEG!
KREE-EEG!
KREE-EE
BUR-R-RG
A-A-AY!

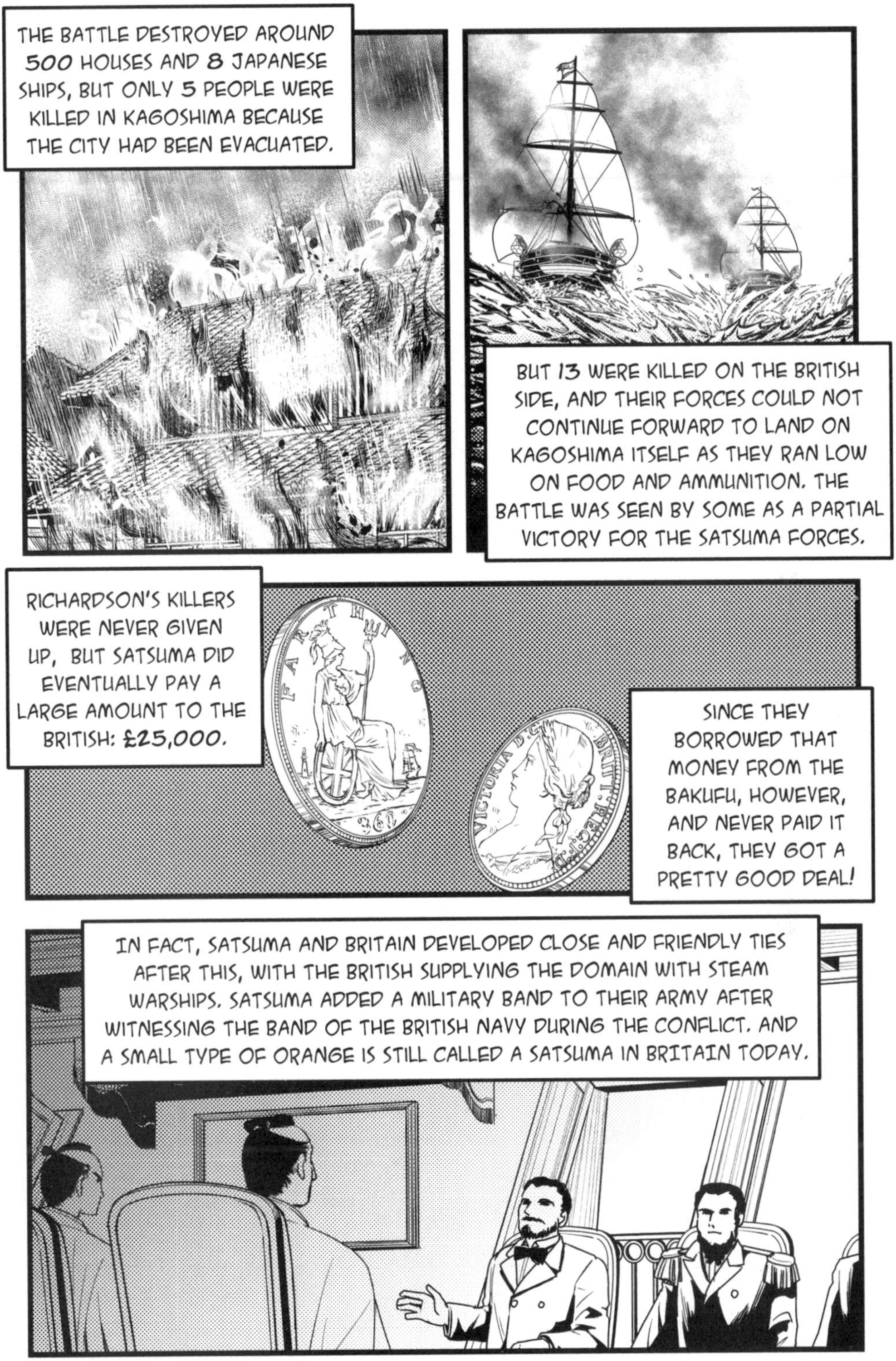

THE BATTLE DESTROYED AROUND 500 HOUSES AND 8 JAPANESE SHIPS, BUT ONLY 5 PEOPLE WERE KILLED IN KAGOSHIMA BECAUSE THE CITY HAD BEEN EVACUATED.

BUT 13 WERE KILLED ON THE BRITISH SIDE, AND THEIR FORCES COULD NOT CONTINUE FORWARD TO LAND ON KAGOSHIMA ITSELF AS THEY RAN LOW ON FOOD AND AMMUNITION. THE BATTLE WAS SEEN BY SOME AS A PARTIAL VICTORY FOR THE SATSUMA FORCES.

RICHARDSON'S KILLERS WERE NEVER GIVEN UP, BUT SATSUMA DID EVENTUALLY PAY A LARGE AMOUNT TO THE BRITISH: £25,000.

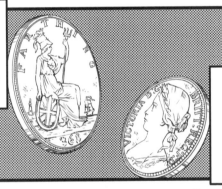

SINCE THEY BORROWED THAT MONEY FROM THE BAKUFU, HOWEVER, AND NEVER PAID IT BACK, THEY GOT A PRETTY GOOD DEAL!

IN FACT, SATSUMA AND BRITAIN DEVELOPED CLOSE AND FRIENDLY TIES AFTER THIS, WITH THE BRITISH SUPPLYING THE DOMAIN WITH STEAM WARSHIPS. SATSUMA ADDED A MILITARY BAND TO THEIR ARMY AFTER WITNESSING THE BAND OF THE BRITISH NAVY DURING THE CONFLICT. AND A SMALL TYPE OF ORANGE IS STILL CALLED A SATSUMA IN BRITAIN TODAY.

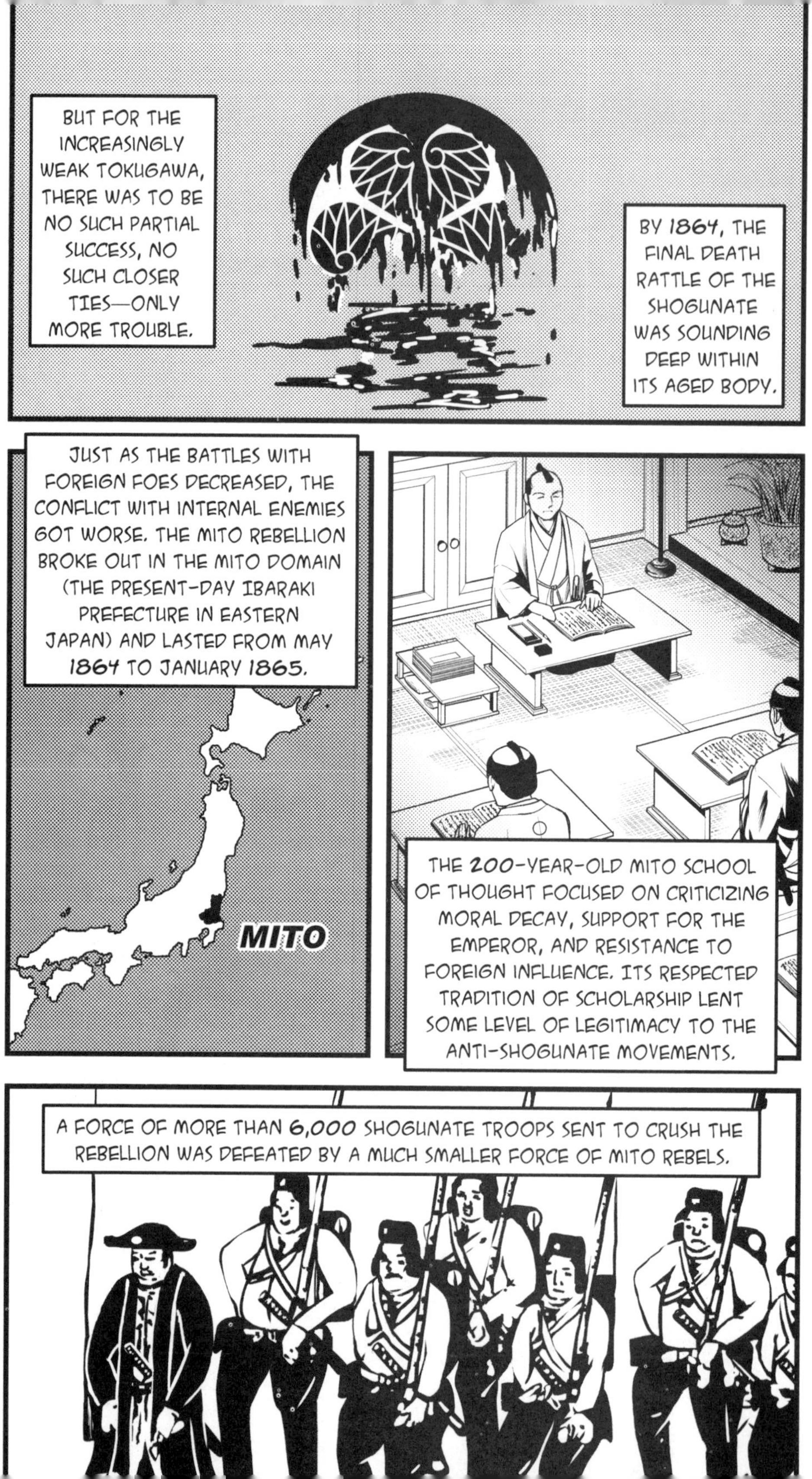

BUT FOR THE INCREASINGLY WEAK TOKUGAWA, THERE WAS TO BE NO SUCH PARTIAL SUCCESS, NO SUCH CLOSER TIES—ONLY MORE TROUBLE.
BY 1864, THE FINAL DEATH RATTLE OF THE SHOGUNATE WAS SOUNDING DEEP WITHIN ITS AGED BODY.
JUST AS THE BATTLES WITH FOREIGN FOES DECREASED, THE CONFLICT WITH INTERNAL ENEMIES GOT WORSE. THE MITO REBELLION BROKE OUT IN THE MITO DOMAIN (THE PRESENT-DAY IBARAKI PREFECTURE IN EASTERN JAPAN) AND LASTED FROM MAY 1864 TO JANUARY 1865.
MITO
THE 200-YEAR-OLD MITO SCHOOL OF THOUGHT FOCUSED ON CRITICIZING MORAL DECAY, SUPPORT FOR THE EMPEROR, AND RESISTANCE TO FOREIGN INFLUENCE. ITS RESPECTED TRADITION OF SCHOLARSHIP LENT SOME LEVEL OF LEGITIMACY TO THE ANTI-SHOGUNATE MOVEMENTS.
A FORCE OF MORE THAN 6,000 SHOGUNATE TROOPS SENT TO CRUSH THE REBELLION WAS DEFEATED BY A MUCH SMALLER FORCE OF MITO REBELS.

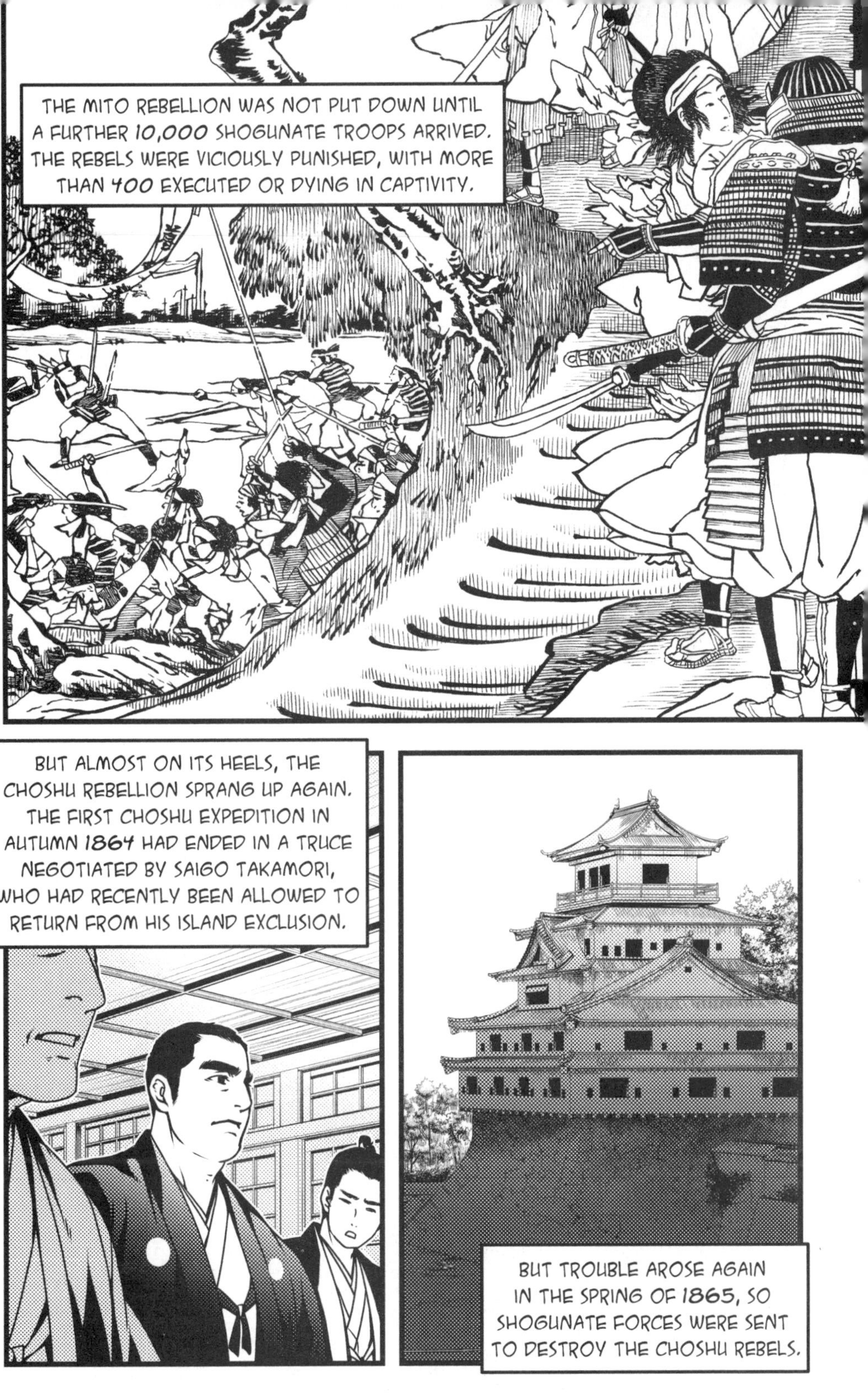
THE MITO REBELLION WAS NOT PUT DOWN UNTIL A FURTHER 10,000 SHOGUNATE TROOPS ARRIVED. THE REBELS WERE VICIOUSLY PUNISHED, WITH MORE THAN 400 EXECUTED OR DYING IN CAPTIVITY.
BUT ALMOST ON ITS HEELS, THE CHOSHU REBELLION SPRANG UP AGAIN. THE FIRST CHOSHU EXPEDITION IN AUTUMN 1864 HAD ENDED IN A TRUCE NEGOTIATED BY SAIGO TAKAMORI, WHO HAD RECENTLY BEEN ALLOWED TO RETURN FROM HIS ISLAND EXCLUSION.
BUT TROUBLE AROSE AGAIN IN THE SPRING OF 1865, SO SHOGUNATE FORCES WERE SENT TO DESTROY THE CHOSHU REBELS.

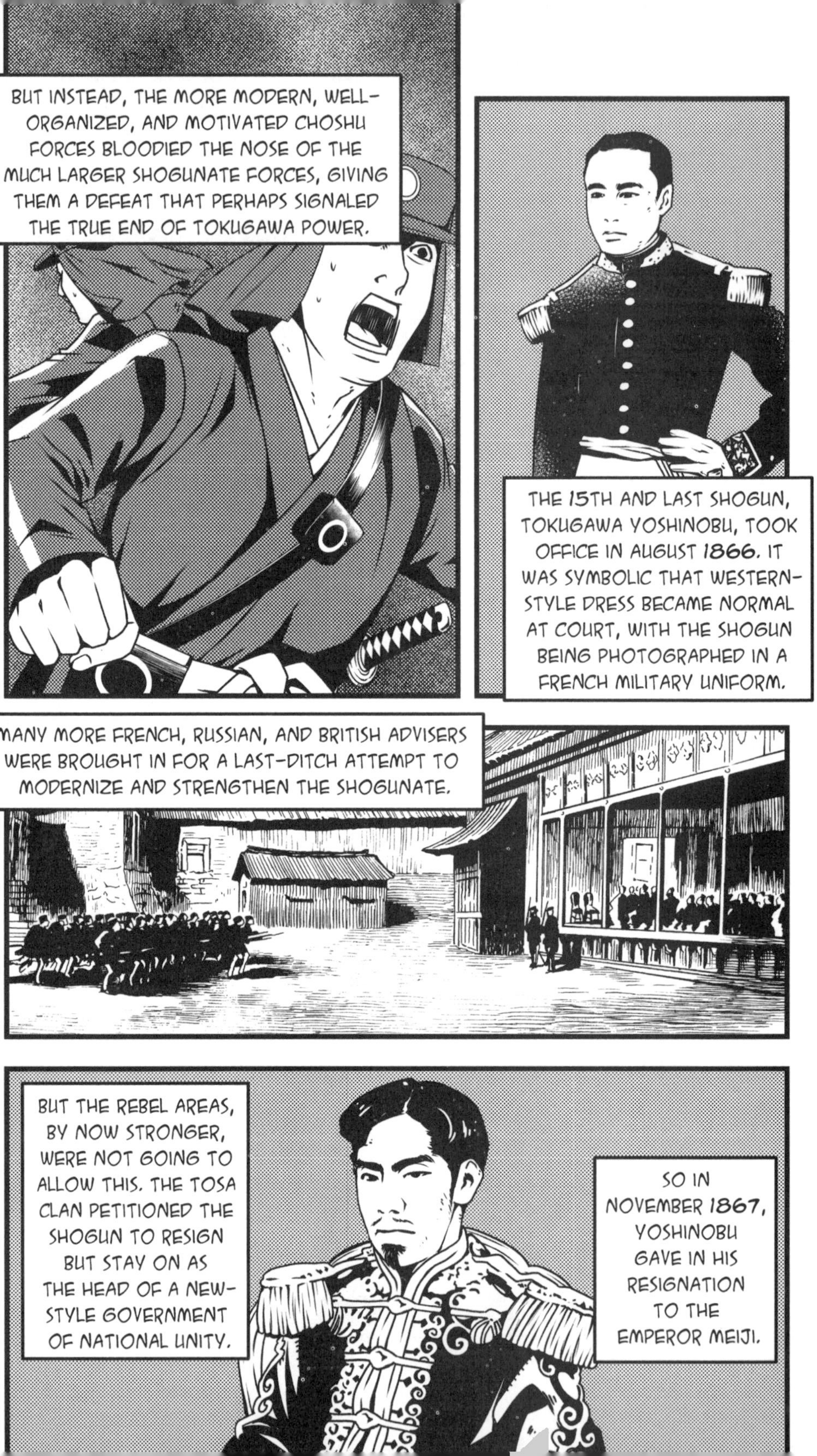
BUT INSTEAD, THE MORE MODERN, WELL-ORGANIZED, AND MOTIVATED CHOSHU FORCES BLOODIED THE NOSE OF THE MUCH LARGER SHOGUNATE FORCES, GIVING THEM A DEFEAT THAT PERHAPS SIGNALED THE TRUE END OF TOKUGAWA POWER.
THE 15TH AND LAST SHOGUN, TOKUGAWA YOSHINOBU, TOOK OFFICE IN AUGUST 1866. IT WAS SYMBOLIC THAT WESTERN-STYLE DRESS BECAME NORMAL AT COURT, WITH THE SHOGUN BEING PHOTOGRAPHED IN A FRENCH MILITARY UNIFORM.
MANY MORE FRENCH, RUSSIAN, AND BRITISH ADVISERS WERE BROUGHT IN FOR A LAST-DITCH ATTEMPT TO MODERNIZE AND STRENGTHEN THE SHOGUNATE.
BUT THE REBEL AREAS, BY NOW STRONGER, WERE NOT GOING TO ALLOW THIS. THE TOSA CLAN PETITIONED THE SHOGUN TO RESIGN BUT STAY ON AS THE HEAD OF A NEW-STYLE GOVERNMENT OF NATIONAL UNITY.
SO IN NOVEMBER 1867, YOSHINOBU GAVE IN HIS RESIGNATION TO THE EMPEROR MEIJI.

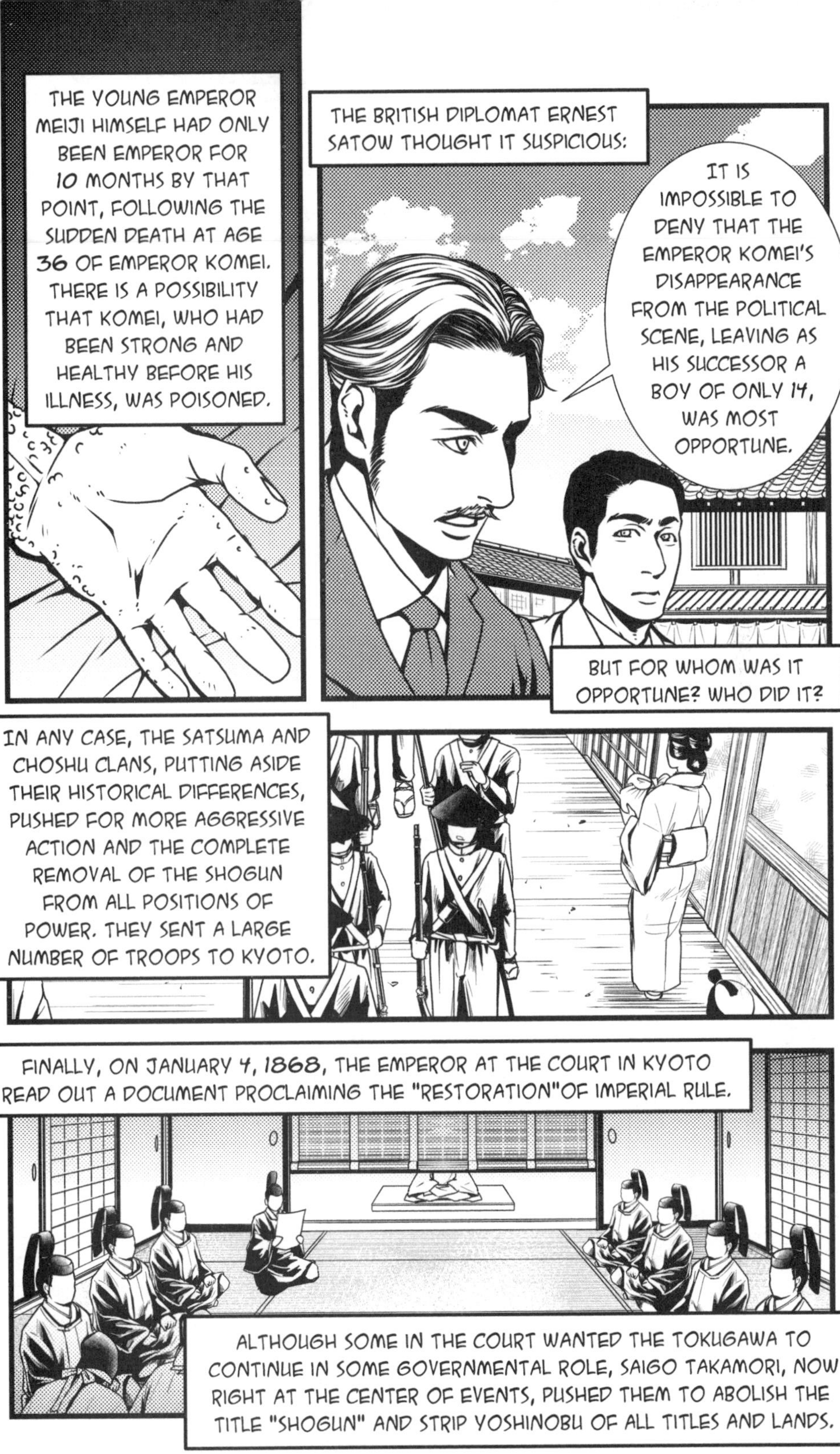
THE YOUNG EMPEROR MEIJI HIMSELF HAD ONLY BEEN EMPEROR FOR 10 MONTHS BY THAT POINT, FOLLOWING THE SUDDEN DEATH AT AGE 36 OF EMPEROR KOMEI. THERE IS A POSSIBILITY THAT KOMEI, WHO HAD BEEN STRONG AND HEALTHY BEFORE HIS ILLNESS, WAS POISONED.
THE BRITISH DIPLOMAT ERNEST SATOW THOUGHT IT SUSPICIOUS:
IT IS IMPOSSIBLE TO DENY THAT THE EMPEROR KOMEI'S DISAPPEARANCE FROM THE POLITICAL SCENE, LEAVING AS HIS SUCCESSOR A BOY OF ONLY 14, WAS MOST OPPORTUNE.
BUT FOR WHOM WAS IT OPPORTUNE? WHO DID IT?
IN ANY CASE, THE SATSUMA AND CHOSHU CLANS, PUTTING ASIDE THEIR HISTORICAL DIFFERENCES, PUSHED FOR MORE AGGRESSIVE ACTION AND THE COMPLETE REMOVAL OF THE SHOGUN FROM ALL POSITIONS OF POWER. THEY SENT A LARGE NUMBER OF TROOPS TO KYOTO.
FINALLY, ON JANUARY 4, 1868, THE EMPEROR AT THE COURT IN KYOTO READ OUT A DOCUMENT PROCLAIMING THE "RESTORATION" OF IMPERIAL RULE.
ALTHOUGH SOME IN THE COURT WANTED THE TOKUGAWA TO CONTINUE IN SOME GOVERNMENTAL ROLE, SAIGO TAKAMORI, NOW RIGHT AT THE CENTER OF EVENTS, PUSHED THEM TO ABOLISH THE TITLE "SHOGUN" AND STRIP YOSHINOBU OF ALL TITLES AND LANDS.

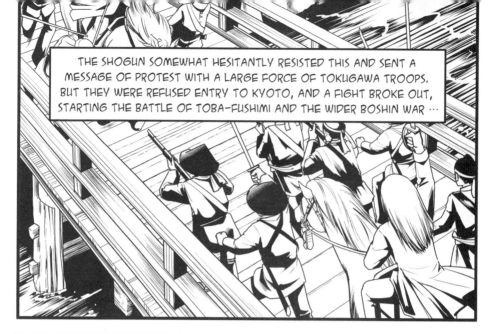

THE SHOGUN SOMEWHAT HESITANTLY RESISTED THIS AND SENT A MESSAGE OF PROTEST WITH A LARGE FORCE OF TOKUGAWA TROOPS. BUT THEY WERE REFUSED ENTRY TO KYOTO, AND A FIGHT BROKE OUT, STARTING THE BATTLE OF TOBA–FUSHIMI AND THE WIDER BOSHIN WAR ...

THE SHOGUNATE FORCES WERE MORE NUMEROUS, BUT THE CHOSHU AND SATSUMA MORE MODERN, WITH WESTERN ARMS SUCH AS ARMSTRONG HOWITZERS, MINIÉ RIFLES, AND GATLING GUNS.

ON THE SECOND DAY OF BATTLE, THE EMPEROR'S BANNER WAS PRESENTED TO THE TROOPS, AND A RELATIVE OF THE EMPEROR, NINNAJINOMIYA YOSHIAKI, WAS NAMED COMMANDER IN CHIEF. THIS TURNED A FORCE OF REBELS INTO THE OFFICIAL IMPERIAL ARMY!

AT THIS POINT, SEVERAL LORDS DEFECTED TO THE IMPERIAL SIDE, BRINGING THEIR FORCES WITH THEM—SO A DEMORALIZED YOSHINOBU FLED OSAKA ON THE SHIP KAIYO MARU.

SAIGO TAKAMORI TOOK THE LEADERSHIP OF THE IMPERIAL FORCES AND CHASED THE SHOGUNATE TROOPS FARTHER AND FARTHER NORTH, EVENTUALLY SURROUNDING EDO ITSELF IN MAY 1868.

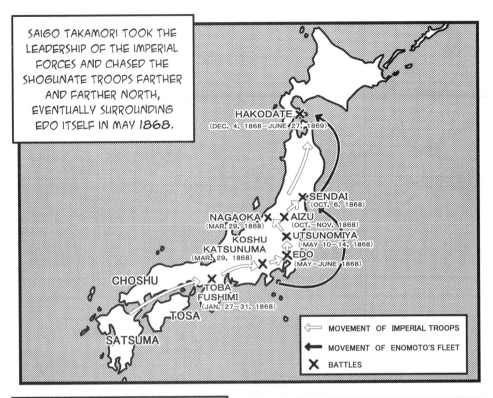

HAKODATE
(DEC. 4, 1868–JUNE 27, 1869)

SENDAI
(OCT. 6, 1868)

NAGAOKA
(MAR. 29, 1868)

AIZU
(OCT.–NOV. 1868)

KOSHU
KATSUNUMA
(MAR. 29, 1868)

UTSUNOMIYA
(MAY 10–14, 1868)

EDO
(MAY–JUNE 1868)

CHOSHU

TOBA
FUSHIMI
(JAN. 27–31, 1868)

TOSA

SATSUMA

MOVEMENT OF IMPERIAL TROOPS

MOVEMENT OF ENOMOTO'S FLEET

X BATTLES

STILL, SOME SHOGUNATE FORCES CONTINUED TO FIGHT. THE LEADER OF THE SHOGUN'S NAVY, ENOMOTO TAKEAKI, SAILED NORTH WITH 8 SHIPS, 2,000 SAILORS, AND WHAT REMAINED OF THE MUCH FEARED SPECIAL POLICE FORCE, THE SHINSENGUMI.

THEY JOINED UP WITH SOME LOYAL NORTHERN LORDS AND A HANDFUL OF FRENCH ADVISERS, ESTABLISHING THE SHORT-LIVED EZO REPUBLIC, WITH ENOMOTO AS ITS PRESIDENT.

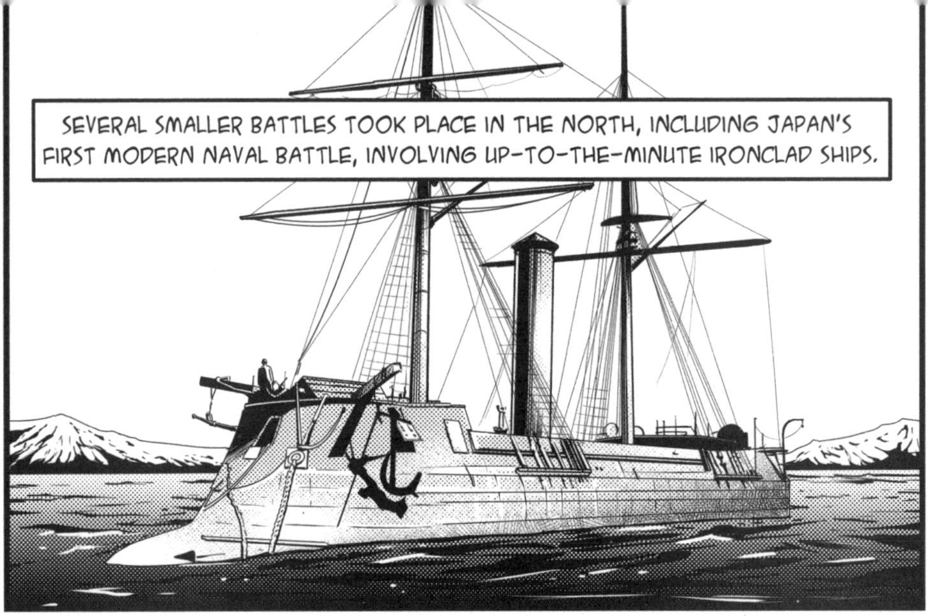
SEVERAL SMALLER BATTLES TOOK PLACE IN THE NORTH, INCLUDING JAPAN'S FIRST MODERN NAVAL BATTLE, INVOLVING UP-TO-THE-MINUTE IRONCLAD SHIPS.

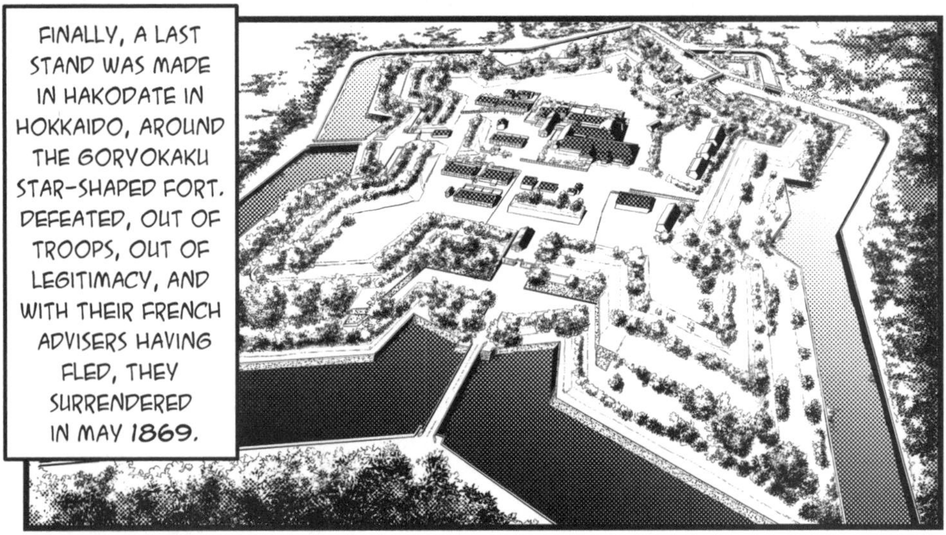
FINALLY, A LAST STAND WAS MADE IN HAKODATE IN HOKKAIDO, AROUND THE GORYOKAKU STAR-SHAPED FORT. DEFEATED, OUT OF TROOPS, OUT OF LEGITIMACY, AND WITH THEIR FRENCH ADVISERS HAVING FLED, THEY SURRENDERED IN MAY 1869.

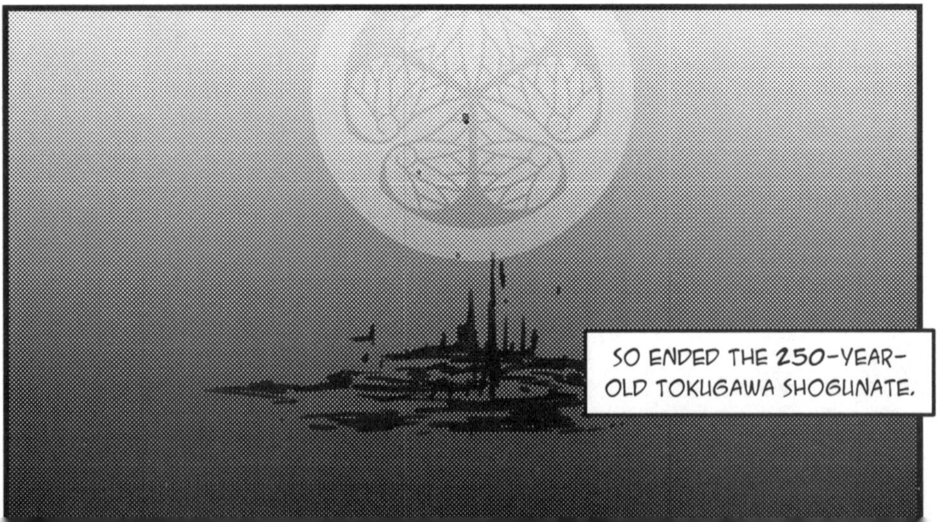
SO ENDED THE 250-YEAR-OLD TOKUGAWA SHOGUNATE.

CHAPTER 2

THE NEW JAPAN

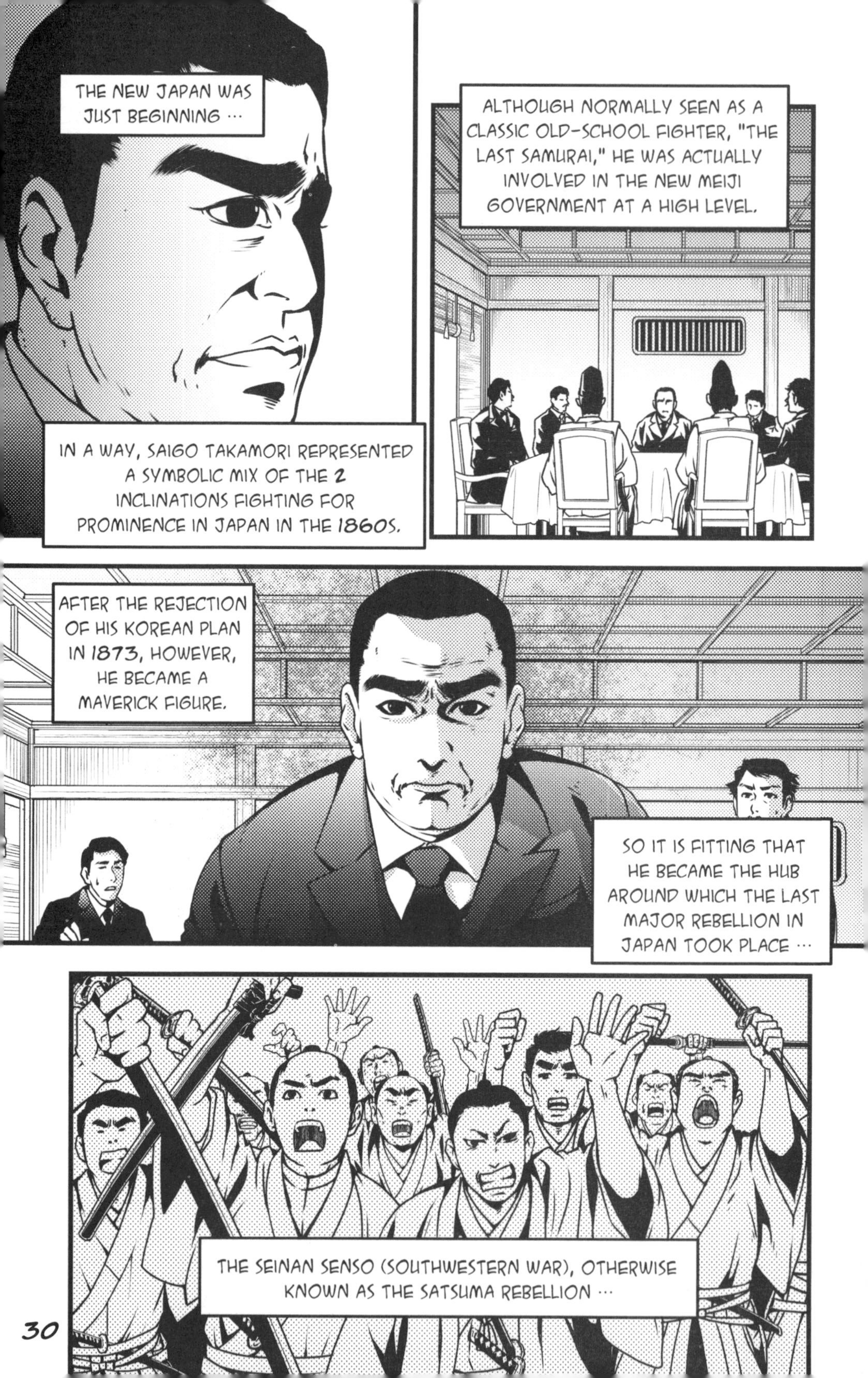
THE NEW JAPAN WAS JUST BEGINNING …
IN A WAY, SAIGO TAKAMORI REPRESENTED A SYMBOLIC MIX OF THE 2 INCLINATIONS FIGHTING FOR PROMINENCE IN JAPAN IN THE 1860S.
ALTHOUGH NORMALLY SEEN AS A CLASSIC OLD-SCHOOL FIGHTER, "THE LAST SAMURAI," HE WAS ACTUALLY INVOLVED IN THE NEW MEIJI GOVERNMENT AT A HIGH LEVEL.
AFTER THE REJECTION OF HIS KOREAN PLAN IN 1873, HOWEVER, HE BECAME A MAVERICK FIGURE.
SO IT IS FITTING THAT HE BECAME THE HUB AROUND WHICH THE LAST MAJOR REBELLION IN JAPAN TOOK PLACE …
THE SEINAN SENSO (SOUTHWESTERN WAR), OTHERWISE KNOWN AS THE SATSUMA REBELLION …

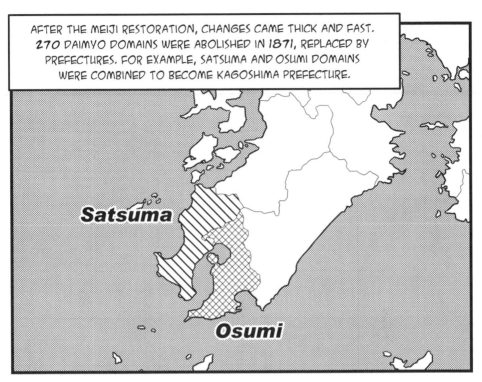

AFTER THE MEIJI RESTORATION, CHANGES CAME THICK AND FAST. 270 DAIMYO DOMAINS WERE ABOLISHED IN 1871, REPLACED BY PREFECTURES. FOR EXAMPLE, SATSUMA AND OSUMI DOMAINS WERE COMBINED TO BECOME KAGOSHIMA PREFECTURE.

Satsuma

Osumi

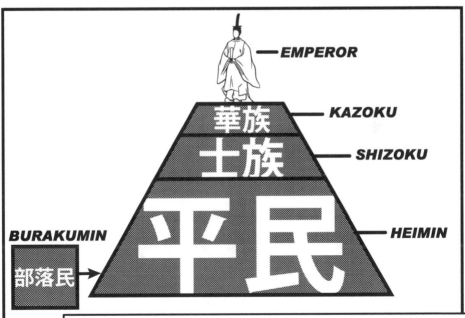

— EMPEROR

華族 — *KAZOKU*

士族 — *SHIZOKU*

平民 — *HEIMIN*

BURAKUMIN

部落民 →

IN A LARGE CHANGE OF SOCIAL STRUCTURE, SAMURAI WERE RECLASSIFIED AS SHIZOKU (WARRIOR FAMILIES), WITH KAZOKU (HEREDITARY PEERS AND LORDS) AT THE TOP AND THE HEIMIN (COMMONERS) AT THE BOTTOM. THE BURAKUMIN UNDERCLASS WAS "PROMOTED" INTO THE HEIMIN GROUP TOO.

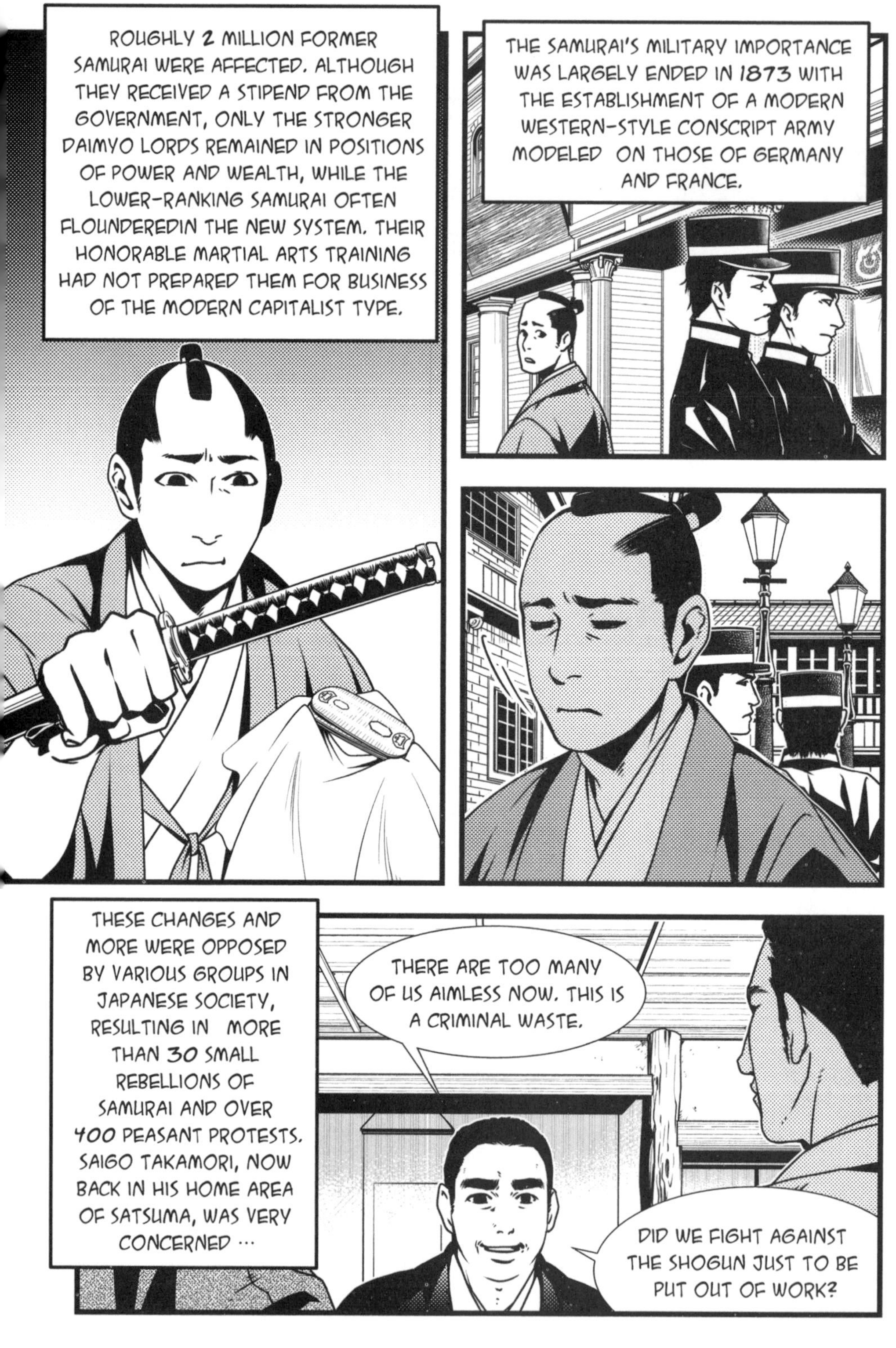
ROUGHLY 2 MILLION FORMER SAMURAI WERE AFFECTED. ALTHOUGH THEY RECEIVED A STIPEND FROM THE GOVERNMENT, ONLY THE STRONGER DAIMYO LORDS REMAINED IN POSITIONS OF POWER AND WEALTH, WHILE THE LOWER-RANKING SAMURAI OFTEN FLOUNDEREDIN THE NEW SYSTEM. THEIR HONORABLE MARTIAL ARTS TRAINING HAD NOT PREPARED THEM FOR BUSINESS OF THE MODERN CAPITALIST TYPE.
THE SAMURAI'S MILITARY IMPORTANCE WAS LARGELY ENDED IN 1873 WITH THE ESTABLISHMENT OF A MODERN WESTERN-STYLE CONSCRIPT ARMY MODELED ON THOSE OF GERMANY AND FRANCE.
THESE CHANGES AND MORE WERE OPPOSED BY VARIOUS GROUPS IN JAPANESE SOCIETY, RESULTING IN MORE THAN 30 SMALL REBELLIONS OF SAMURAI AND OVER 400 PEASANT PROTESTS. SAIGO TAKAMORI, NOW BACK IN HIS HOME AREA OF SATSUMA, WAS VERY CONCERNED ...
THERE ARE TOO MANY OF US AIMLESS NOW. THIS IS A CRIMINAL WASTE.
DID WE FIGHT AGAINST THE SHOGUN JUST TO BE PUT OUT OF WORK?

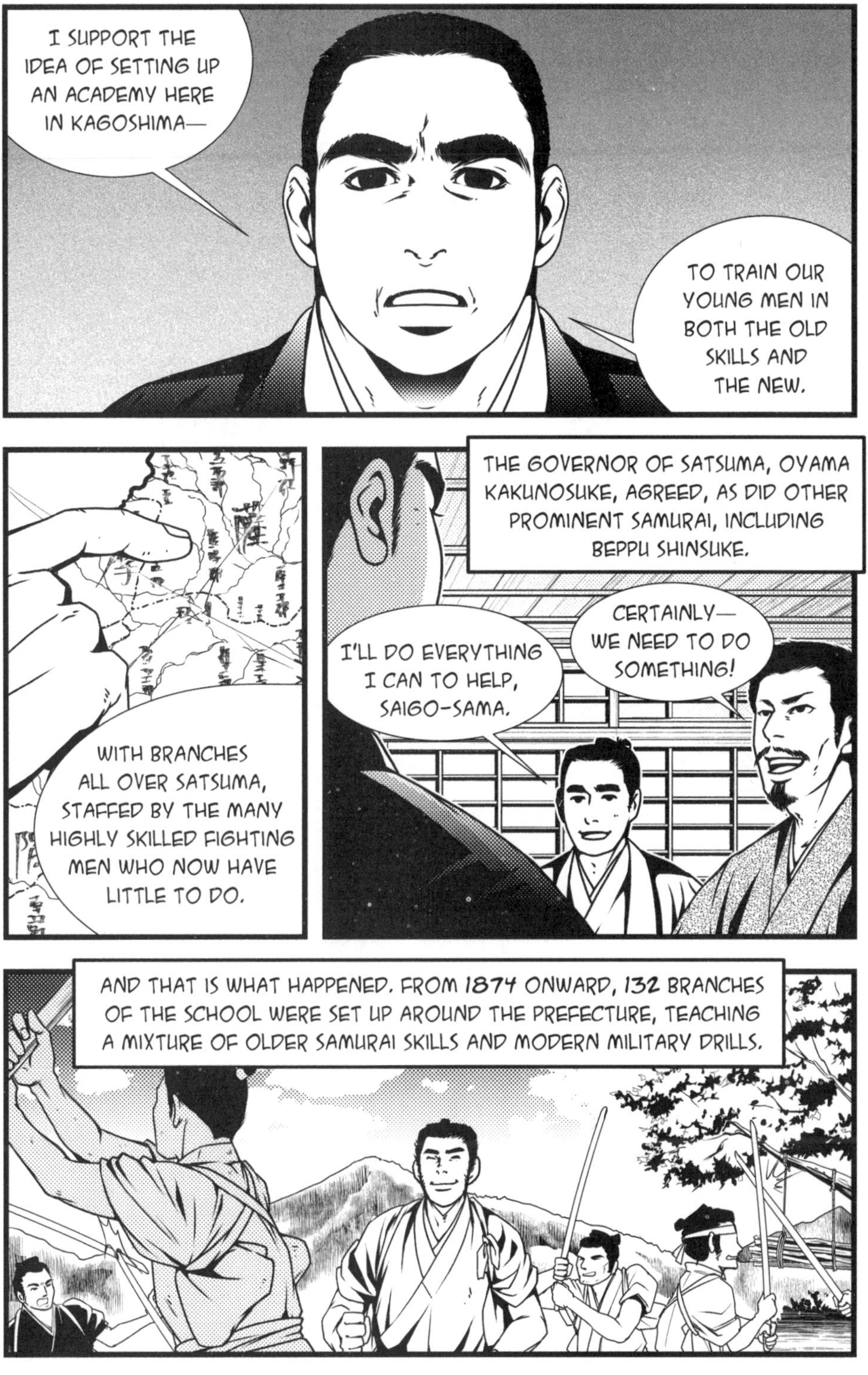
I SUPPORT THE IDEA OF SETTING UP AN ACADEMY HERE IN KAGOSHIMA—
TO TRAIN OUR YOUNG MEN IN BOTH THE OLD SKILLS AND THE NEW.
WITH BRANCHES ALL OVER SATSUMA, STAFFED BY THE MANY HIGHLY SKILLED FIGHTING MEN WHO NOW HAVE LITTLE TO DO.
THE GOVERNOR OF SATSUMA, OYAMA KAKUNOSUKE, AGREED, AS DID OTHER PROMINENT SAMURAI, INCLUDING BEPPU SHINSUKE.
CERTAINLY— WE NEED TO DO SOMETHING!
I'LL DO EVERYTHING I CAN TO HELP, SAIGO-SAMA.
AND THAT IS WHAT HAPPENED. FROM 1874 ONWARD, 132 BRANCHES OF THE SCHOOL WERE SET UP AROUND THE PREFECTURE, TEACHING A MIXTURE OF OLDER SAMURAI SKILLS AND MODERN MILITARY DRILLS.

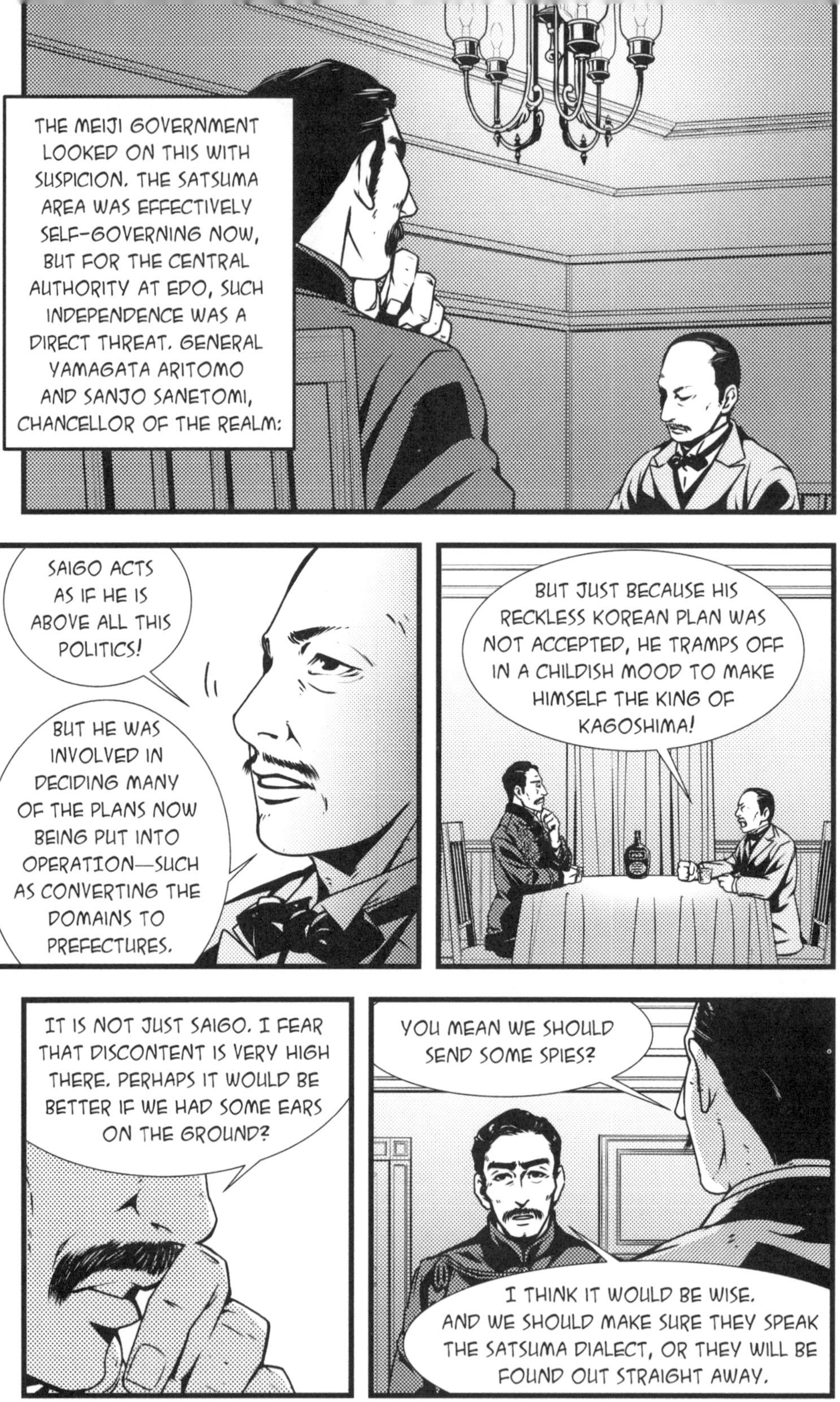
THE MEIJI GOVERNMENT LOOKED ON THIS WITH SUSPICION. THE SATSUMA AREA WAS EFFECTIVELY SELF-GOVERNING NOW, BUT FOR THE CENTRAL AUTHORITY AT EDO, SUCH INDEPENDENCE WAS A DIRECT THREAT. GENERAL YAMAGATA ARITOMO AND SANJO SANETOMI, CHANCELLOR OF THE REALM:
SAIGO ACTS AS IF HE IS ABOVE ALL THIS POLITICS!
BUT HE WAS INVOLVED IN DECIDING MANY OF THE PLANS NOW BEING PUT INTO OPERATION—SUCH AS CONVERTING THE DOMAINS TO PREFECTURES.
BUT JUST BECAUSE HIS RECKLESS KOREAN PLAN WAS NOT ACCEPTED, HE TRAMPS OFF IN A CHILDISH MOOD TO MAKE HIMSELF THE KING OF KAGOSHIMA!
IT IS NOT JUST SAIGO. I FEAR THAT DISCONTENT IS VERY HIGH THERE. PERHAPS IT WOULD BE BETTER IF WE HAD SOME EARS ON THE GROUND?
YOU MEAN WE SHOULD SEND SOME SPIES?
I THINK IT WOULD BE WISE. AND WE SHOULD MAKE SURE THEY SPEAK THE SATSUMA DIALECT, OR THEY WILL BE FOUND OUT STRAIGHT AWAY.

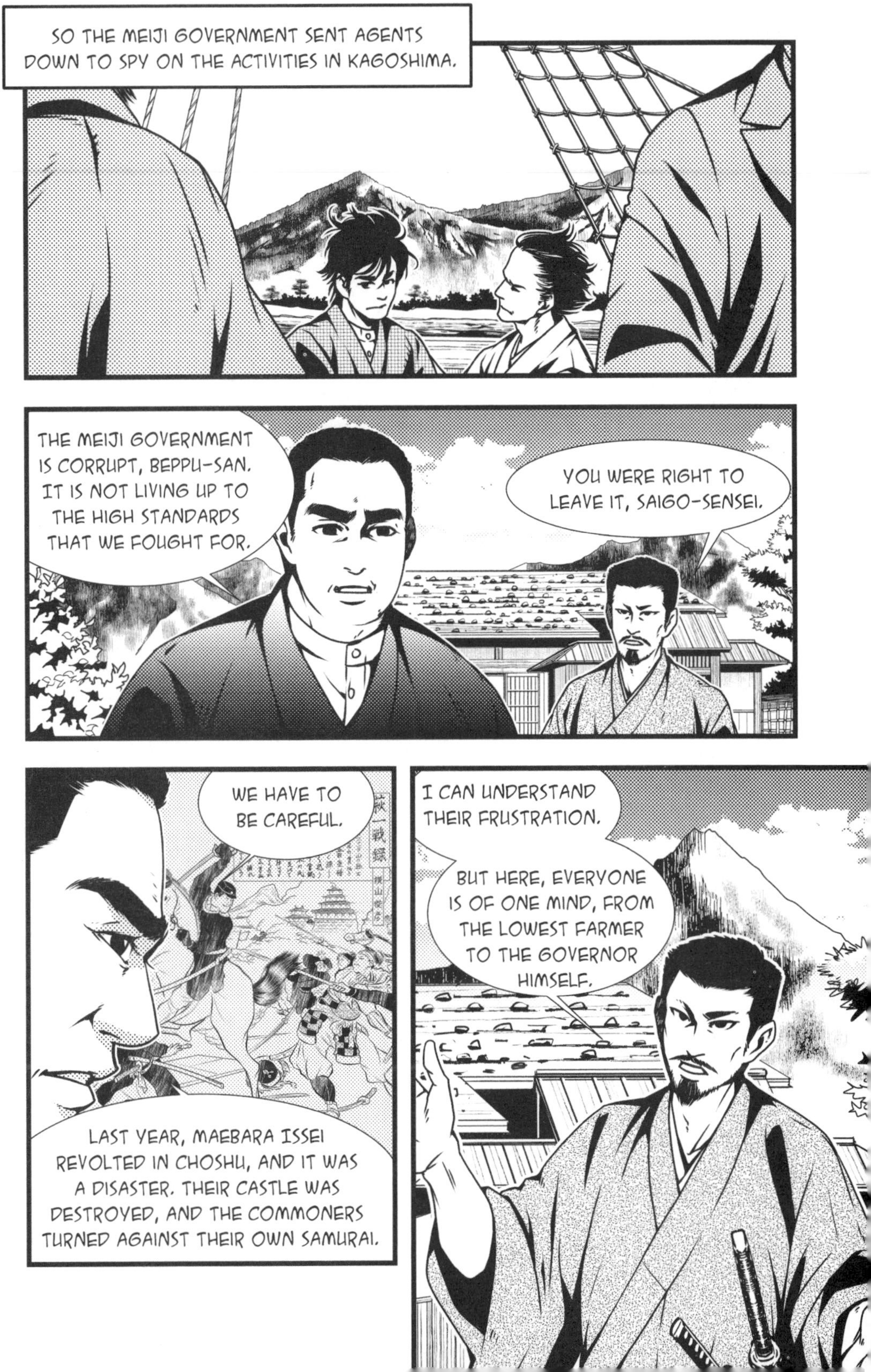
SO THE MEIJI GOVERNMENT SENT AGENTS DOWN TO SPY ON THE ACTIVITIES IN KAGOSHIMA.
THE MEIJI GOVERNMENT IS CORRUPT, BEPPU-SAN. IT IS NOT LIVING UP TO THE HIGH STANDARDS THAT WE FOUGHT FOR.
YOU WERE RIGHT TO LEAVE IT, SAIGO-SENSEI.
WE HAVE TO BE CAREFUL.
LAST YEAR, MAEBARA ISSEI REVOLTED IN CHOSHU, AND IT WAS A DISASTER. THEIR CASTLE WAS DESTROYED, AND THE COMMONERS TURNED AGAINST THEIR OWN SAMURAI.
I CAN UNDERSTAND THEIR FRUSTRATION.
BUT HERE, EVERYONE IS OF ONE MIND, FROM THE LOWEST FARMER TO THE GOVERNOR HIMSELF.

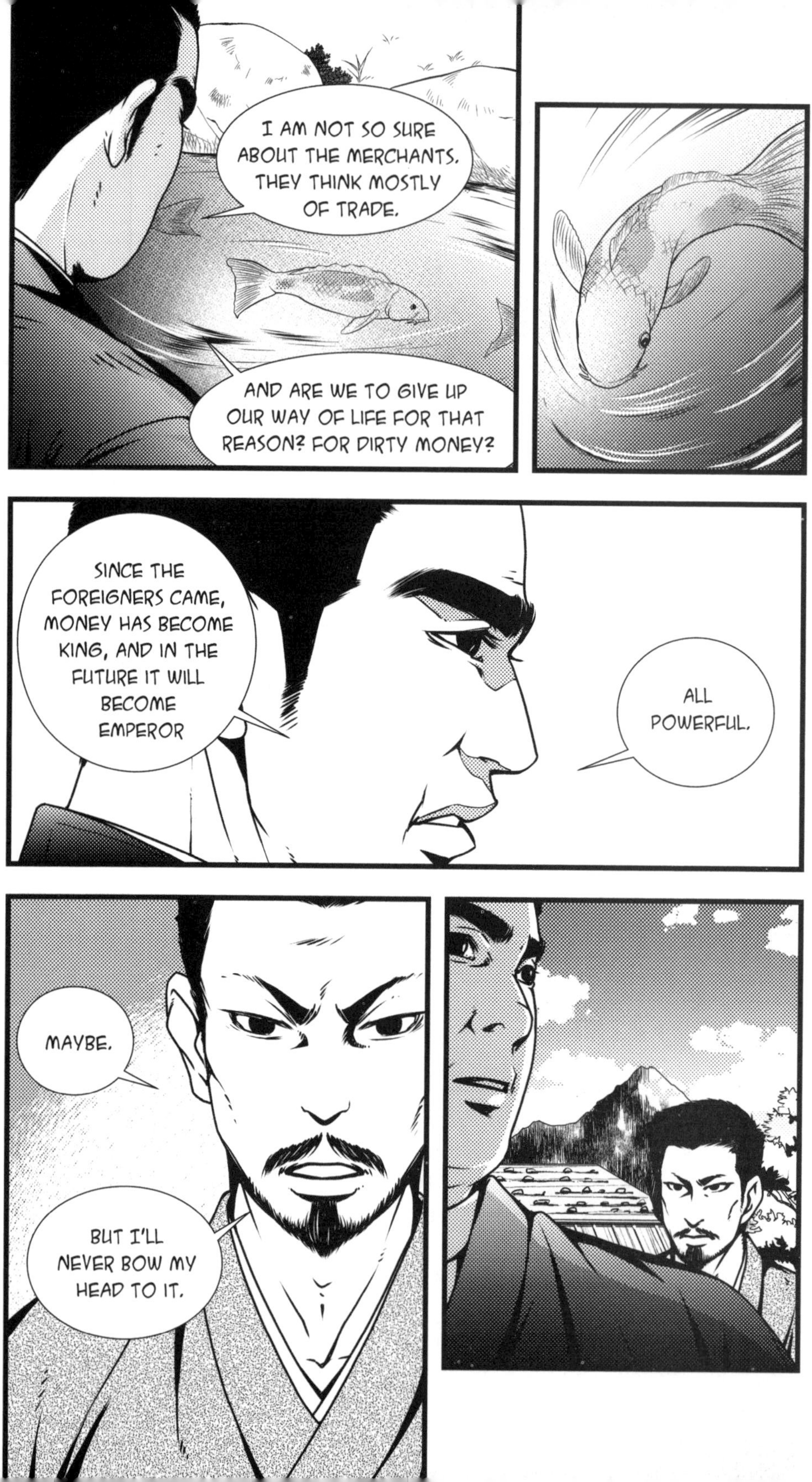
I AM NOT SO SURE ABOUT THE MERCHANTS. THEY THINK MOSTLY OF TRADE.
AND ARE WE TO GIVE UP OUR WAY OF LIFE FOR THAT REASON? FOR DIRTY MONEY?
SINCE THE FOREIGNERS CAME, MONEY HAS BECOME KING, AND IN THE FUTURE IT WILL BECOME EMPEROR
ALL POWERFUL.
MAYBE.
BUT I'LL NEVER BOW MY HEAD TO IT.

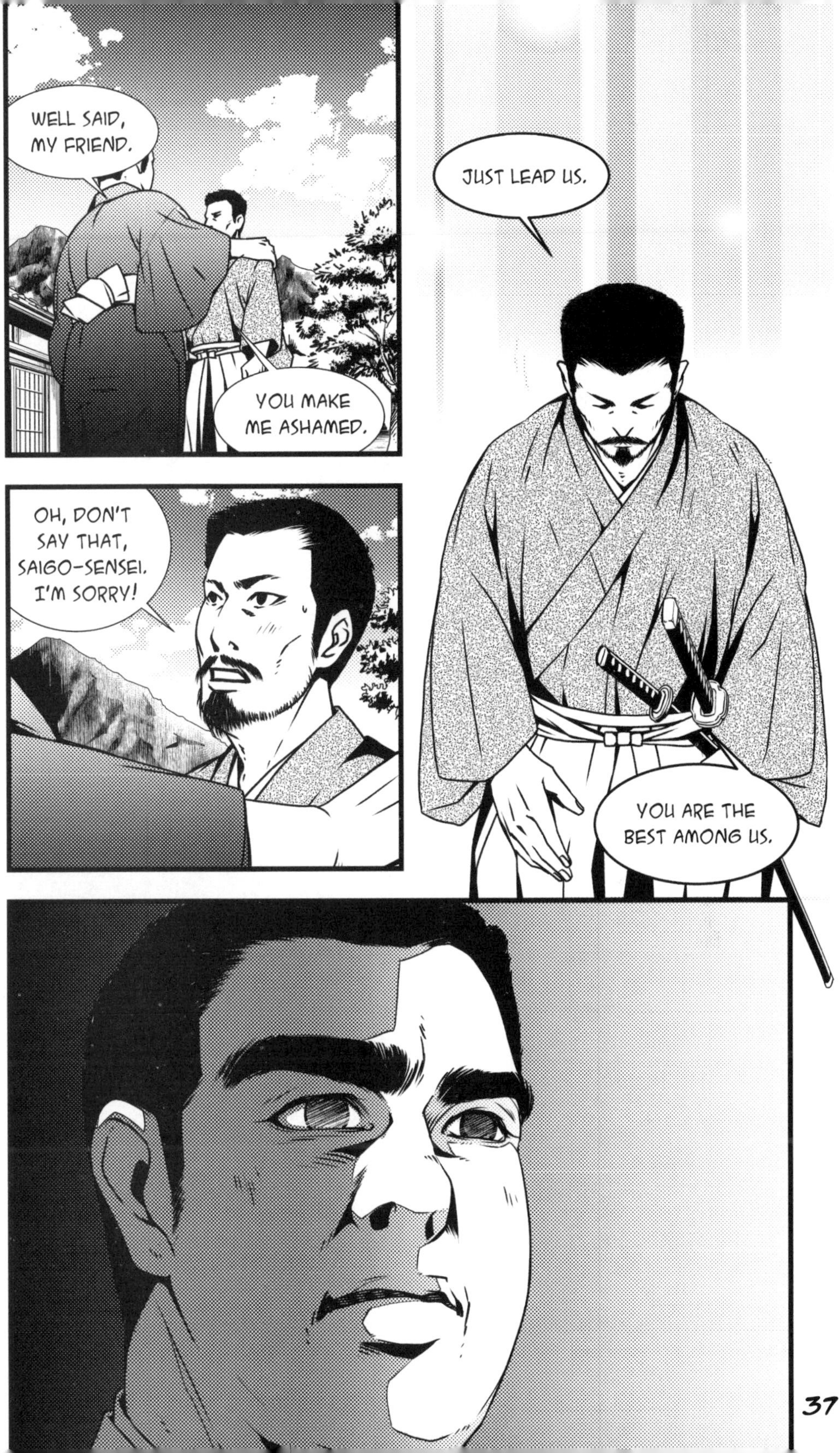
WELL SAID, MY FRIEND.
YOU MAKE ME ASHAMED.
JUST LEAD US.
OH, DON'T SAY THAT, SAIGO-SENSEI. I'M SORRY!
YOU ARE THE BEST AMONG US.

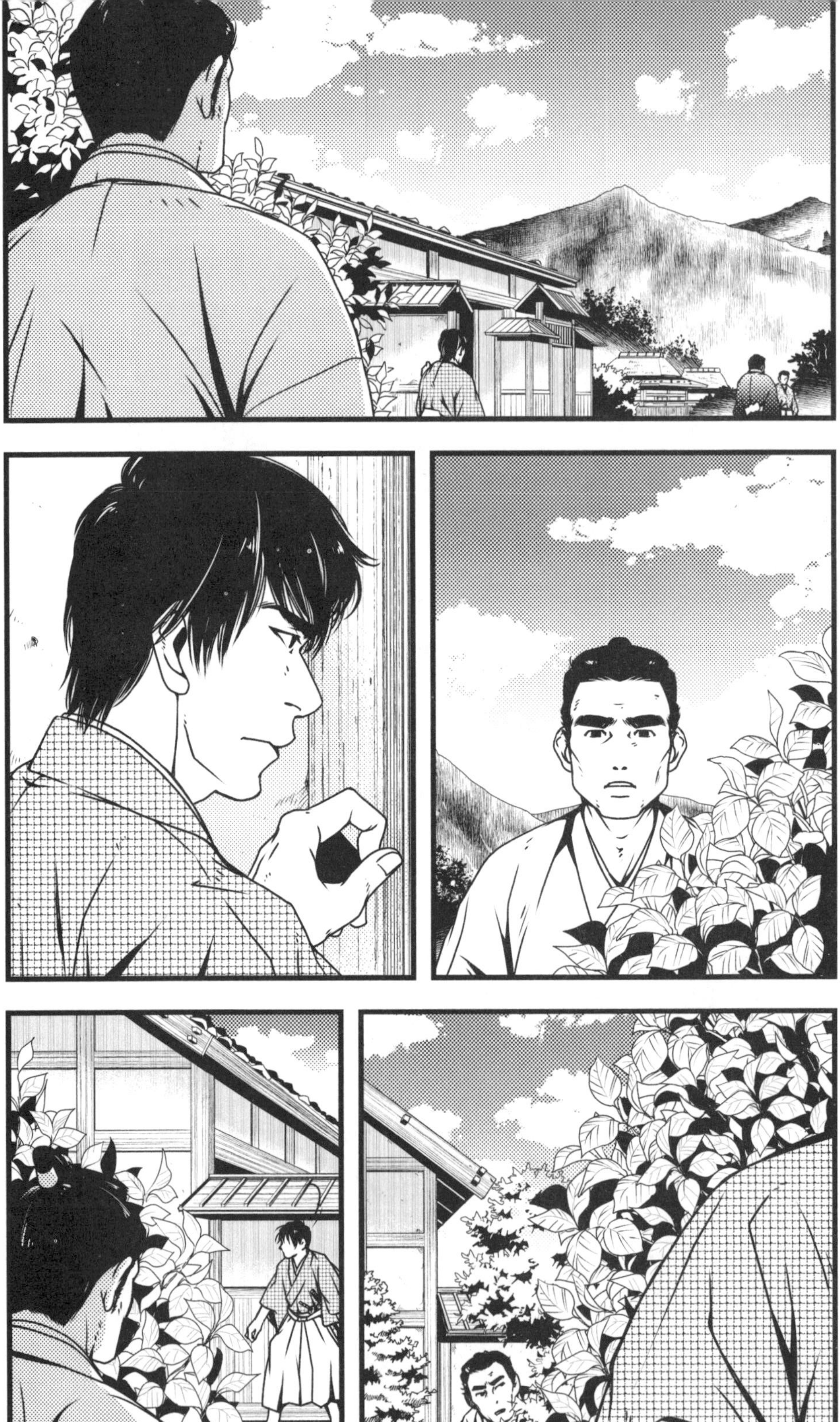

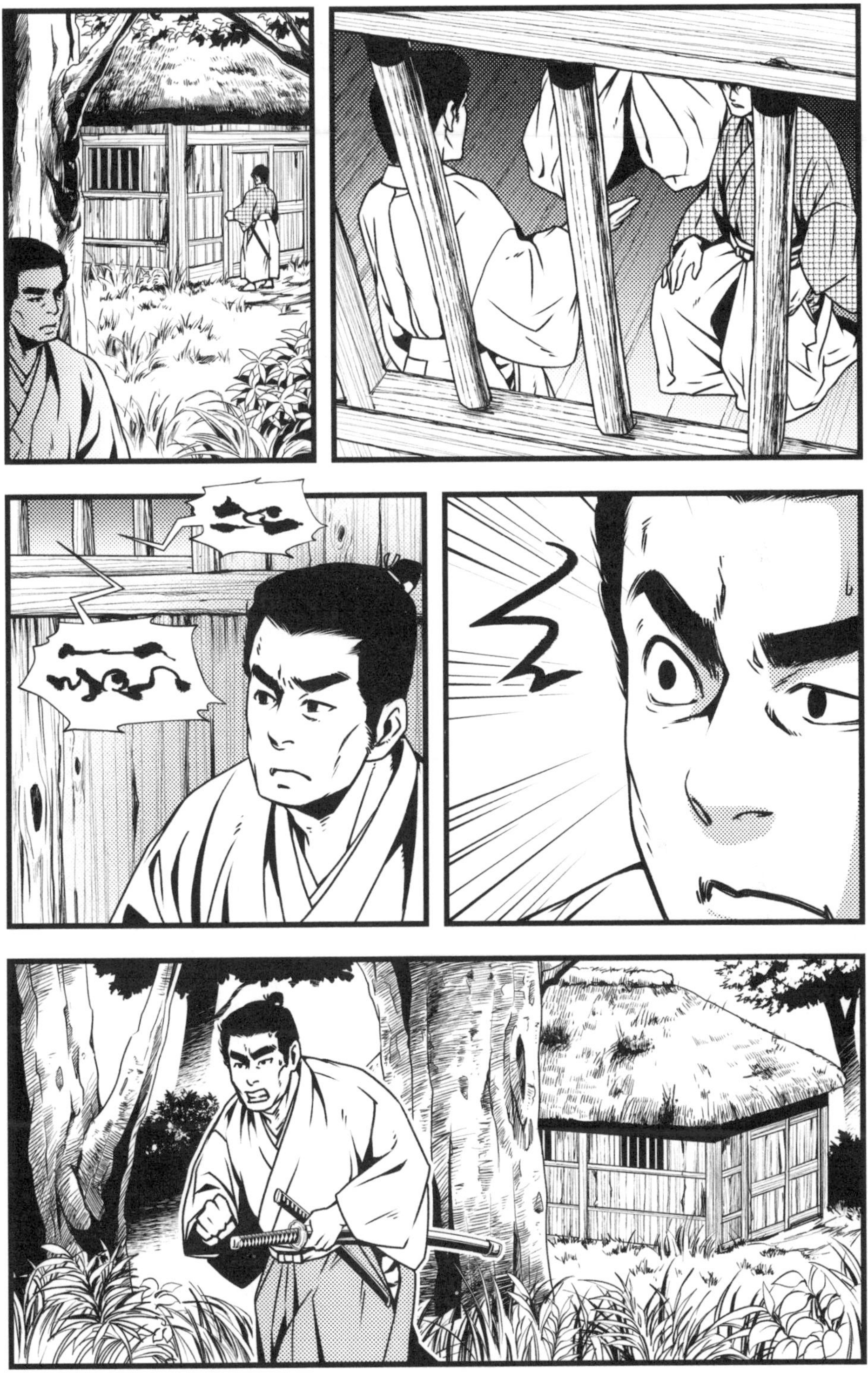

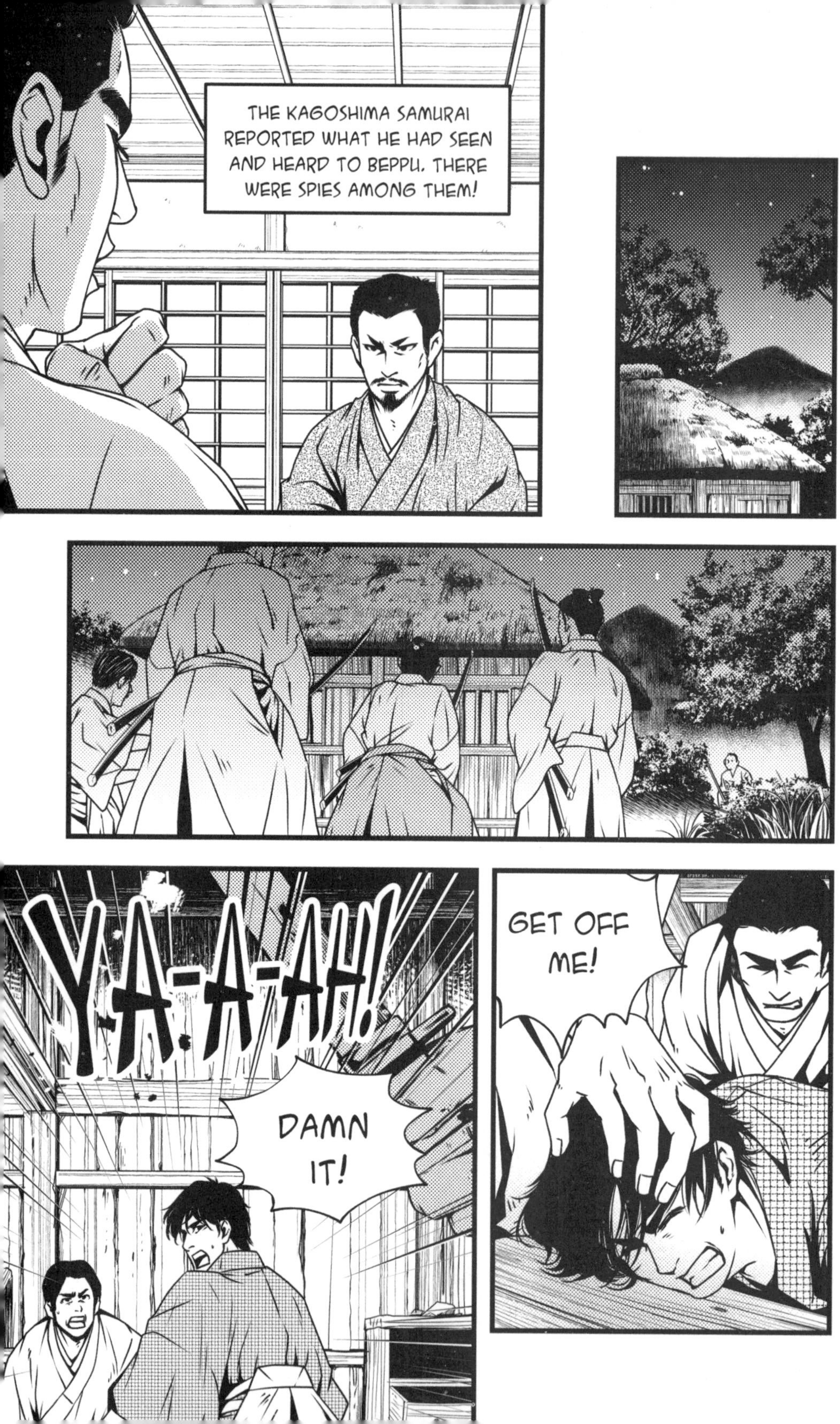
THE KAGOSHIMA SAMURAI REPORTED WHAT HE HAD SEEN AND HEARD TO BEPPU. THERE WERE SPIES AMONG THEM!
YA-A-AH!
DAMN IT!
GET OFF ME!

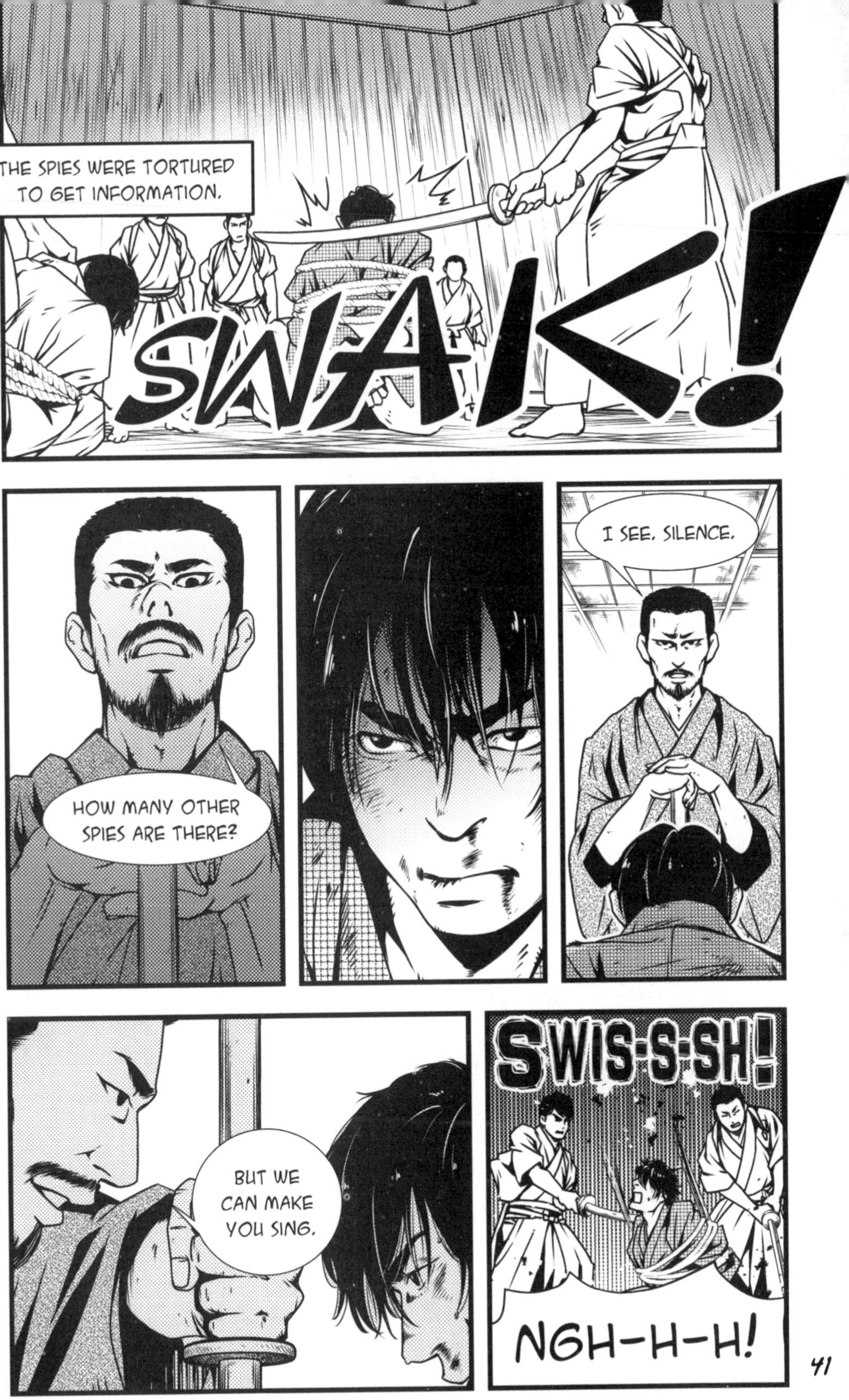
THE SPIES WERE TORTURED TO GET INFORMATION.
SWAK!
HOW MANY OTHER SPIES ARE THERE?
I SEE. SILENCE.
BUT WE CAN MAKE YOU SING.
SWIS-S-SH!
NGH-H-H!

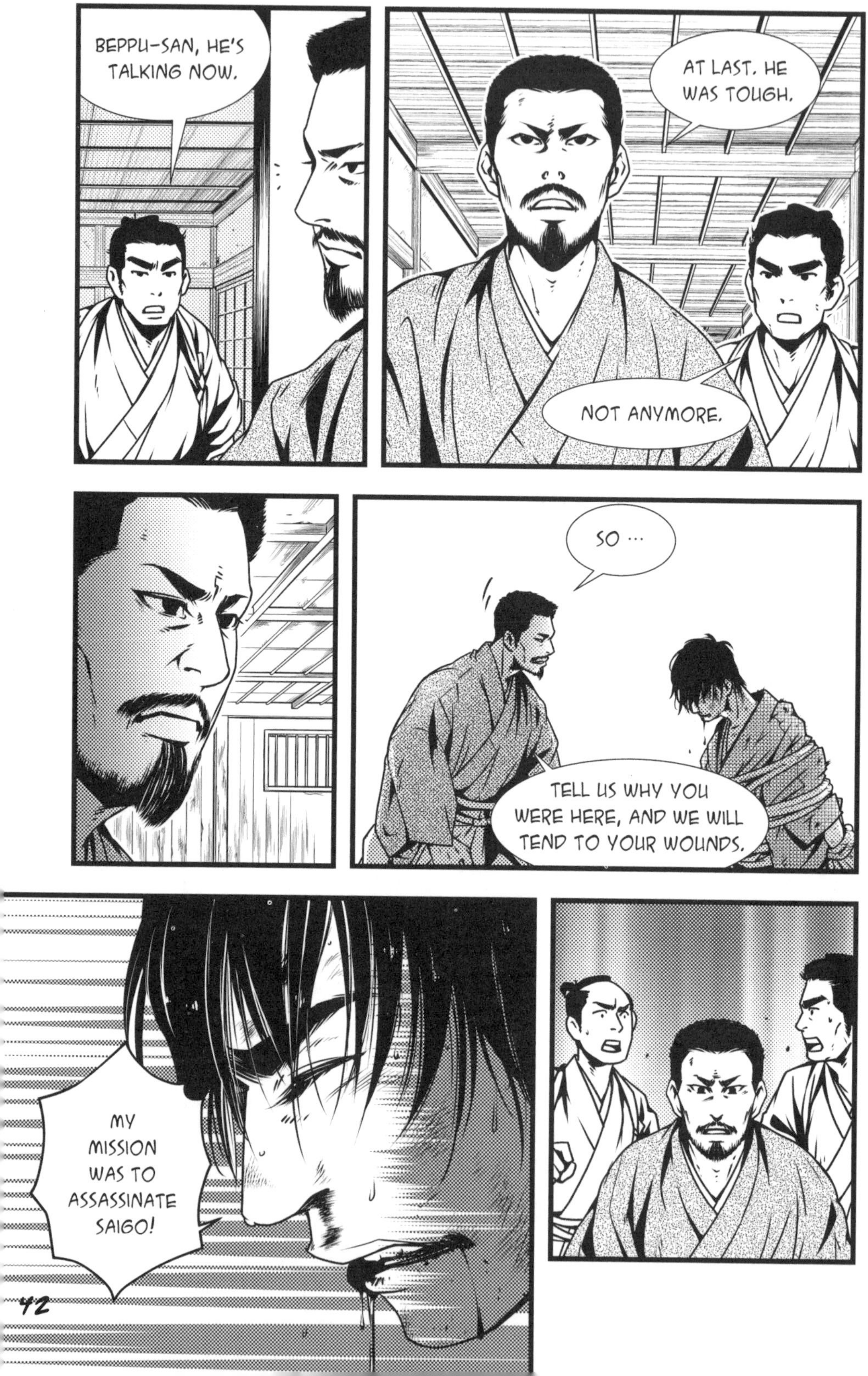
BEPPU-SAN, HE'S TALKING NOW.
AT LAST. HE WAS TOUGH.
NOT ANYMORE.
SO ...
TELL US WHY YOU WERE HERE, AND WE WILL TEND TO YOUR WOUNDS.
MY MISSION WAS TO ASSASSINATE SAIGO!

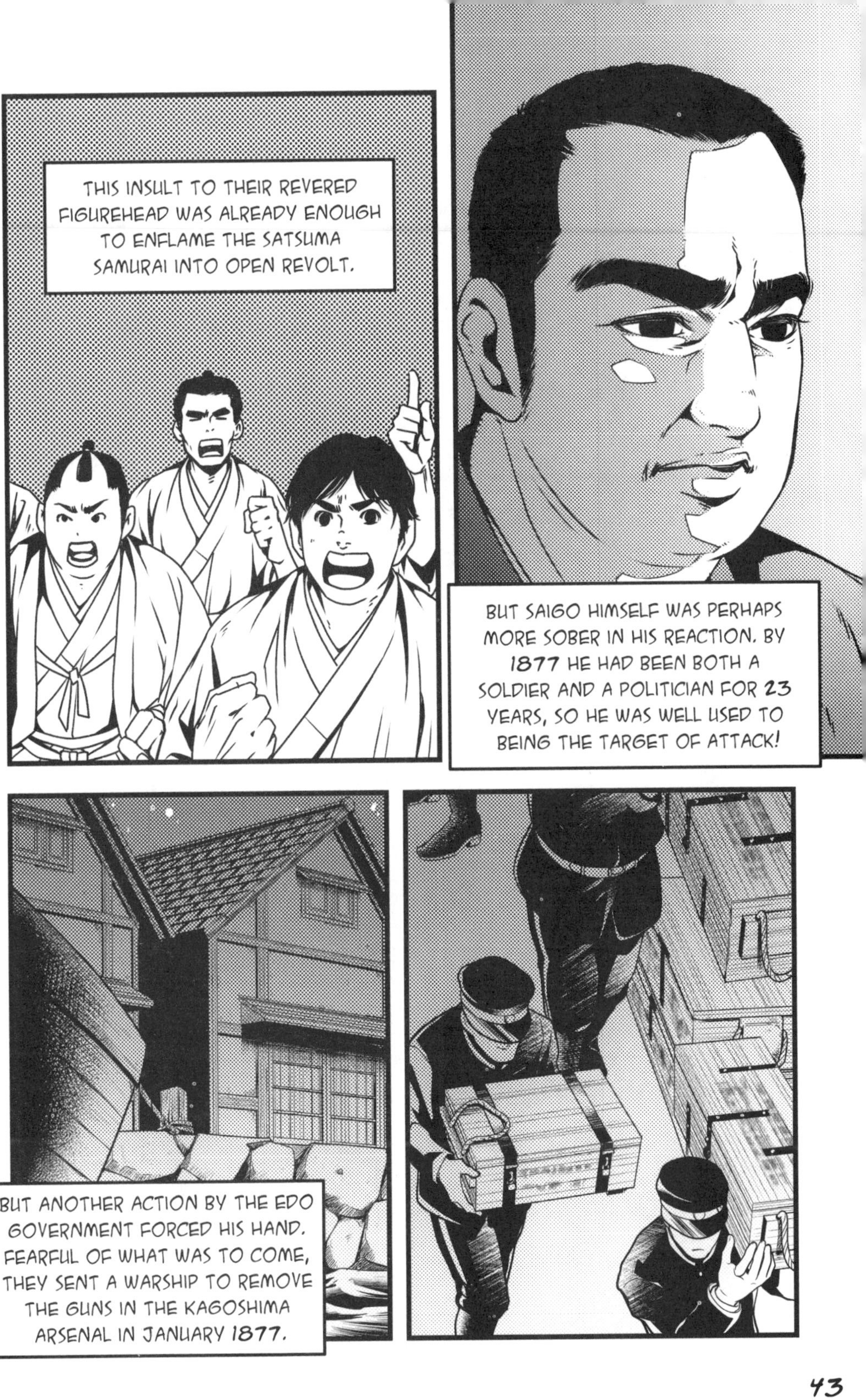
THIS INSULT TO THEIR REVERED FIGUREHEAD WAS ALREADY ENOUGH TO ENFLAME THE SATSUMA SAMURAI INTO OPEN REVOLT.
BUT SAIGO HIMSELF WAS PERHAPS MORE SOBER IN HIS REACTION. BY 1877 HE HAD BEEN BOTH A SOLDIER AND A POLITICIAN FOR 23 YEARS, SO HE WAS WELL USED TO BEING THE TARGET OF ATTACK!
BUT ANOTHER ACTION BY THE EDO GOVERNMENT FORCED HIS HAND. FEARFUL OF WHAT WAS TO COME, THEY SENT A WARSHIP TO REMOVE THE GUNS IN THE KAGOSHIMA ARSENAL IN JANUARY 1877.

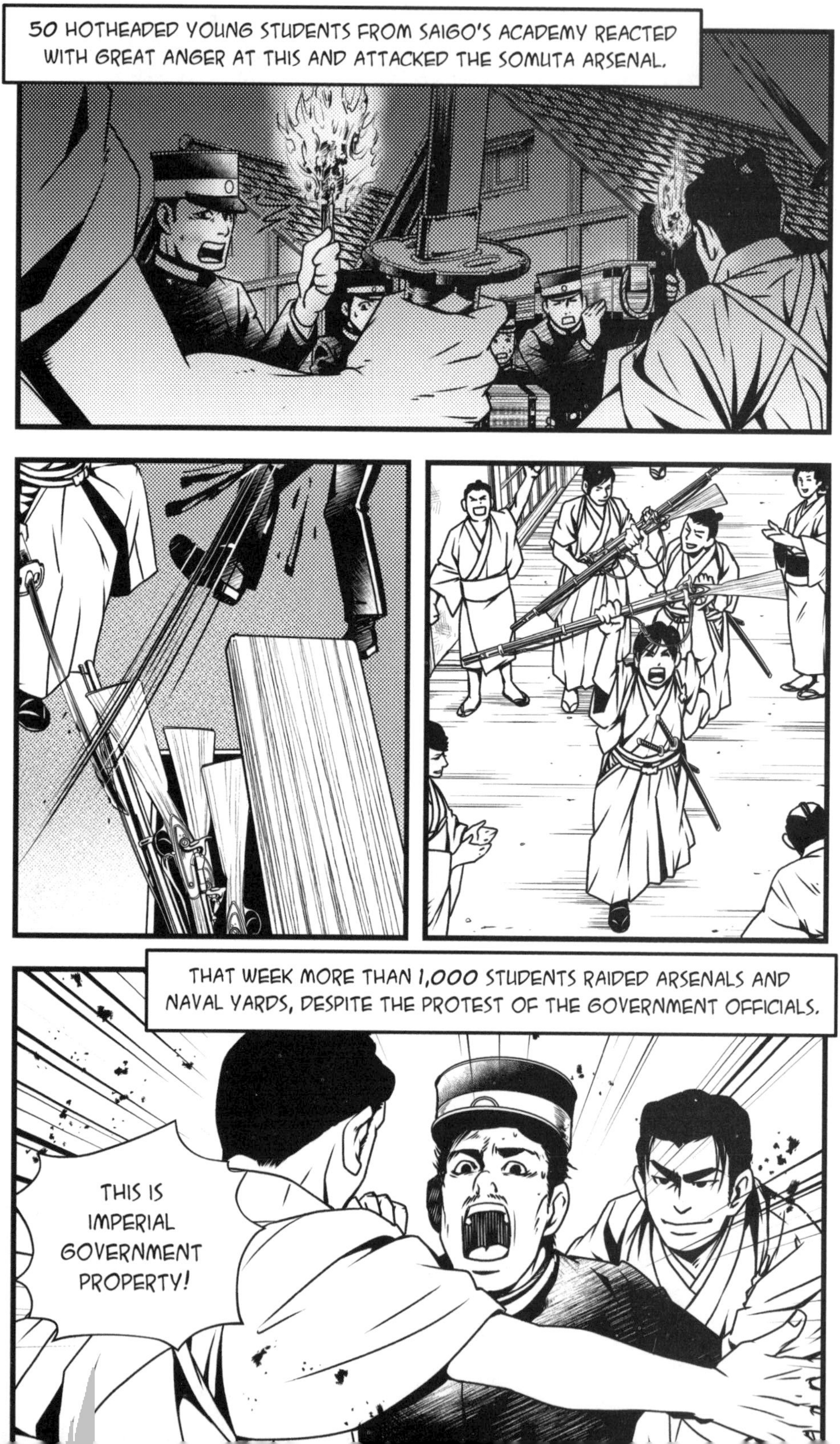
50 HOTHEADED YOUNG STUDENTS FROM SAIGO'S ACADEMY REACTED WITH GREAT ANGER AT THIS AND ATTACKED THE SOMUTA ARSENAL.
THAT WEEK MORE THAN 1,000 STUDENTS RAIDED ARSENALS AND NAVAL YARDS, DESPITE THE PROTEST OF THE GOVERNMENT OFFICIALS.
THIS IS IMPERIAL GOVERNMENT PROPERTY!

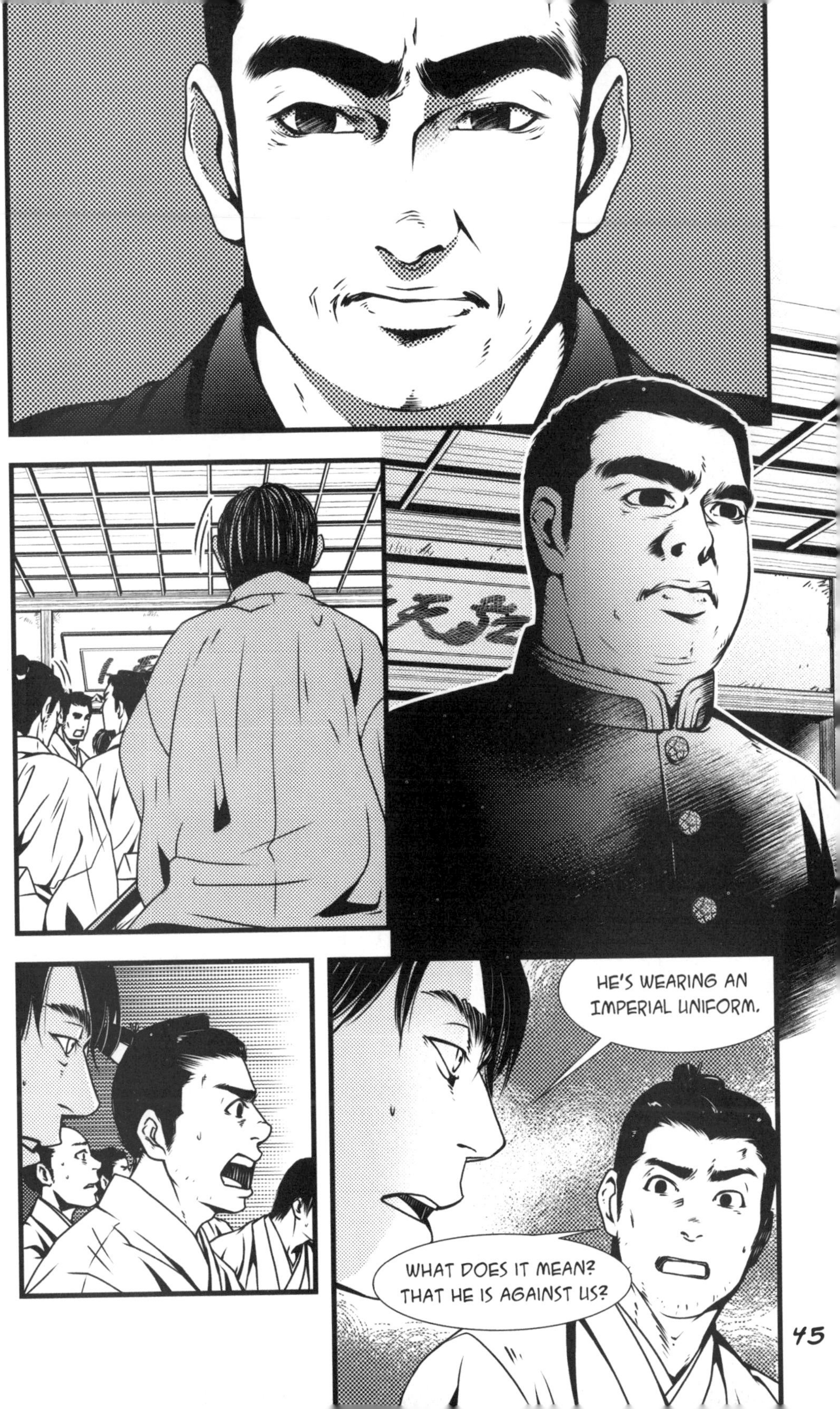
HE'S WEARING AN IMPERIAL UNIFORM.
WHAT DOES IT MEAN? THAT HE IS AGAINST US?

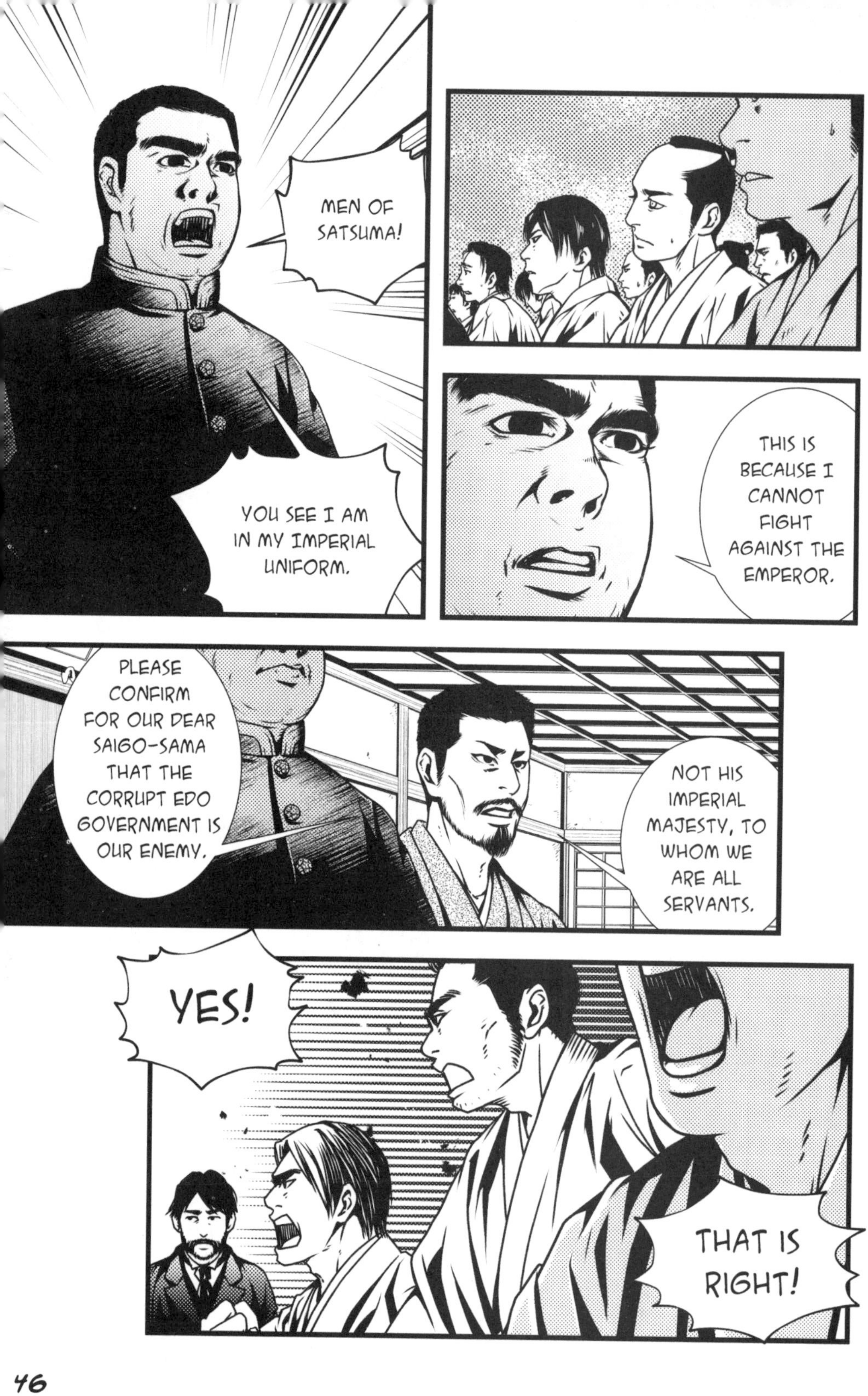
MEN OF SATSUMA!
YOU SEE I AM IN MY IMPERIAL UNIFORM.
THIS IS BECAUSE I CANNOT FIGHT AGAINST THE EMPEROR.
PLEASE CONFIRM FOR OUR DEAR SAIGO-SAMA THAT THE CORRUPT EDO GOVERNMENT IS OUR ENEMY.
NOT HIS IMPERIAL MAJESTY, TO WHOM WE ARE ALL SERVANTS.
YES!
THAT IS RIGHT!

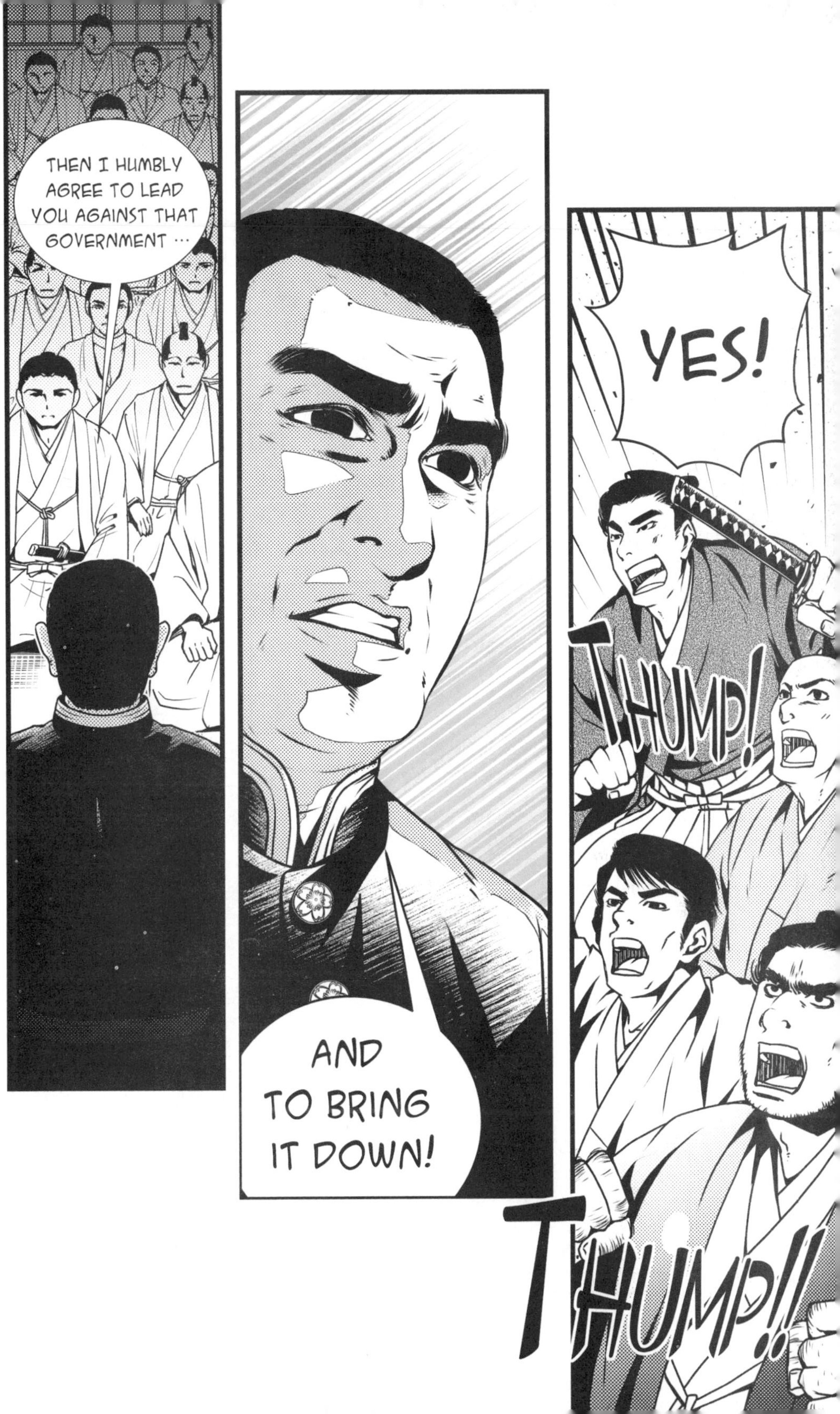
THEN I HUMBLY AGREE TO LEAD YOU AGAINST THAT GOVERNMENT ...
AND TO BRING IT DOWN!
YES!
THUMP!
THUMP!!

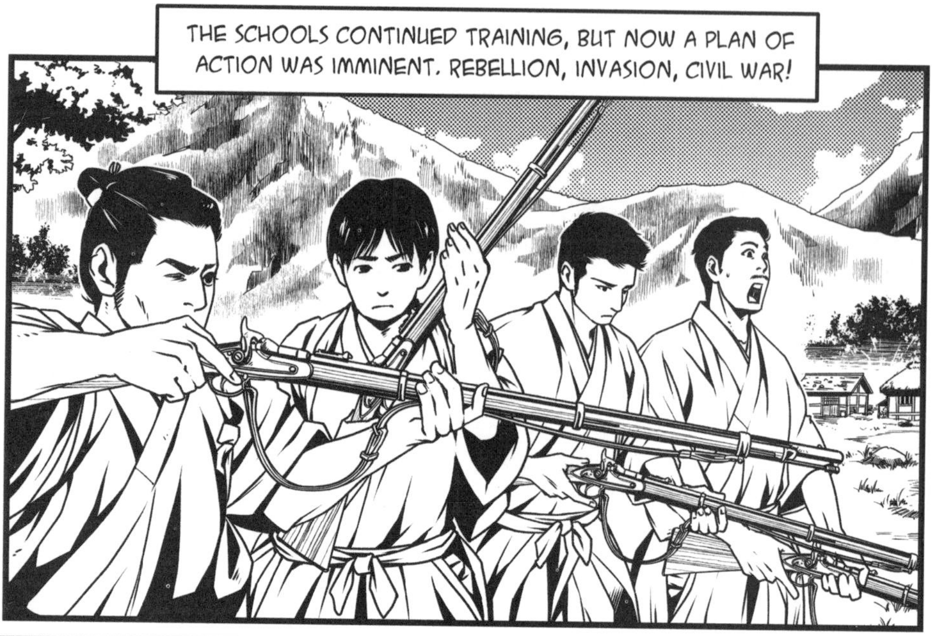
THE SCHOOLS CONTINUED TRAINING, BUT NOW A PLAN OF ACTION WAS IMMINENT. REBELLION, INVASION, CIVIL WAR!

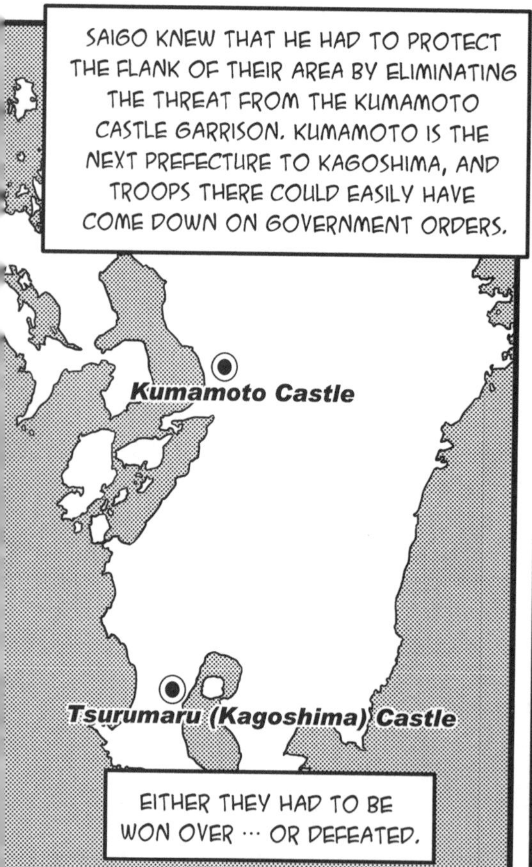
SAIGO KNEW THAT HE HAD TO PROTECT THE FLANK OF THEIR AREA BY ELIMINATING THE THREAT FROM THE KUMAMOTO CASTLE GARRISON. KUMAMOTO IS THE NEXT PREFECTURE TO KAGOSHIMA, AND TROOPS THERE COULD EASILY HAVE COME DOWN ON GOVERNMENT ORDERS.
Kumamoto Castle
Tsurumaru (Kagoshima) Castle
EITHER THEY HAD TO BE WON OVER … OR DEFEATED.

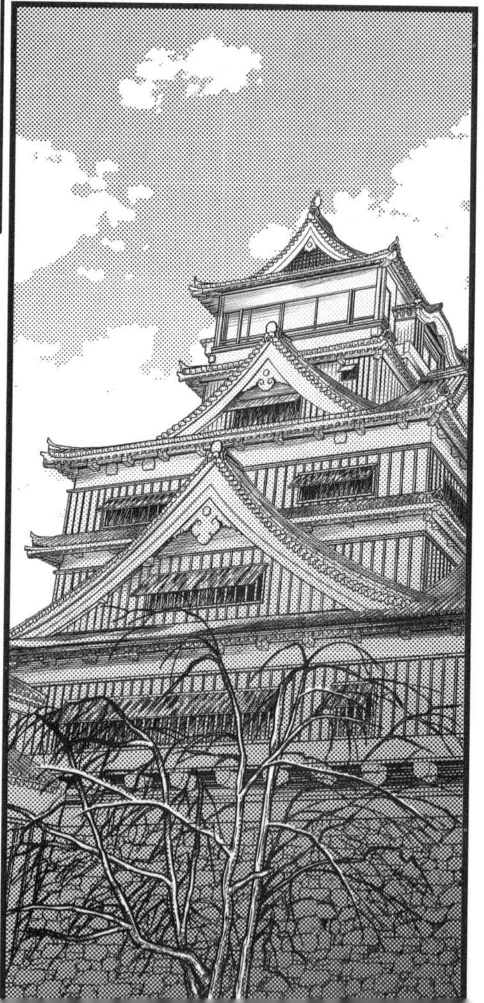

CHAPTER 3

REBELLION!

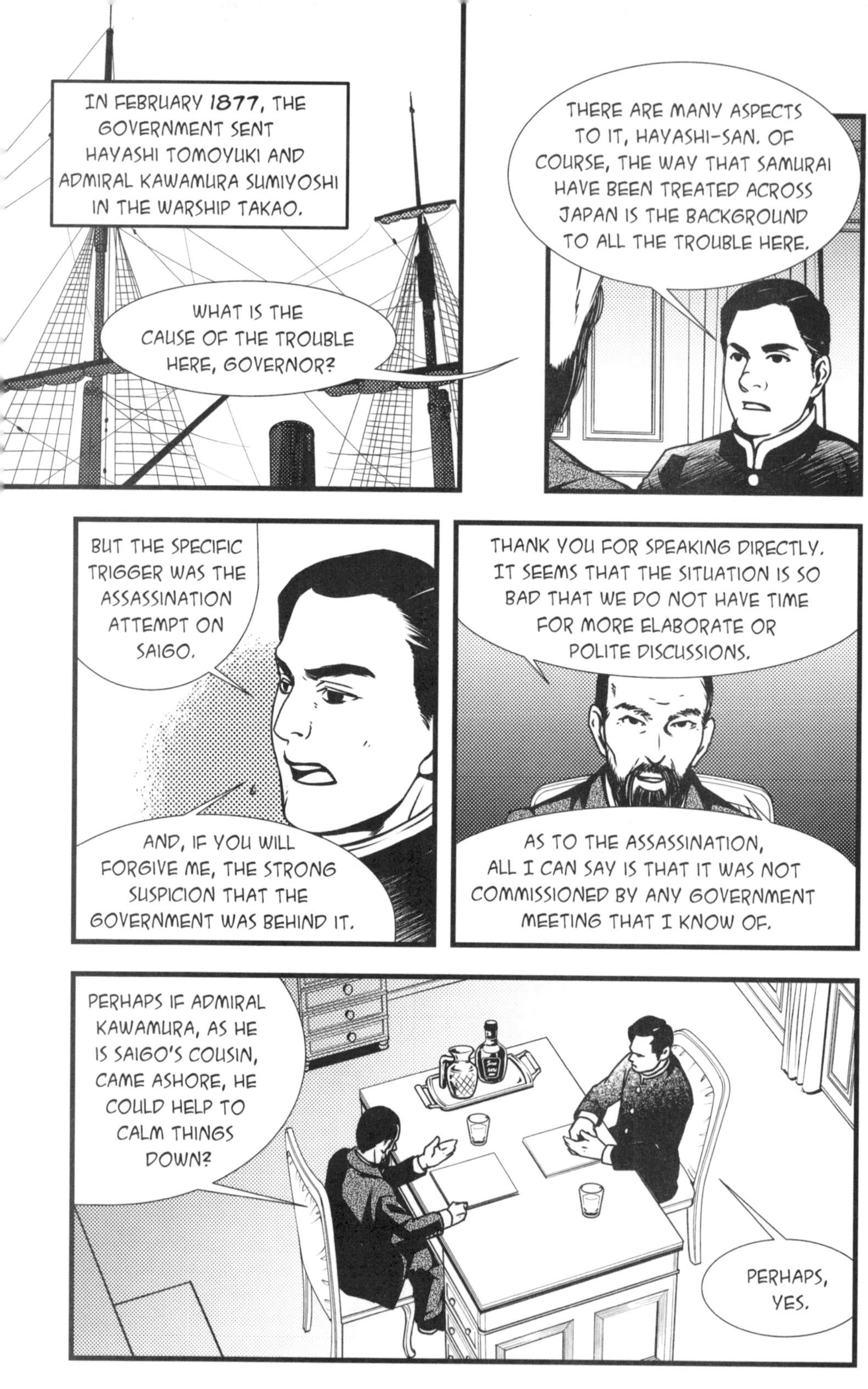
IN FEBRUARY 1877, THE GOVERNMENT SENT HAYASHI TOMOYUKI AND ADMIRAL KAWAMURA SUMIYOSHI IN THE WARSHIP TAKAO.
WHAT IS THE CAUSE OF THE TROUBLE HERE, GOVERNOR?
THERE ARE MANY ASPECTS TO IT, HAYASHI-SAN. OF COURSE, THE WAY THAT SAMURAI HAVE BEEN TREATED ACROSS JAPAN IS THE BACKGROUND TO ALL THE TROUBLE HERE.
BUT THE SPECIFIC TRIGGER WAS THE ASSASSINATION ATTEMPT ON SAIGO.
AND, IF YOU WILL FORGIVE ME, THE STRONG SUSPICION THAT THE GOVERNMENT WAS BEHIND IT.
THANK YOU FOR SPEAKING DIRECTLY. IT SEEMS THAT THE SITUATION IS SO BAD THAT WE DO NOT HAVE TIME FOR MORE ELABORATE OR POLITE DISCUSSIONS.
AS TO THE ASSASSINATION, ALL I CAN SAY IS THAT IT WAS NOT COMMISSIONED BY ANY GOVERNMENT MEETING THAT I KNOW OF.
PERHAPS IF ADMIRAL KAWAMURA, AS HE IS SAIGO'S COUSIN, CAME ASHORE, HE COULD HELP TO CALM THINGS DOWN?
PERHAPS, YES.

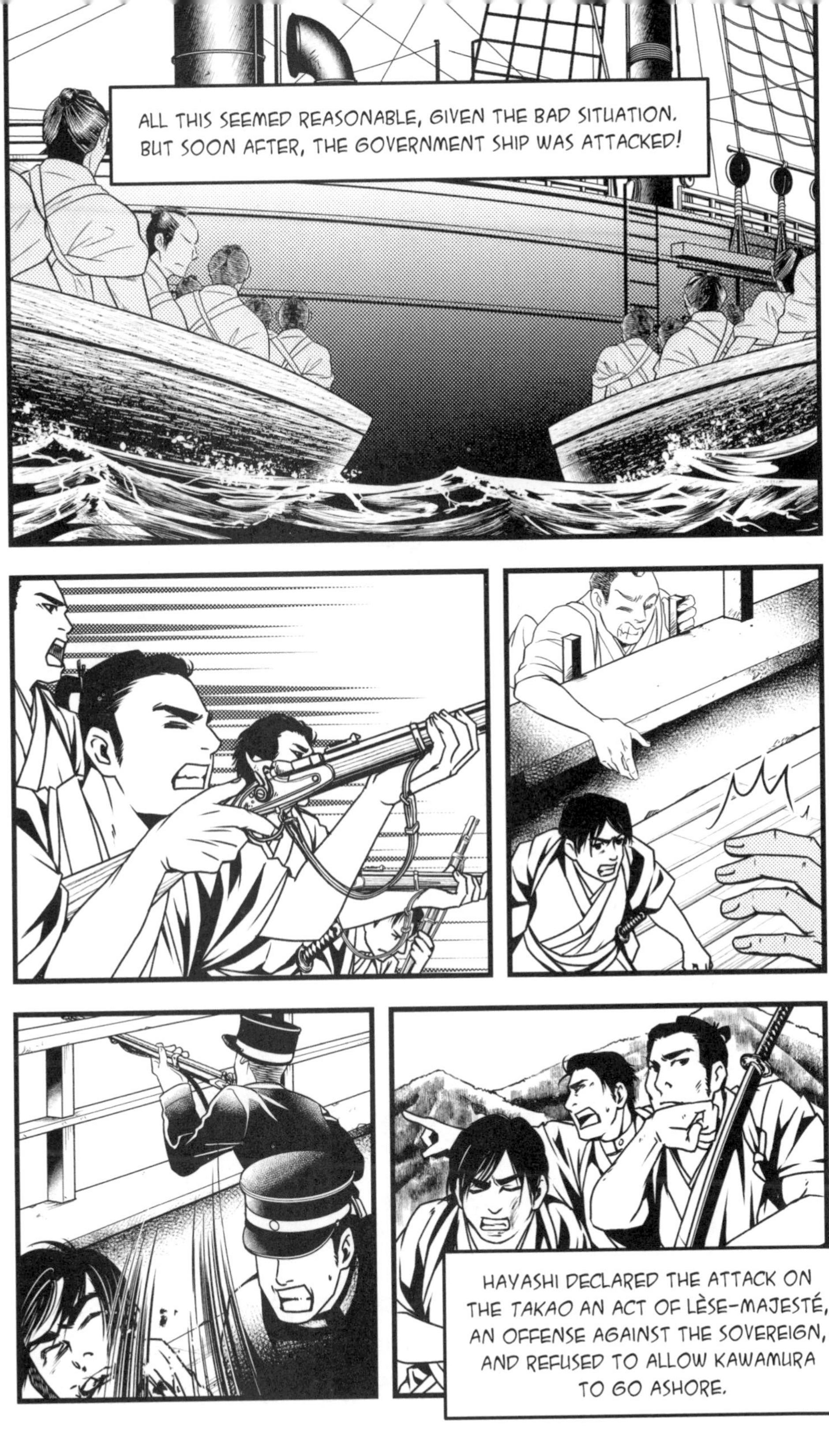
ALL THIS SEEMED REASONABLE, GIVEN THE BAD SITUATION. BUT SOON AFTER, THE GOVERNMENT SHIP WAS ATTACKED!
HAYASHI DECLARED THE ATTACK ON THE TAKAO AN ACT OF LÈSE-MAJESTÉ, AN OFFENSE AGAINST THE SOVEREIGN, AND REFUSED TO ALLOW KAWAMURA TO GO ASHORE.

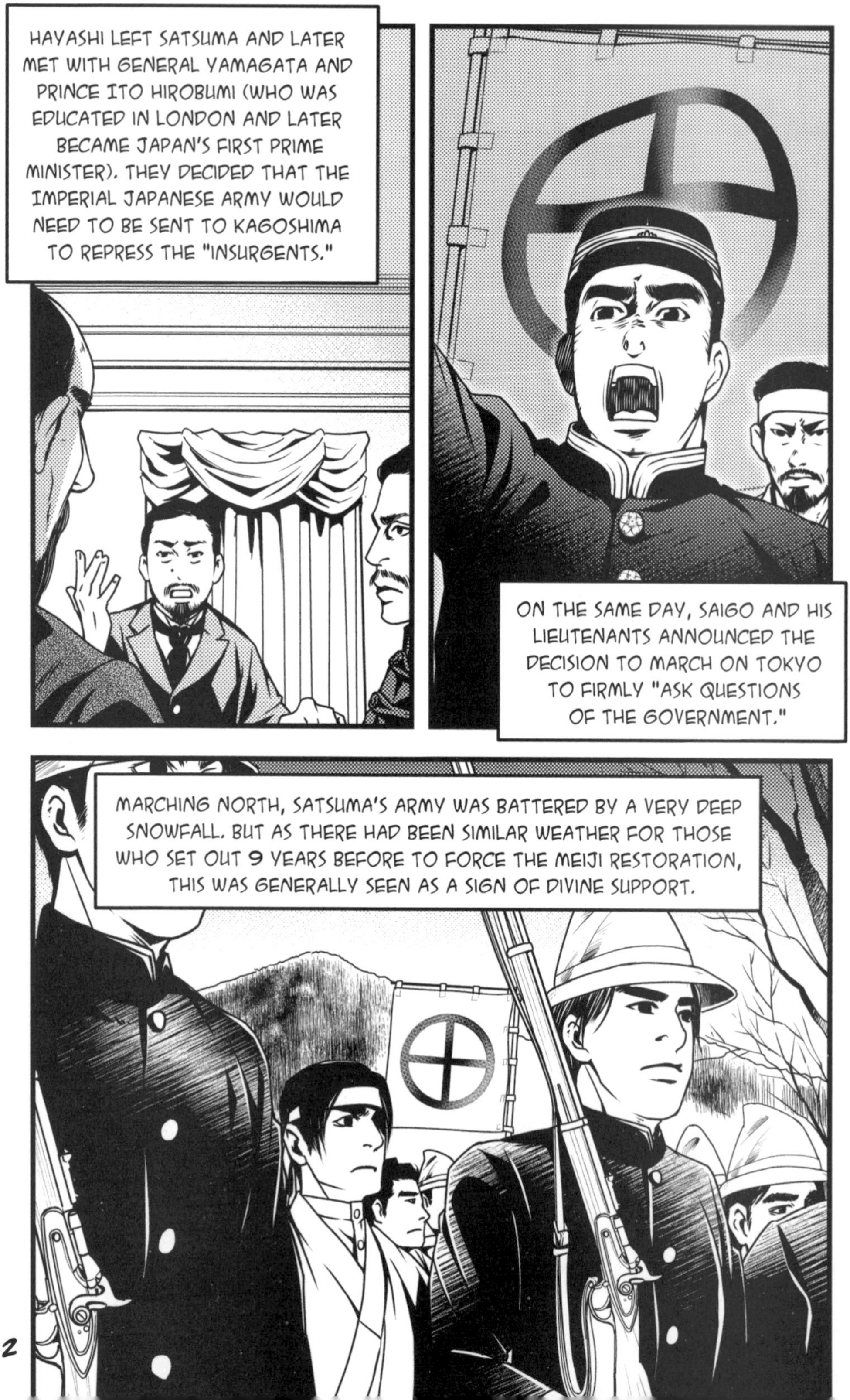
HAYASHI LEFT SATSUMA AND LATER MET WITH GENERAL YAMAGATA AND PRINCE ITO HIROBUMI (WHO WAS EDUCATED IN LONDON AND LATER BECAME JAPAN'S FIRST PRIME MINISTER). THEY DECIDED THAT THE IMPERIAL JAPANESE ARMY WOULD NEED TO BE SENT TO KAGOSHIMA TO REPRESS THE "INSURGENTS."
ON THE SAME DAY, SAIGO AND HIS LIEUTENANTS ANNOUNCED THE DECISION TO MARCH ON TOKYO TO FIRMLY "ASK QUESTIONS OF THE GOVERNMENT."
MARCHING NORTH, SATSUMA'S ARMY WAS BATTERED BY A VERY DEEP SNOWFALL. BUT AS THERE HAD BEEN SIMILAR WEATHER FOR THOSE WHO SET OUT 9 YEARS BEFORE TO FORCE THE MEIJI RESTORATION, THIS WAS GENERALLY SEEN AS A SIGN OF DIVINE SUPPORT.

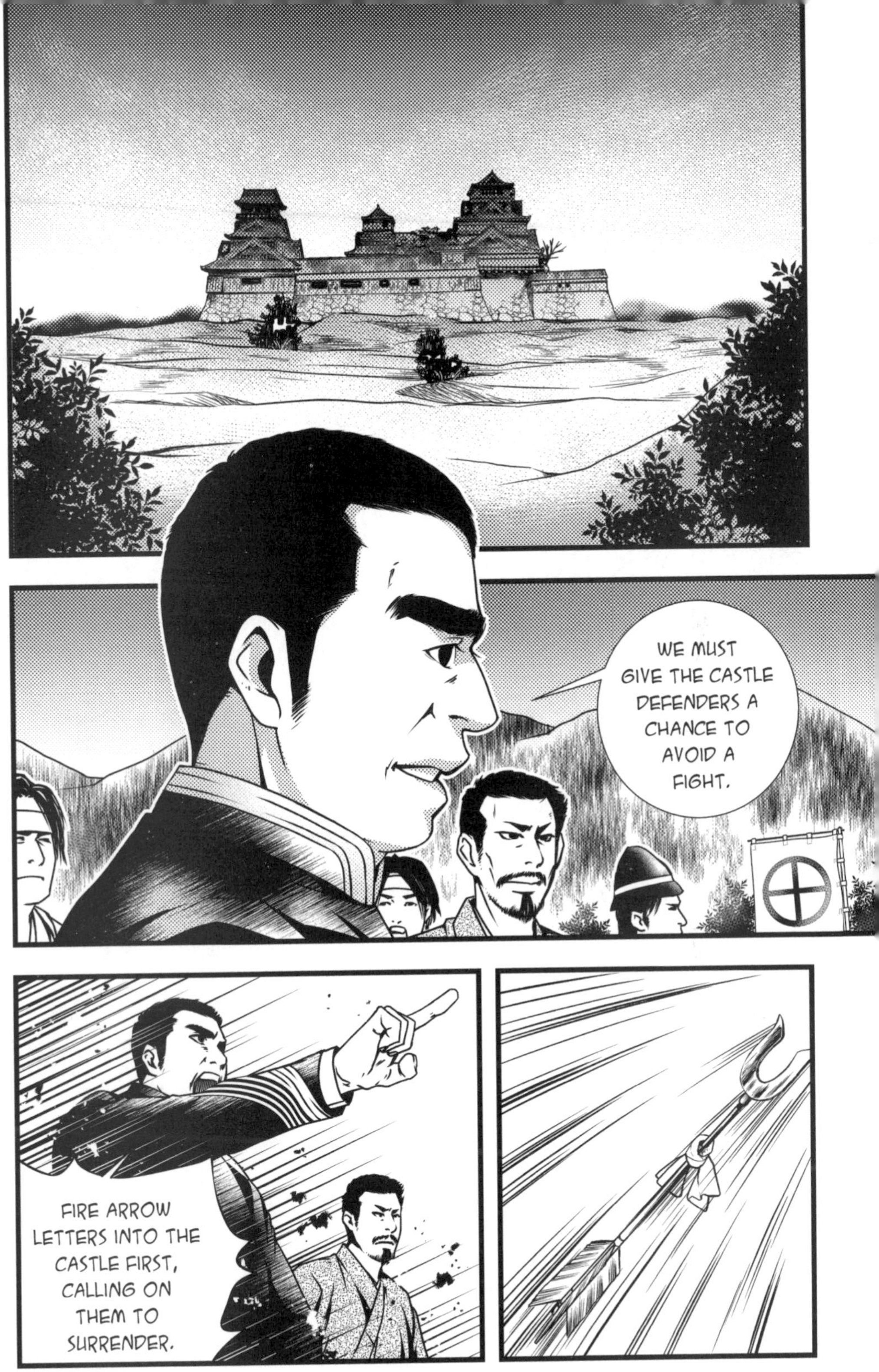
WE MUST GIVE THE CASTLE DEFENDERS A CHANCE TO AVOID A FIGHT.
FIRE ARROW LETTERS INTO THE CASTLE FIRST, CALLING ON THEM TO SURRENDER.

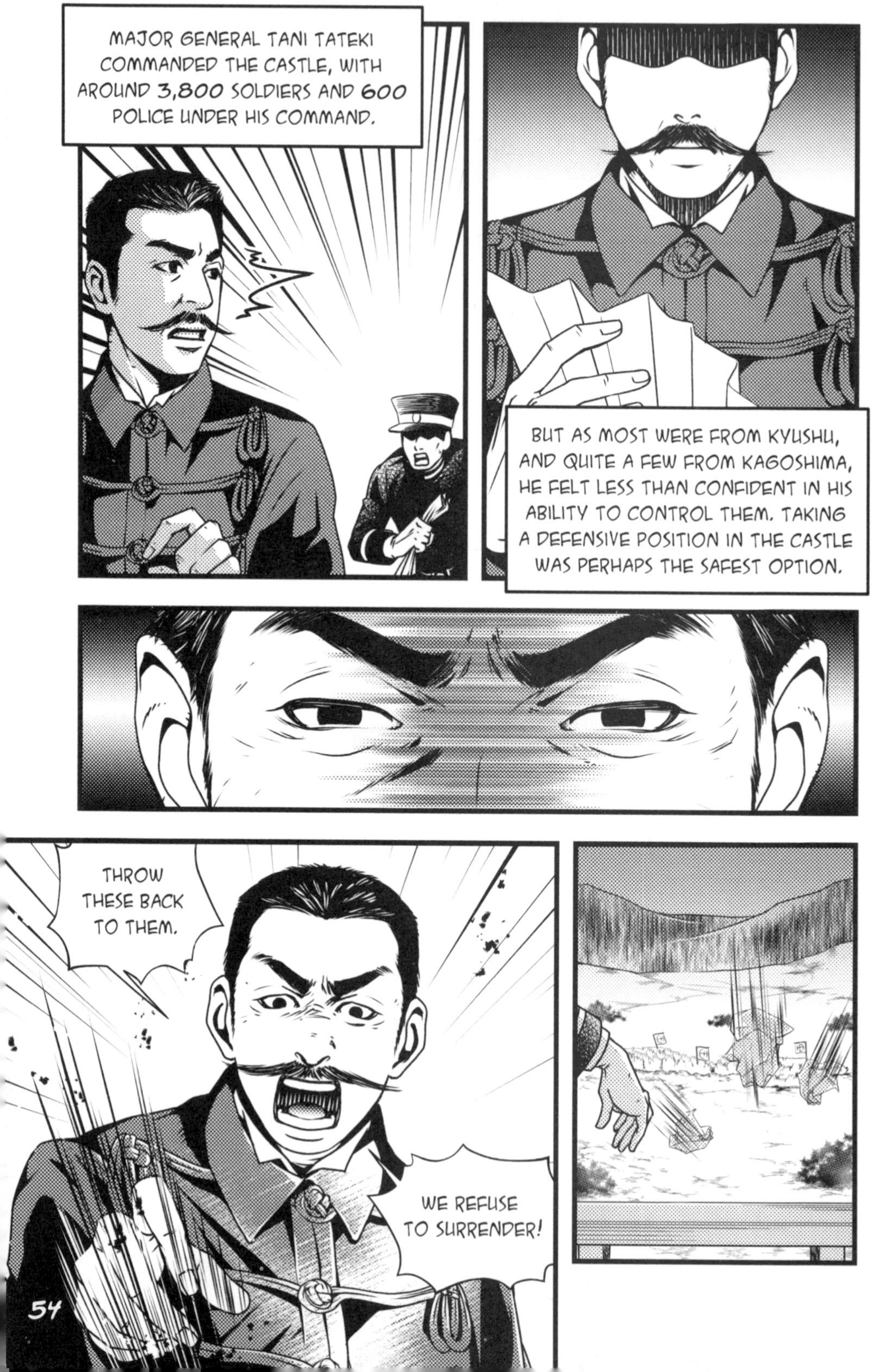
MAJOR GENERAL TANI TATEKI COMMANDED THE CASTLE, WITH AROUND 3,800 SOLDIERS AND 600 POLICE UNDER HIS COMMAND.
BUT AS MOST WERE FROM KYUSHU, AND QUITE A FEW FROM KAGOSHIMA, HE FELT LESS THAN CONFIDENT IN HIS ABILITY TO CONTROL THEM. TAKING A DEFENSIVE POSITION IN THE CASTLE WAS PERHAPS THE SAFEST OPTION.
THROW THESE BACK TO THEM.
WE REFUSE TO SURRENDER!

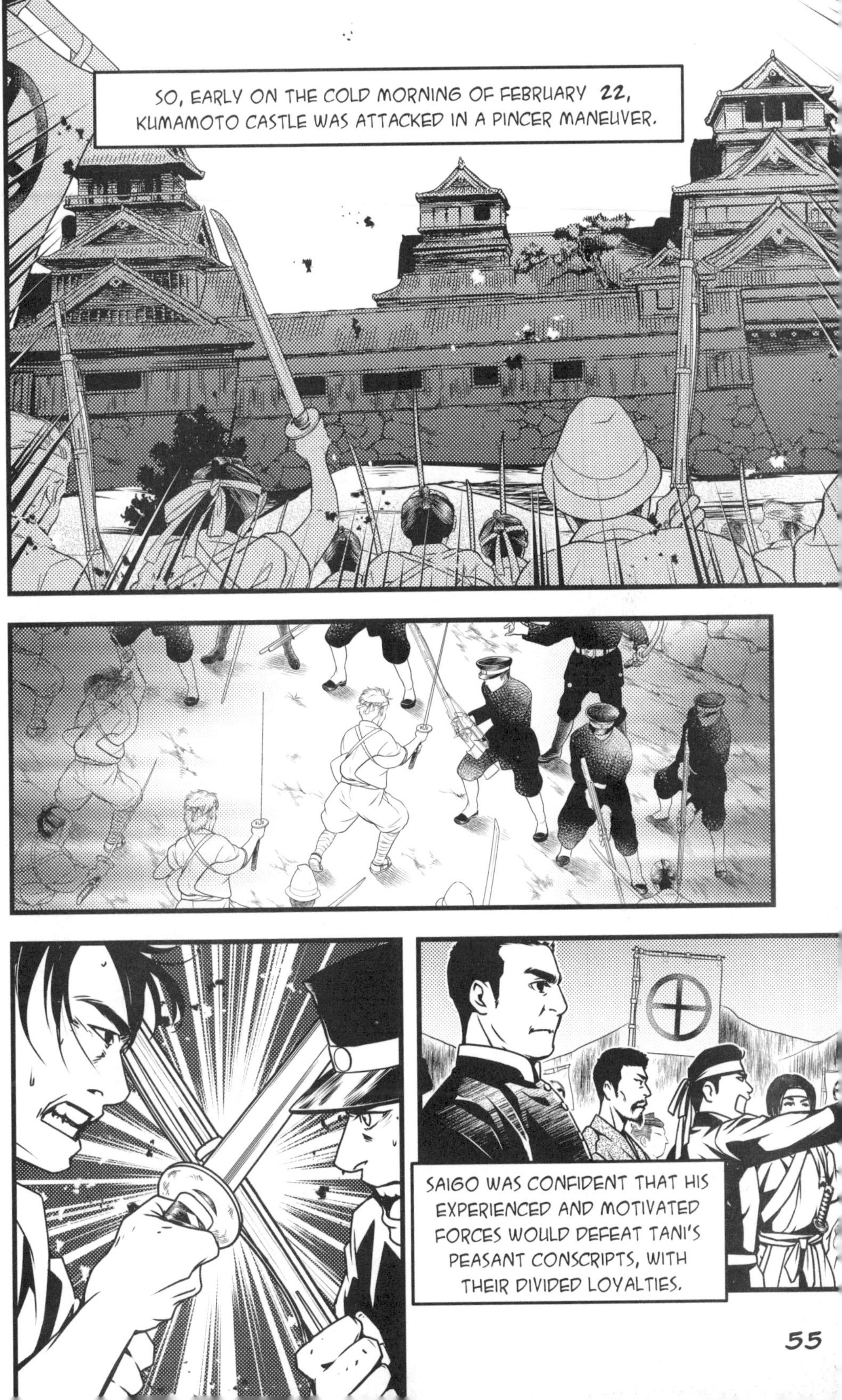
SO, EARLY ON THE COLD MORNING OF FEBRUARY 22, KUMAMOTO CASTLE WAS ATTACKED IN A PINCER MANEUVER.
SAIGO WAS CONFIDENT THAT HIS EXPERIENCED AND MOTIVATED FORCES WOULD DEFEAT TANI'S PEASANT CONSCRIPTS, WITH THEIR DIVIDED LOYALTIES.

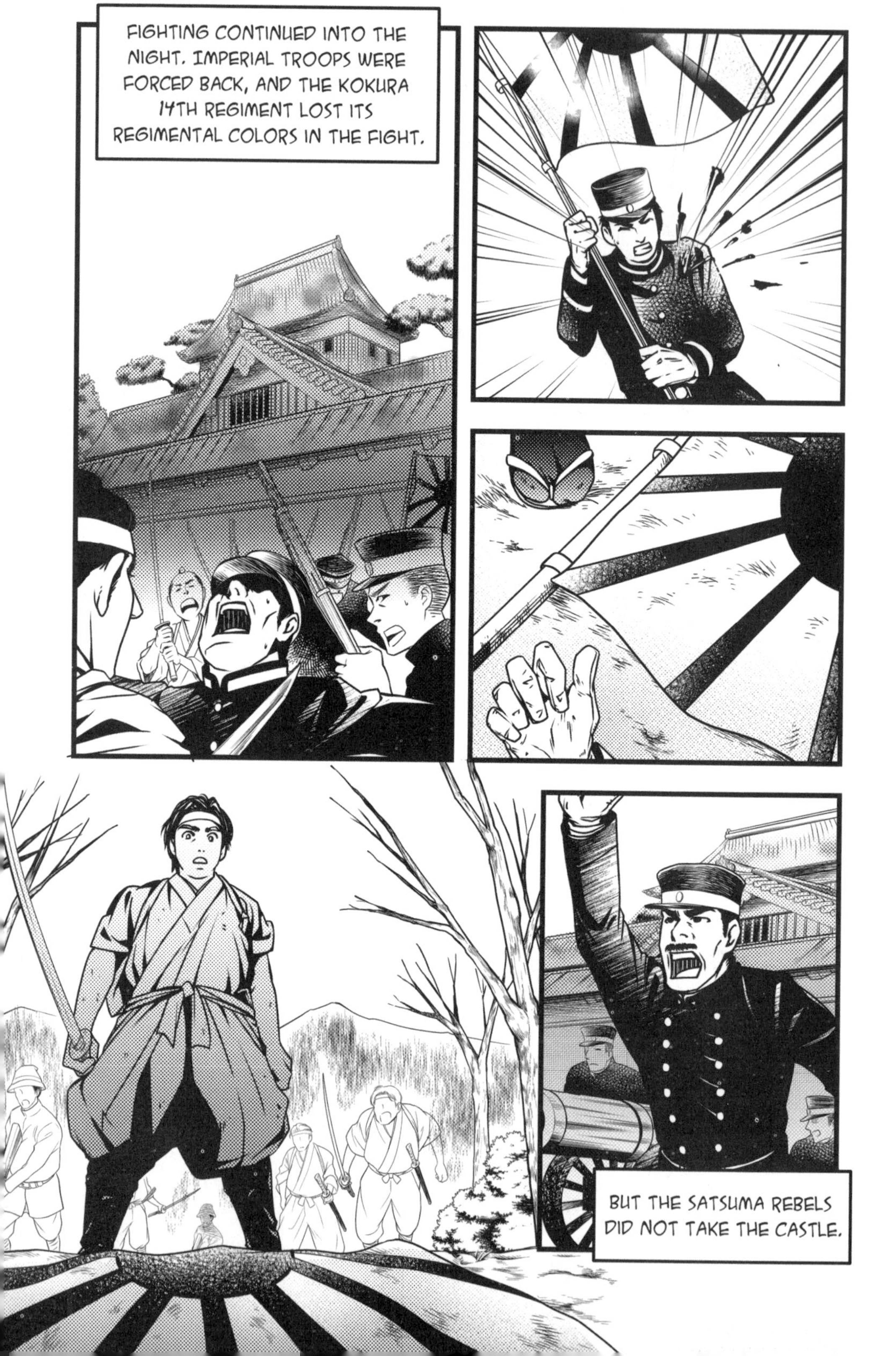
FIGHTING CONTINUED INTO THE NIGHT. IMPERIAL TROOPS WERE FORCED BACK, AND THE KOKURA 14TH REGIMENT LOST ITS REGIMENTAL COLORS IN THE FIGHT.
BUT THE SATSUMA REBELS DID NOT TAKE THE CASTLE.

THE GOVERNMENT'S CONSCRIPT ARMY IS FIGHTING MORE BRAVELY THAN I IMAGINED THEY WOULD. THEIR TRAINING IS SURPRISINGLY GOOD.

YES. WE ARE WINNING, BUT THEY ARE PUTTING UP A GOOD FIGHT.

IT'S A PITY THEY DID NOT SURRENDER THIS MORNING.

I EXPECTED THAT THE SIGHT OF SO MANY ARMED SAMURAI WOULD FRIGHTEN THEM.

ONE OF SAIGO'S LIEUTENANTS, KIRINO TOSHIAKI, WAS ALSO PRESENT:

ON THE OTHER HAND, MANY KUMAMOTO SAMURAI ARE COMING TO OUR SIDE.

YES, KIRINO ... OUR NUMBERS ARE SWELLING.

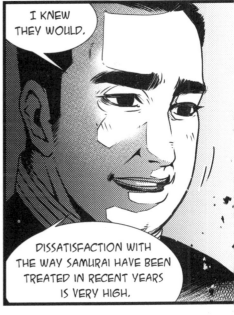

I KNEW THEY WOULD.

DISSATISFACTION WITH THE WAY SAMURAI HAVE BEEN TREATED IN RECENT YEARS IS VERY HIGH.

I'M SURE OUR ARMY WILL BECOME LARGER AND LARGER THE FARTHER NORTH WE MOVE.

BY THE TIME WE REACH OSAKA, OR PERHAPS EVEN BY HIROSHIMA,

THERE WILL BE SO MANY OF US THAT WE WILL BE UNSTOPPABLE.

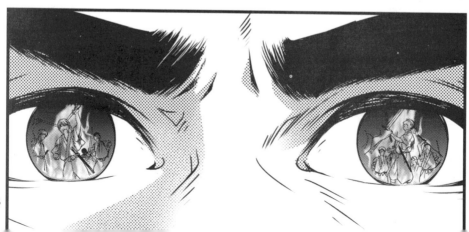

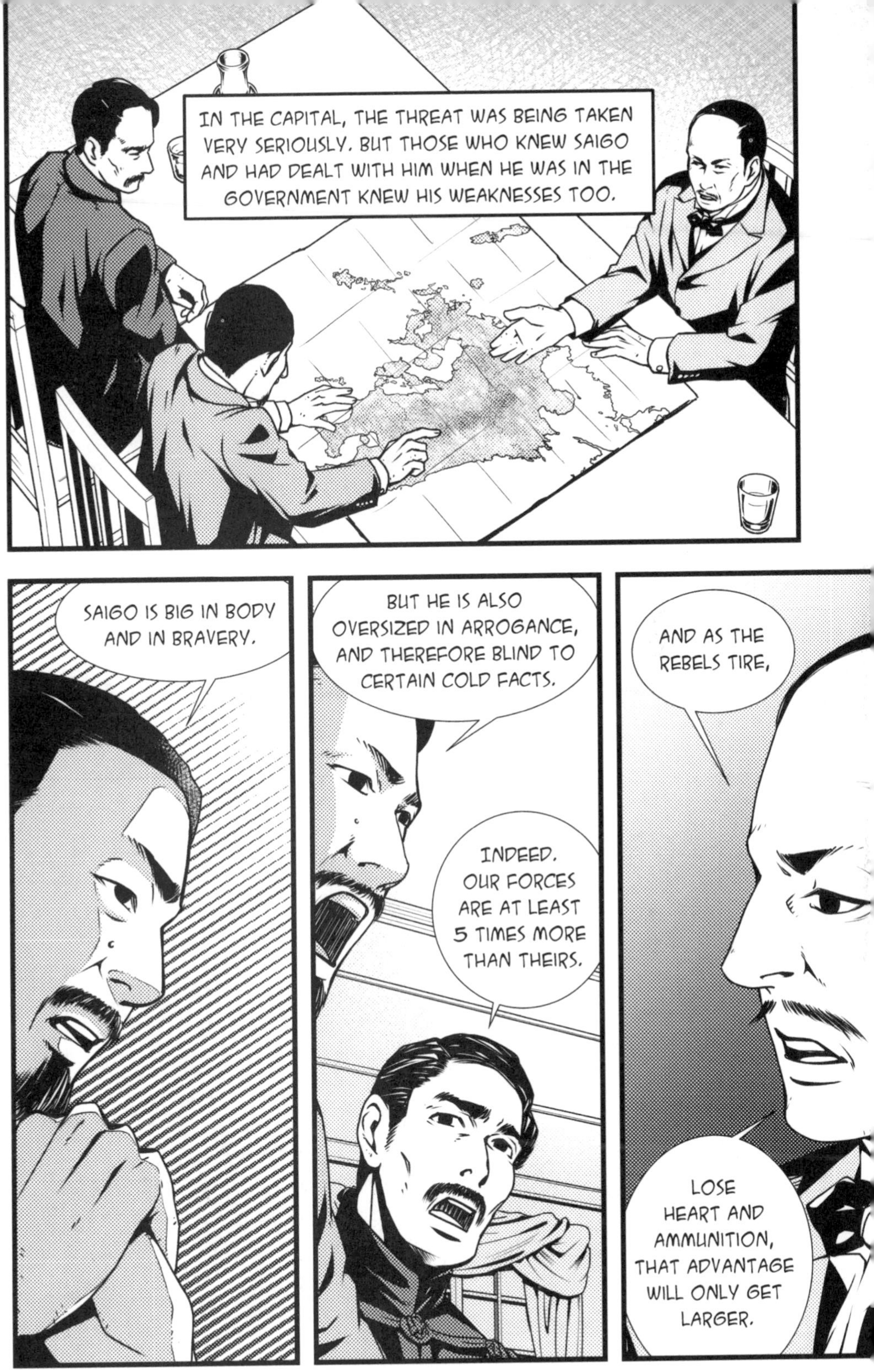
IN THE CAPITAL, THE THREAT WAS BEING TAKEN VERY SERIOUSLY. BUT THOSE WHO KNEW SAIGO AND HAD DEALT WITH HIM WHEN HE WAS IN THE GOVERNMENT KNEW HIS WEAKNESSES TOO.
SAIGO IS BIG IN BODY AND IN BRAVERY.
BUT HE IS ALSO OVERSIZED IN ARROGANCE, AND THEREFORE BLIND TO CERTAIN COLD FACTS.
INDEED. OUR FORCES ARE AT LEAST 5 TIMES MORE THAN THEIRS.
AND AS THE REBELS TIRE,
LOSE HEART AND AMMUNITION, THAT ADVANTAGE WILL ONLY GET LARGER.

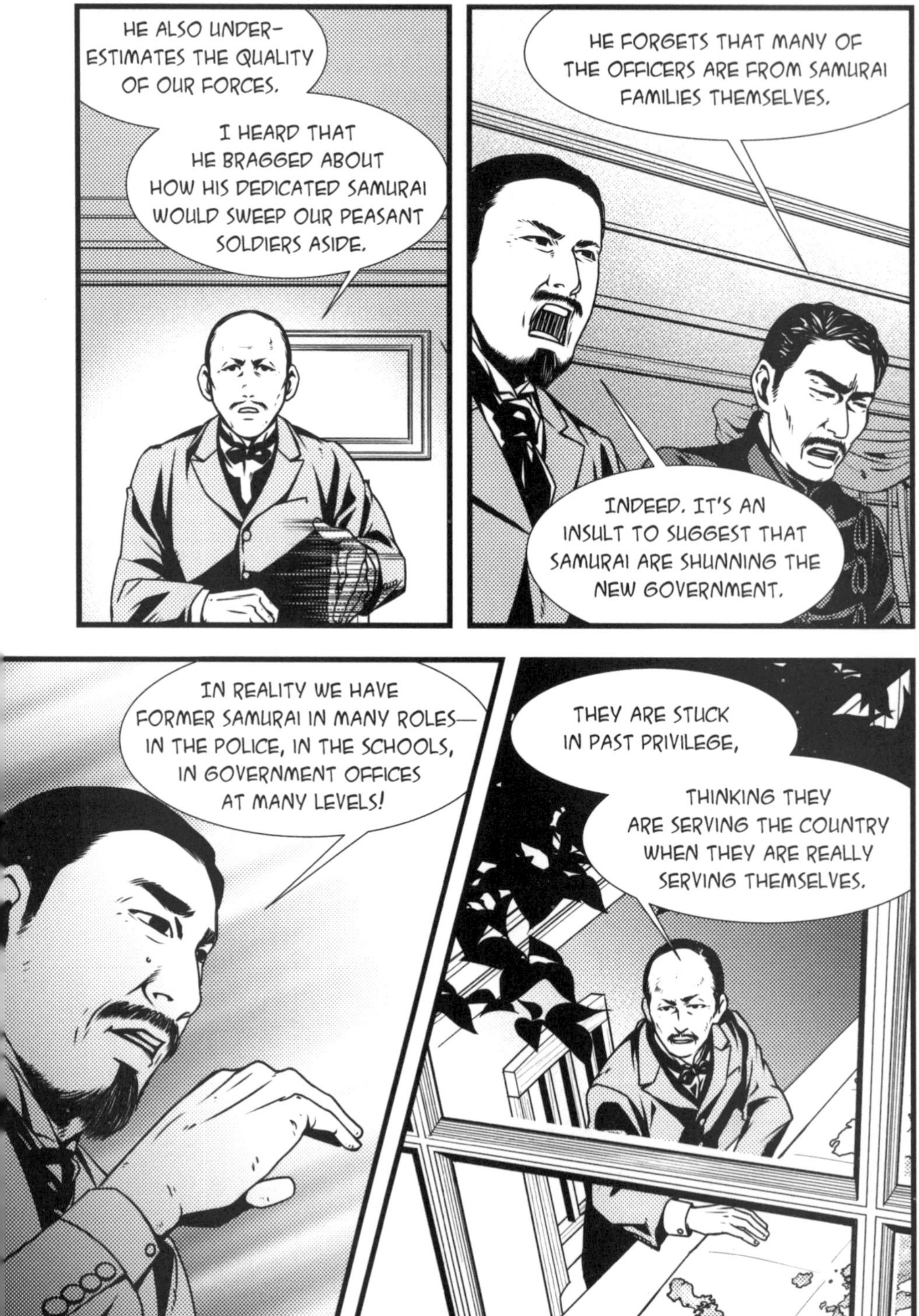
HE ALSO UNDER-ESTIMATES THE QUALITY OF OUR FORCES.
I HEARD THAT HE BRAGGED ABOUT HOW HIS DEDICATED SAMURAI WOULD SWEEP OUR PEASANT SOLDIERS ASIDE.
HE FORGETS THAT MANY OF THE OFFICERS ARE FROM SAMURAI FAMILIES THEMSELVES.
INDEED. IT'S AN INSULT TO SUGGEST THAT SAMURAI ARE SHUNNING THE NEW GOVERNMENT.
IN REALITY WE HAVE FORMER SAMURAI IN MANY ROLES— IN THE POLICE, IN THE SCHOOLS, IN GOVERNMENT OFFICES AT MANY LEVELS!
THEY ARE STUCK IN PAST PRIVILEGE,
THINKING THEY ARE SERVING THE COUNTRY WHEN THEY ARE REALLY SERVING THEMSELVES.

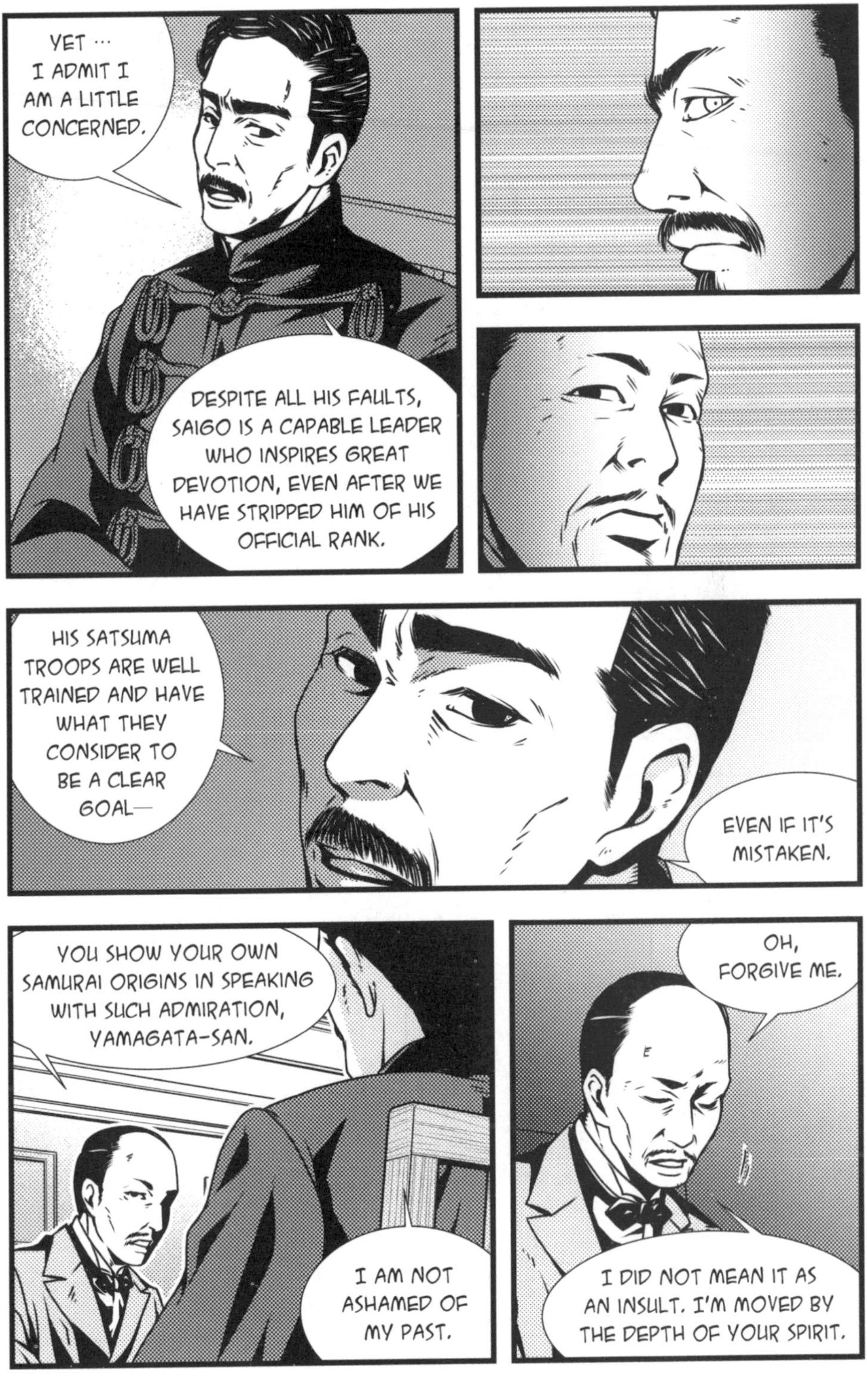
YET ... I ADMIT I AM A LITTLE CONCERNED.
DESPITE ALL HIS FAULTS, SAIGO IS A CAPABLE LEADER WHO INSPIRES GREAT DEVOTION, EVEN AFTER WE HAVE STRIPPED HIM OF HIS OFFICIAL RANK.
HIS SATSUMA TROOPS ARE WELL TRAINED AND HAVE WHAT THEY CONSIDER TO BE A CLEAR GOAL—
EVEN IF IT'S MISTAKEN.
YOU SHOW YOUR OWN SAMURAI ORIGINS IN SPEAKING WITH SUCH ADMIRATION, YAMAGATA-SAN.
I AM NOT ASHAMED OF MY PAST.
OH, FORGIVE ME.
I DID NOT MEAN IT AS AN INSULT. I'M MOVED BY THE DEPTH OF YOUR SPIRIT.

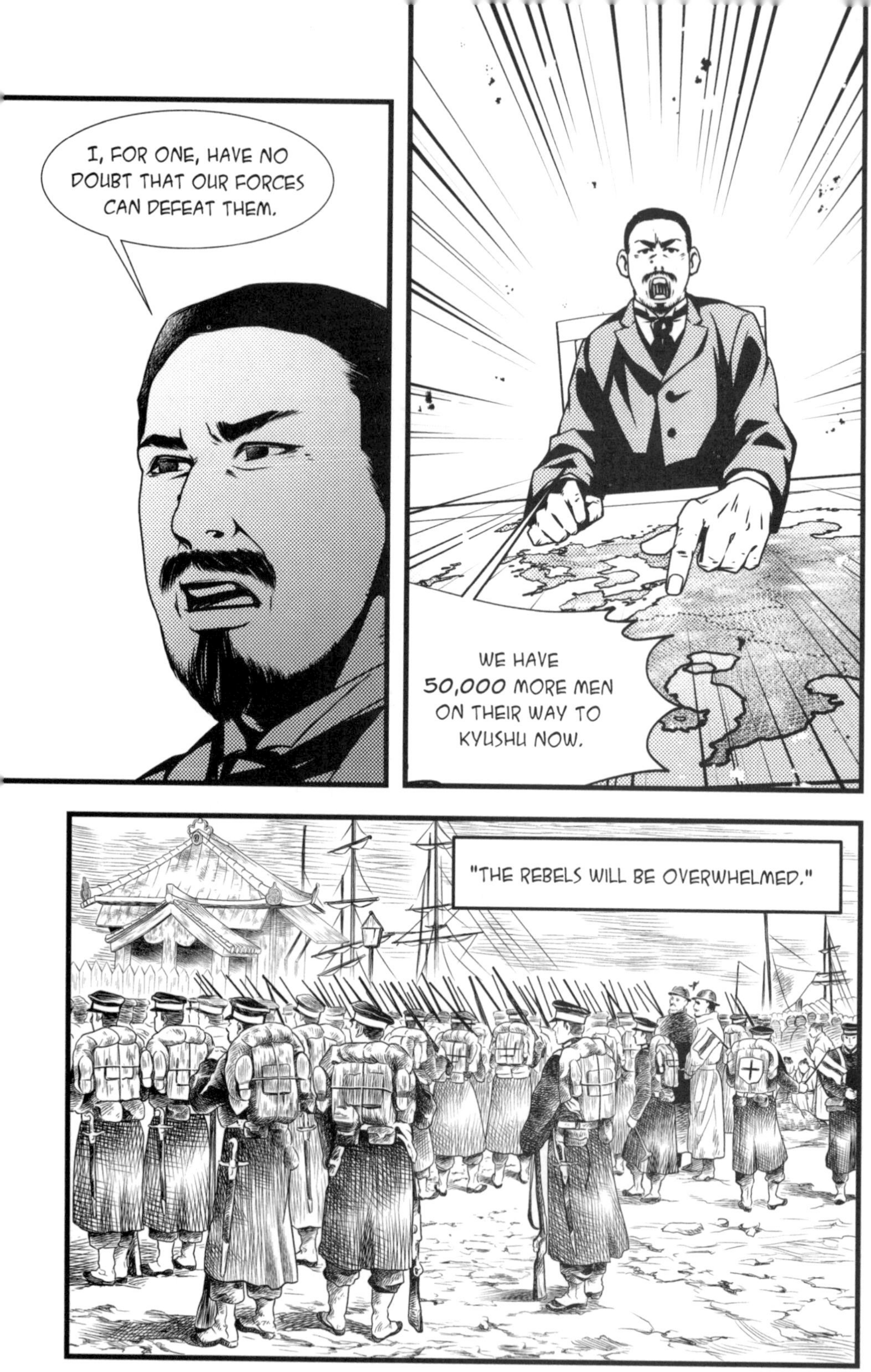
I, FOR ONE, HAVE NO DOUBT THAT OUR FORCES CAN DEFEAT THEM.
WE HAVE 50,000 MORE MEN ON THEIR WAY TO KYUSHU NOW.
"THE REBELS WILL BE OVERWHELMED."

THE REBELLION AFFECTED ASPECTS OF LIFE IN JAPAN BEYOND JUST THE MILITARY. GOVERNMENT SPENDING WAS HIGH AND PLACED A GREAT STRAIN ON THE NEW ADMINISTRATION AND THE NEW SHIPPING AND RAIL TRANSPORTATION SYSTEMS.

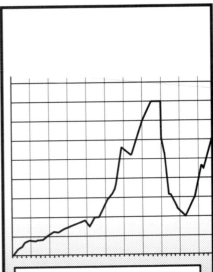

THIS LED TO SERIOUS INFLATION, DECREASED LAND VALUES, AND LESS TAX REVENUE. THEREFORE THE WAR LED TO FURTHER PRESSURE FOR POLITICAL AND ECONOMIC REFORM.

THE REBELS PRINTED SPECIAL MONEY IN KAGOSHIMA TO SUBSIDIZE THEIR FIGHT.

AND THE TELEGRAPH WAS WIDELY USED IN JAPAN FOR THE FIRST TIME, BY THE GOVERNMENT COMMUNICATING WITH THEIR FORCES. BRITISH ENGINEERS ERECTED 900 MILES OF TELEGRAPH LINES IN 1871, AND THE JAPANESE, ORIGINALLY BAFFLED BY THIS MIRACULOUS TECHNOLOGY, NOW SAW ITS VALUE.

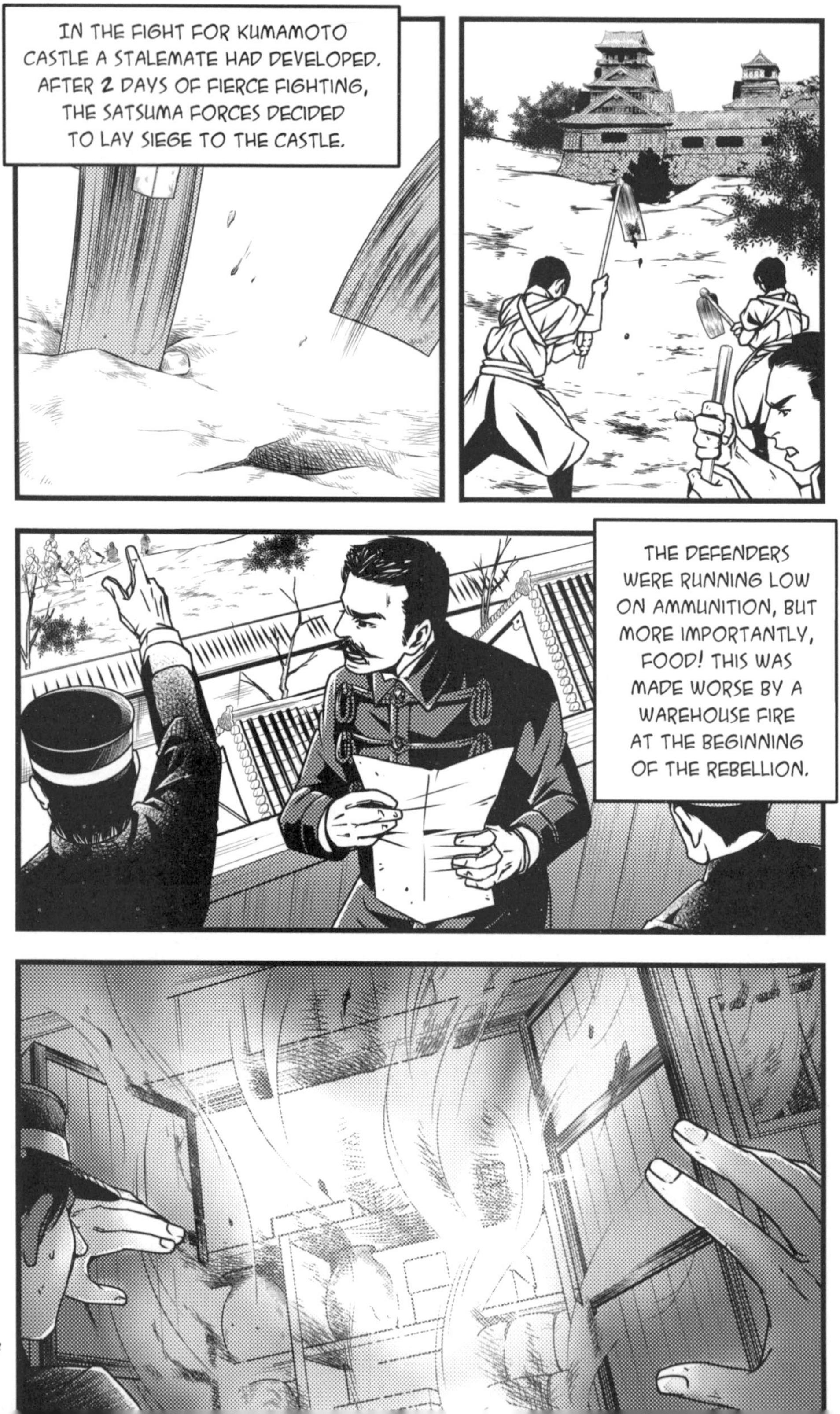
IN THE FIGHT FOR KUMAMOTO CASTLE A STALEMATE HAD DEVELOPED. AFTER 2 DAYS OF FIERCE FIGHTING, THE SATSUMA FORCES DECIDED TO LAY SIEGE TO THE CASTLE.
THE DEFENDERS WERE RUNNING LOW ON AMMUNITION, BUT MORE IMPORTANTLY, FOOD! THIS WAS MADE WORSE BY A WAREHOUSE FIRE AT THE BEGINNING OF THE REBELLION.

AS THE REBELS HAD HOPED, MANY FORMER SAMURAI FROM KUMAMOTO AND HITOYOSHI JOINED THEM. AT THEIR PEAK, THERE WERE AROUND **20,000** ENERGETIC, EXPERIENCED, EMBITTERED SAMURAI.

ENOUGH TO MAKE ANY CORRUPT GOVERNMENT SHUDDER.

BUT AS THE DARK WINTER THAWED INTO EARLY SPRING, NEW POSSIBILITY BLOOMED, AND THE SITUATION CHANGED ...

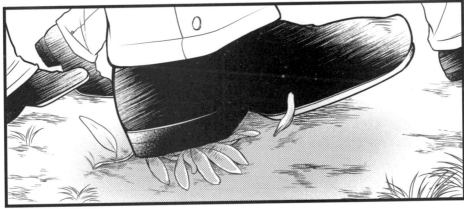

FIRSTLY, GENERAL YAMAGATA ORDERED A FRONTAL ASSAULT FROM TABARUZAKA, NORTH OF KUMAMOTO, ON MARCH 4.

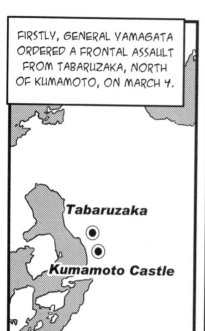

Tabaruzaka

Kumamoto Castle

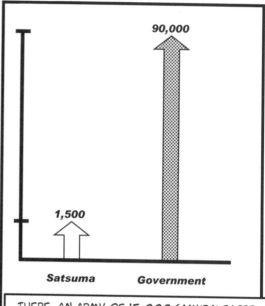

90,000

1,500

Satsuma　　　**Government**

THERE, AN ARMY OF 15,000 SAMURAI FACED THE IMPERIAL ARMY'S 9TH INFANTRY BRIGADE, WHICH WAS 6 TIMES LARGER, AT 90,000 MEN.

AS HISTORY HAS SHOWN, SOMETIMES A MUCH SMALLER ARMY CAN HOLD OUT OR EVEN DEFEAT A LARGER ONE, IF THEY ARE MOTIVATED, WELL LED, WELL EQUIPPED, WELL TRAINED ··· OR JUST LUCKY.

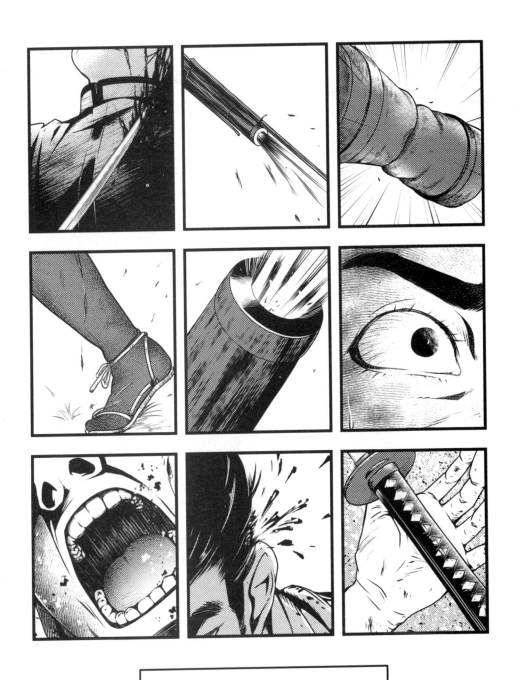

BUT THIS WAS NOT ONE OF THOSE TIMES …

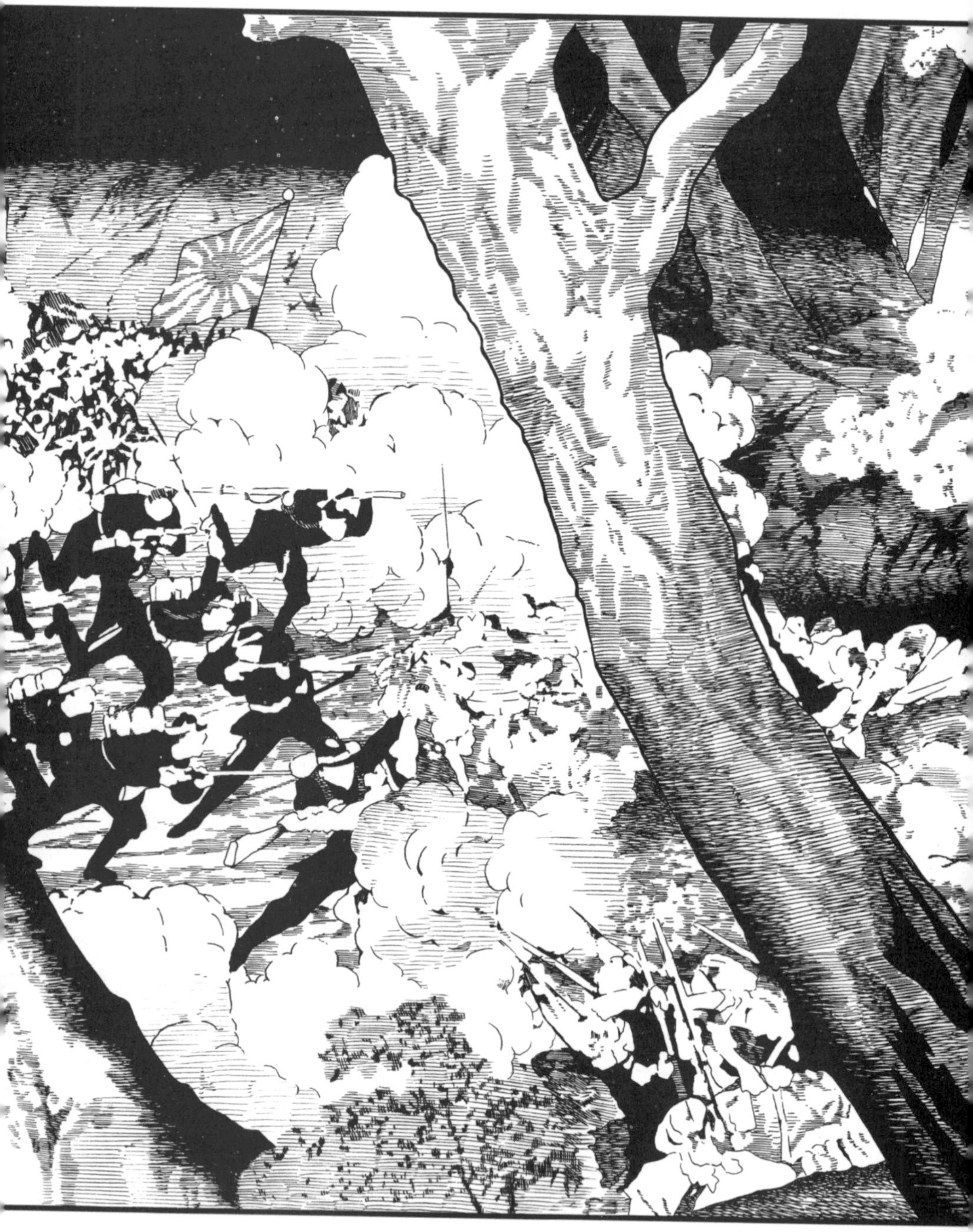

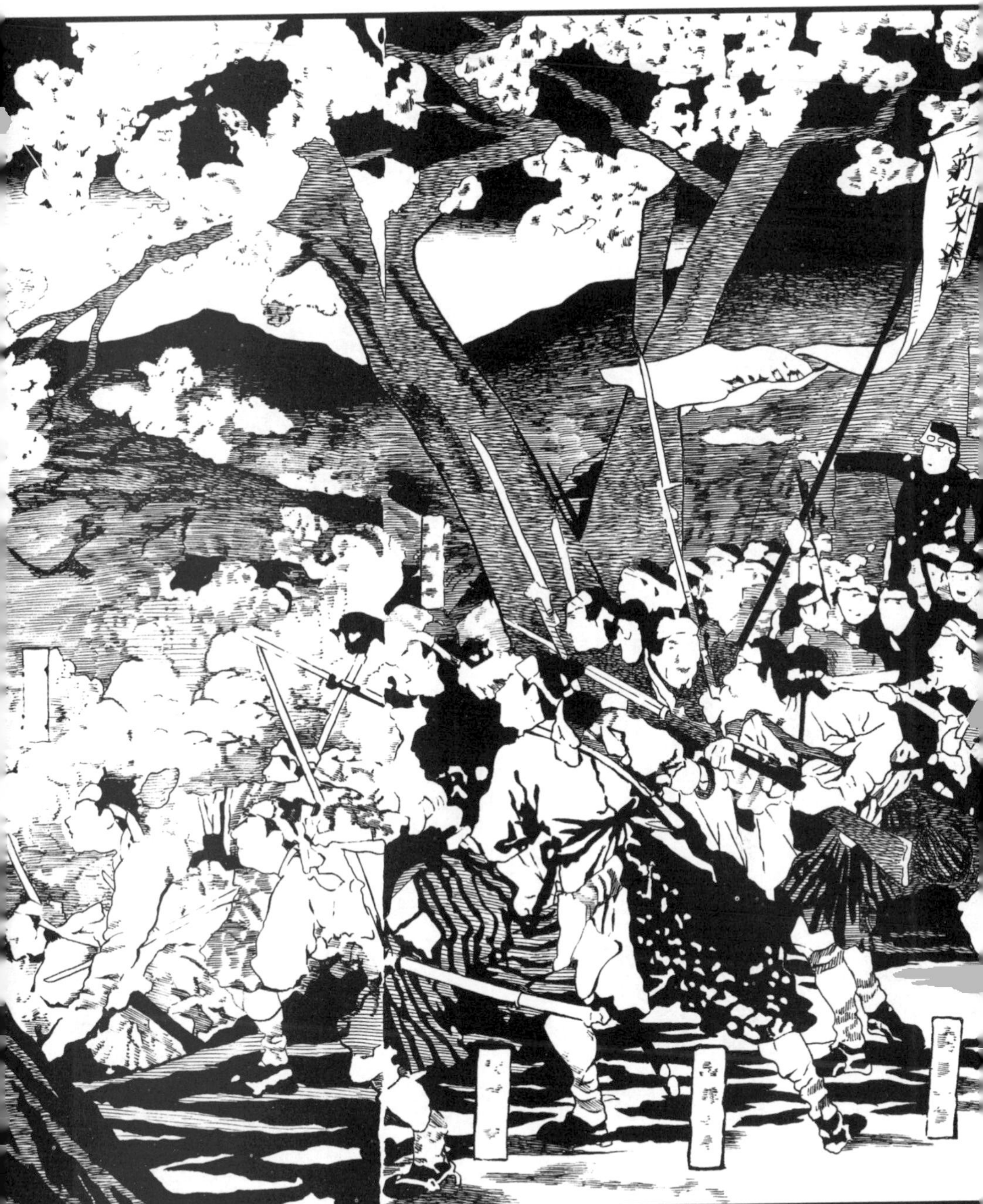

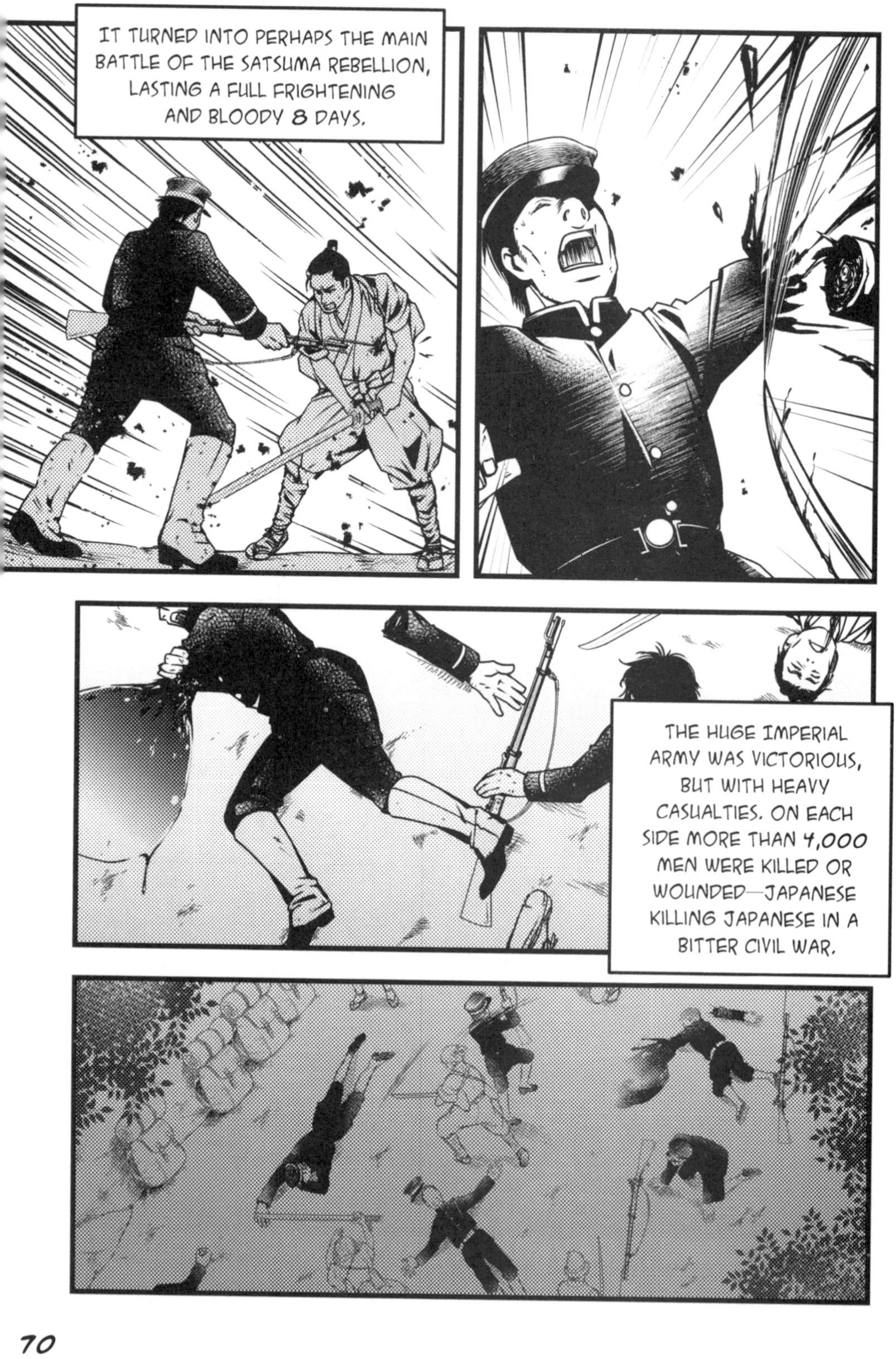
IT TURNED INTO PERHAPS THE MAIN BATTLE OF THE SATSUMA REBELLION, LASTING A FULL FRIGHTENING AND BLOODY 8 DAYS.
THE HUGE IMPERIAL ARMY WAS VICTORIOUS, BUT WITH HEAVY CASUALTIES. ON EACH SIDE MORE THAN 4,000 MEN WERE KILLED OR WOUNDED—JAPANESE KILLING JAPANESE IN A BITTER CIVIL WAR.

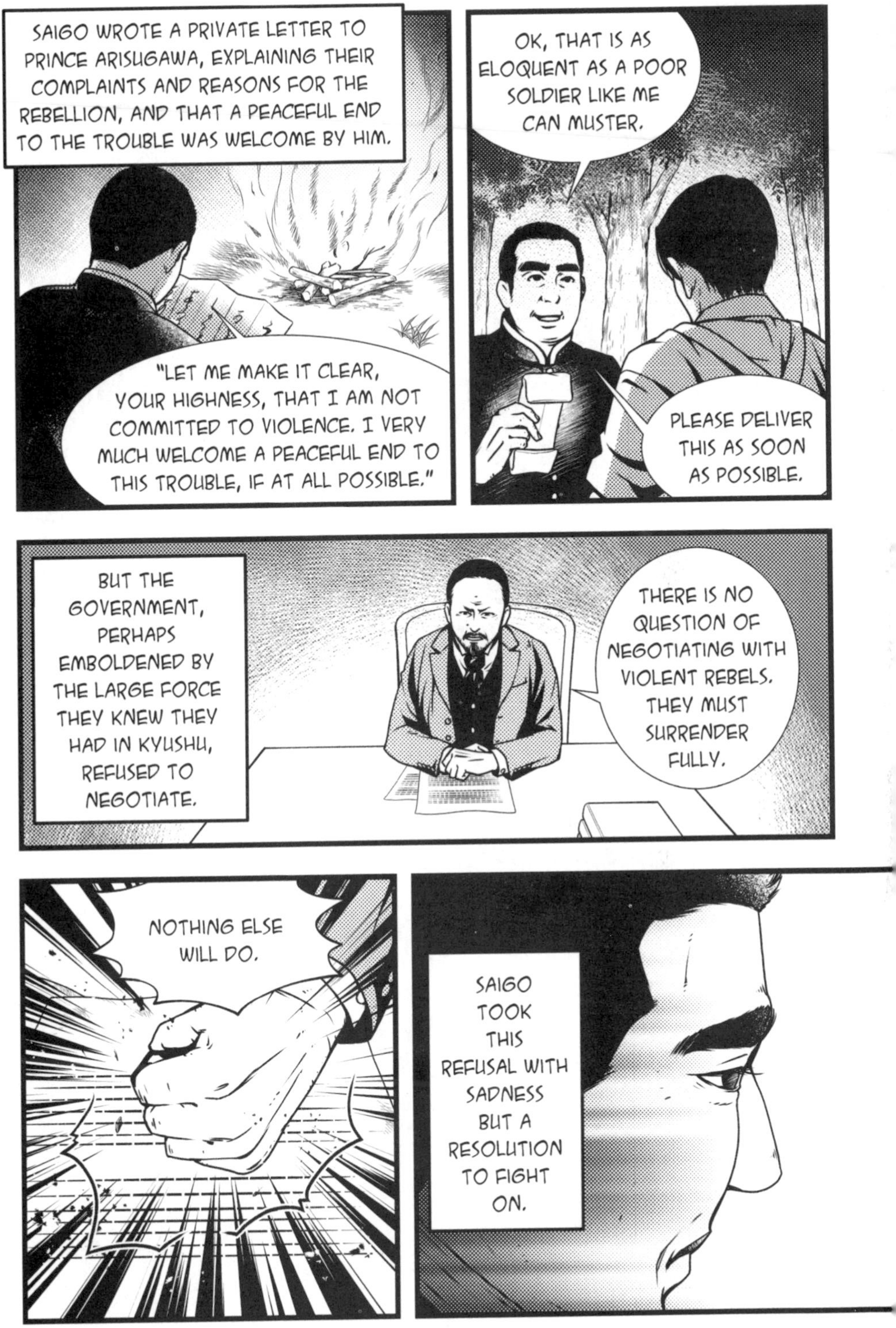
SAIGO WROTE A PRIVATE LETTER TO PRINCE ARISUGAWA, EXPLAINING THEIR COMPLAINTS AND REASONS FOR THE REBELLION, AND THAT A PEACEFUL END TO THE TROUBLE WAS WELCOME BY HIM.
"LET ME MAKE IT CLEAR, YOUR HIGHNESS, THAT I AM NOT COMMITTED TO VIOLENCE. I VERY MUCH WELCOME A PEACEFUL END TO THIS TROUBLE, IF AT ALL POSSIBLE."
OK, THAT IS AS ELOQUENT AS A POOR SOLDIER LIKE ME CAN MUSTER.
PLEASE DELIVER THIS AS SOON AS POSSIBLE.
BUT THE GOVERNMENT, PERHAPS EMBOLDENED BY THE LARGE FORCE THEY KNEW THEY HAD IN KYUSHU, REFUSED TO NEGOTIATE.
THERE IS NO QUESTION OF NEGOTIATING WITH VIOLENT REBELS. THEY MUST SURRENDER FULLY.
NOTHING ELSE WILL DO.
SAIGO TOOK THIS REFUSAL WITH SADNESS BUT A RESOLUTION TO FIGHT ON.

SO, AN IMPERIAL FORCE OF THREE WARSHIPS, WITH AROUND *1,000* MEN, LANDED IN KAGOSHIMA ON MARCH *8*, TO CUT SAIGO OFF FROM FURTHER HELP FROM HOME.

THEY SEIZED ARSENALS ...

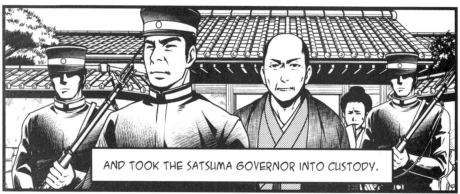

AND TOOK THE SATSUMA GOVERNOR INTO CUSTODY.

TWO INFANTRY BRIGADES AND *1,200* POLICE WERE ALSO LANDED BY SEA FARTHER UP THE COAST, BEHIND THE REBEL LINES, IN ORDER TO ATTACK THEM FROM THE SOUTH, FROM THE YATSUSHIRO AREA. THE ATTACK BEGAN IN MID-MARCH.

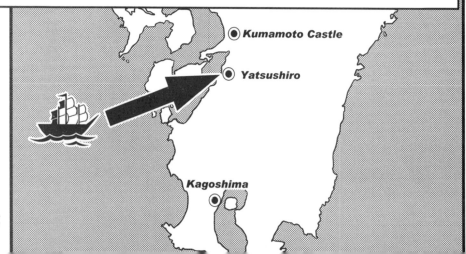

Kumamoto Castle

Yatsushiro

Kagoshima

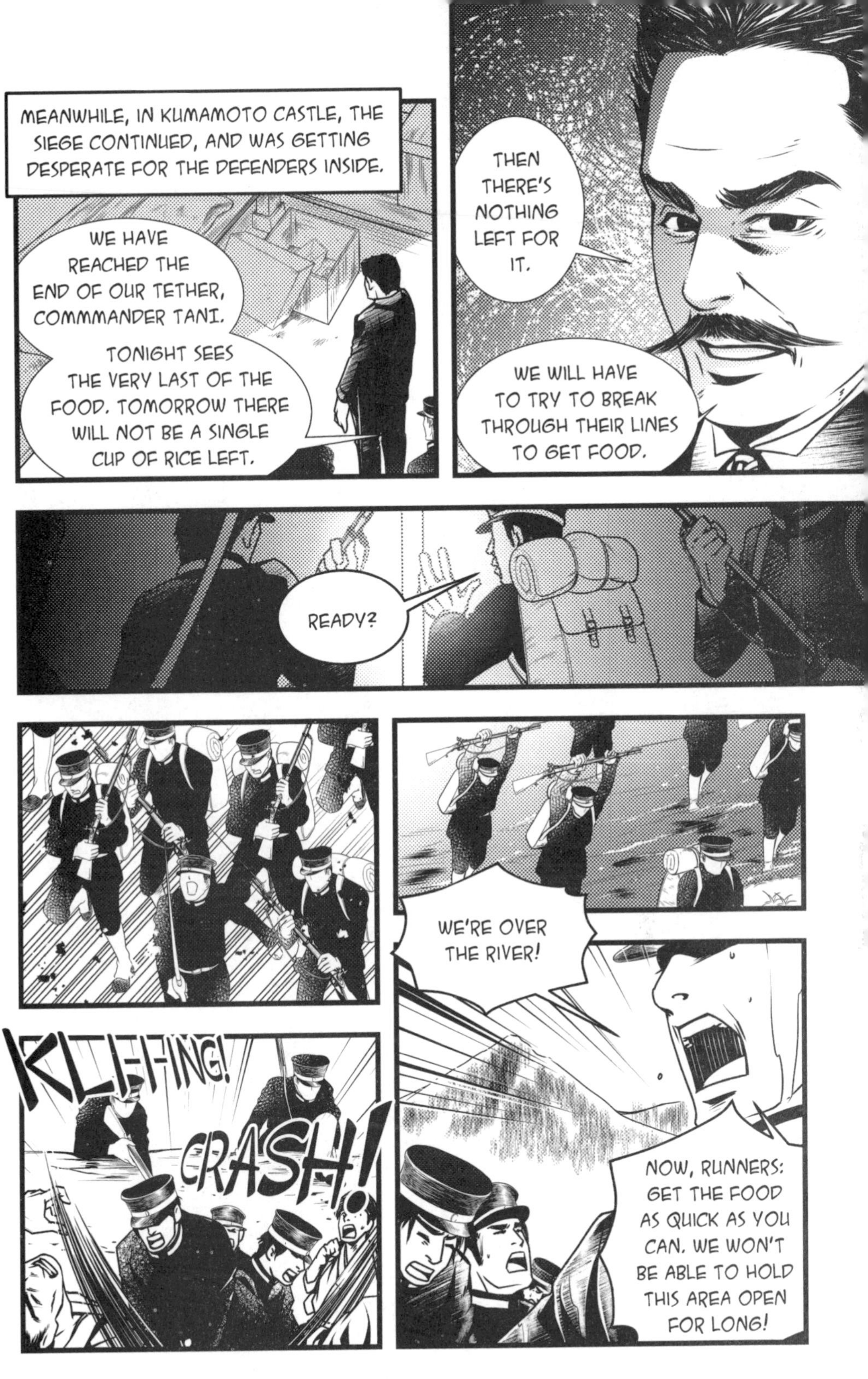
MEANWHILE, IN KUMAMOTO CASTLE, THE SIEGE CONTINUED, AND WAS GETTING DESPERATE FOR THE DEFENDERS INSIDE.
WE HAVE REACHED THE END OF OUR TETHER, COMMMANDER TANI.
TONIGHT SEES THE VERY LAST OF THE FOOD. TOMORROW THERE WILL NOT BE A SINGLE CUP OF RICE LEFT.
THEN THERE'S NOTHING LEFT FOR IT.
WE WILL HAVE TO TRY TO BREAK THROUGH THEIR LINES TO GET FOOD.
READY?
WE'RE OVER THE RIVER!
KLI-I-ING!
CRASH!
NOW, RUNNERS: GET THE FOOD AS QUICK AS YOU CAN. WE WON'T BE ABLE TO HOLD THIS AREA OPEN FOR LONG!

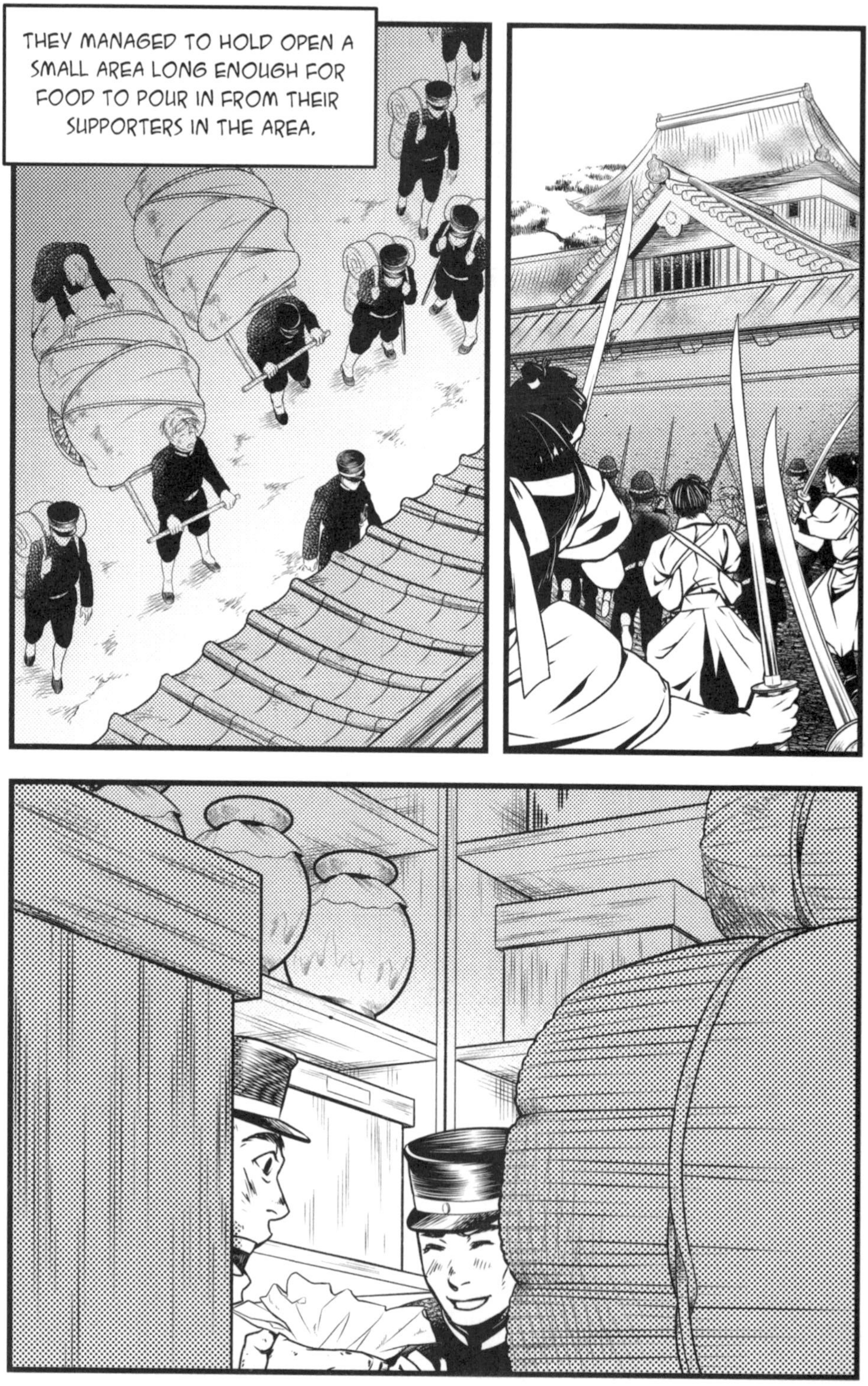
THEY MANAGED TO HOLD OPEN A SMALL AREA LONG ENOUGH FOR FOOD TO POUR IN FROM THEIR SUPPORTERS IN THE AREA.

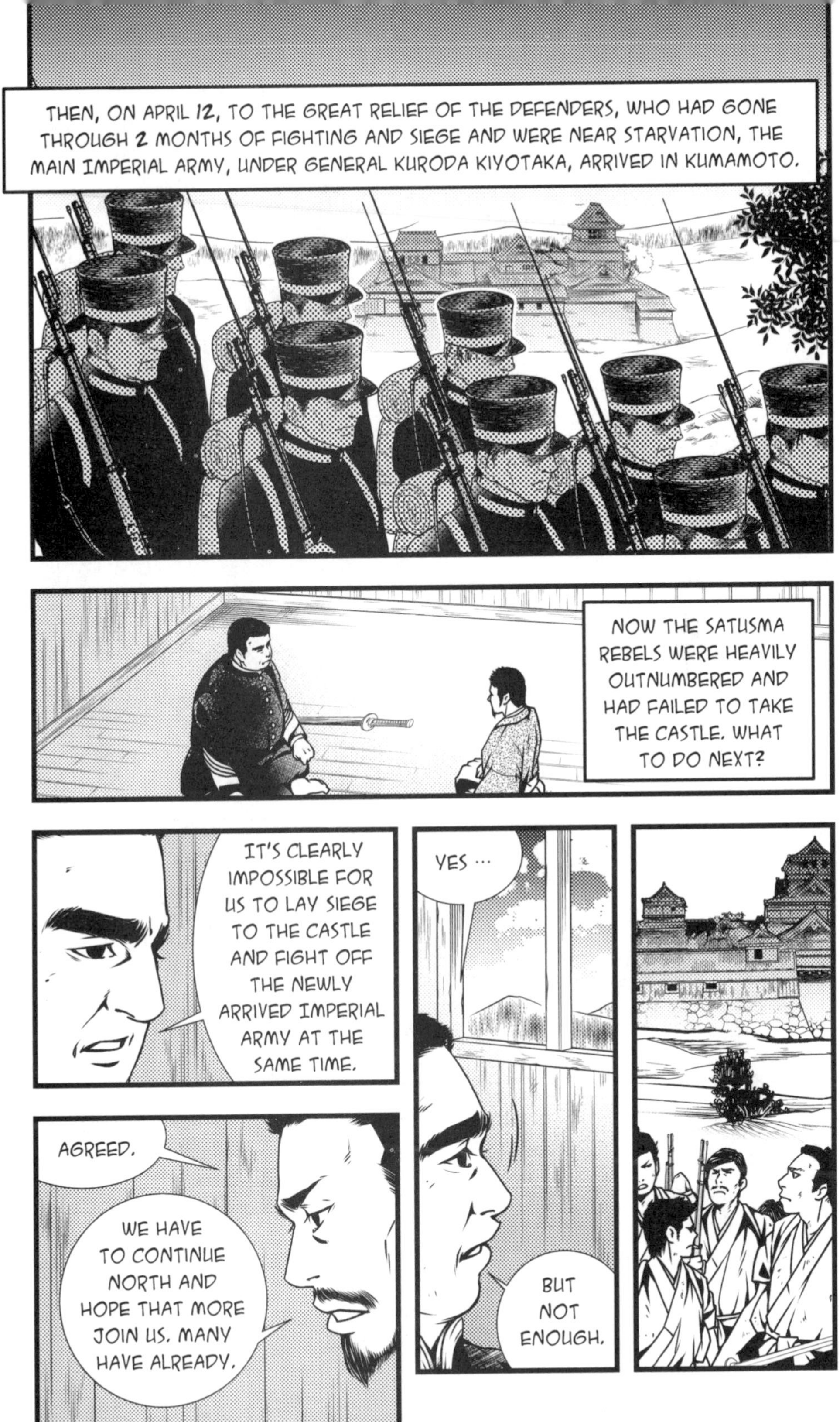

THEN, ON APRIL 12, TO THE GREAT RELIEF OF THE DEFENDERS, WHO HAD GONE THROUGH 2 MONTHS OF FIGHTING AND SIEGE AND WERE NEAR STARVATION, THE MAIN IMPERIAL ARMY, UNDER GENERAL KURODA KIYOTAKA, ARRIVED IN KUMAMOTO.
NOW THE SATUSMA REBELS WERE HEAVILY OUTNUMBERED AND HAD FAILED TO TAKE THE CASTLE. WHAT TO DO NEXT?
IT'S CLEARLY IMPOSSIBLE FOR US TO LAY SIEGE TO THE CASTLE AND FIGHT OFF THE NEWLY ARRIVED IMPERIAL ARMY AT THE SAME TIME.
AGREED.
WE HAVE TO CONTINUE NORTH AND HOPE THAT MORE JOIN US. MANY HAVE ALREADY.
YES ...
BUT NOT ENOUGH.

AFTER THE DEFEATS AT KUMAMOTO, SAIGO LED HIS FOLLOWERS ON A 7-DAY MARCH SOUTH TOWARD THE HITOYOSHI AREA, WHERE THEY HAD CONSIDERABLE SUPPORT.

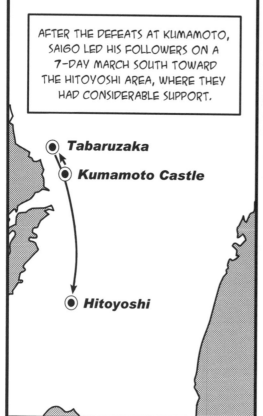

● *Tabaruzaka*

● *Kumamoto Castle*

● *Hitoyoshi*

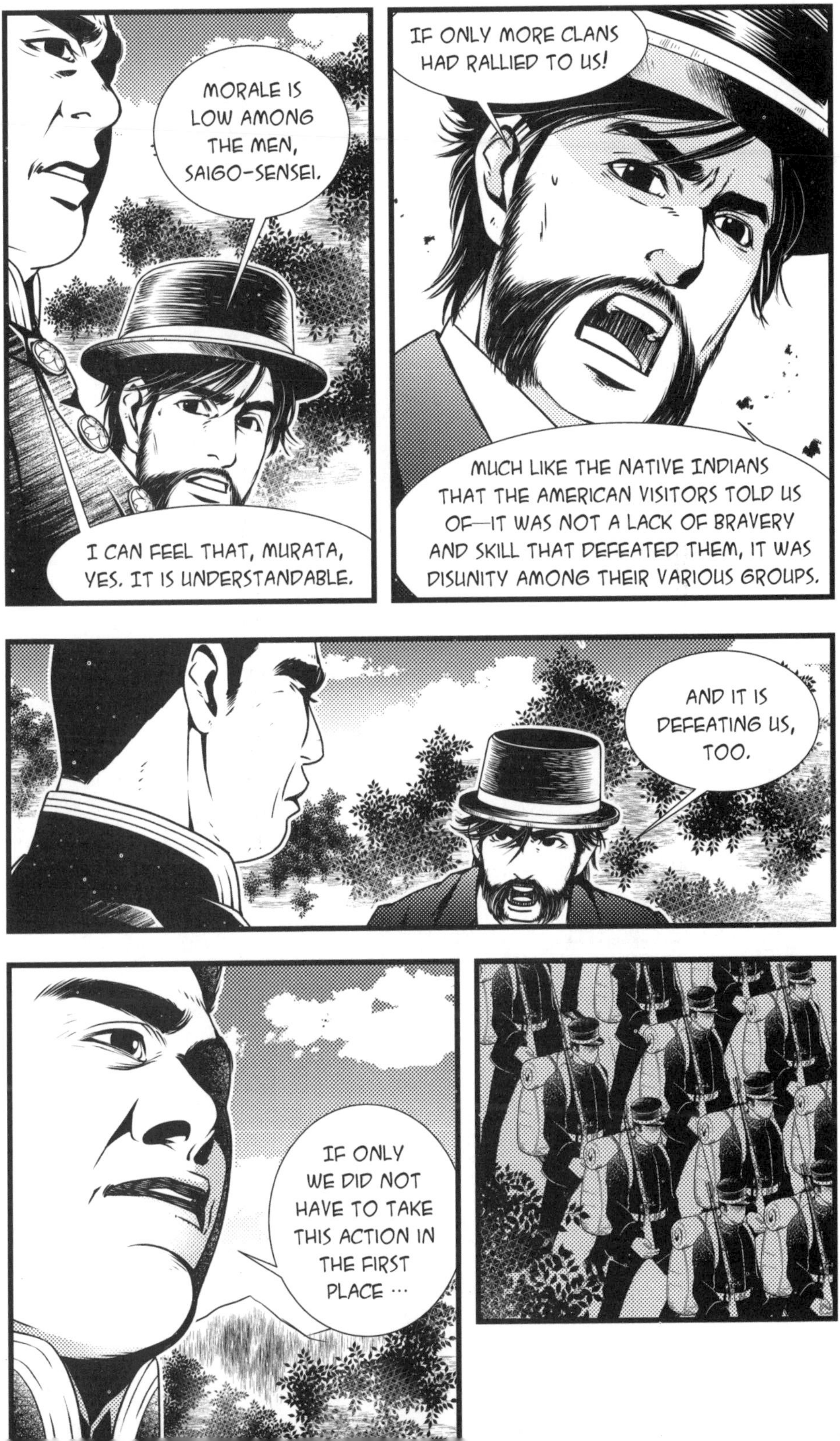
MORALE IS LOW AMONG THE MEN, SAIGO-SENSEI.
I CAN FEEL THAT, MURATA, YES. IT IS UNDERSTANDABLE.
IF ONLY MORE CLANS HAD RALLIED TO US!
MUCH LIKE THE NATIVE INDIANS THAT THE AMERICAN VISITORS TOLD US OF—IT WAS NOT A LACK OF BRAVERY AND SKILL THAT DEFEATED THEM, IT WAS DISUNITY AMONG THEIR VARIOUS GROUPS.
AND IT IS DEFEATING US, TOO.
IF ONLY WE DID NOT HAVE TO TAKE THIS ACTION IN THE FIRST PLACE …

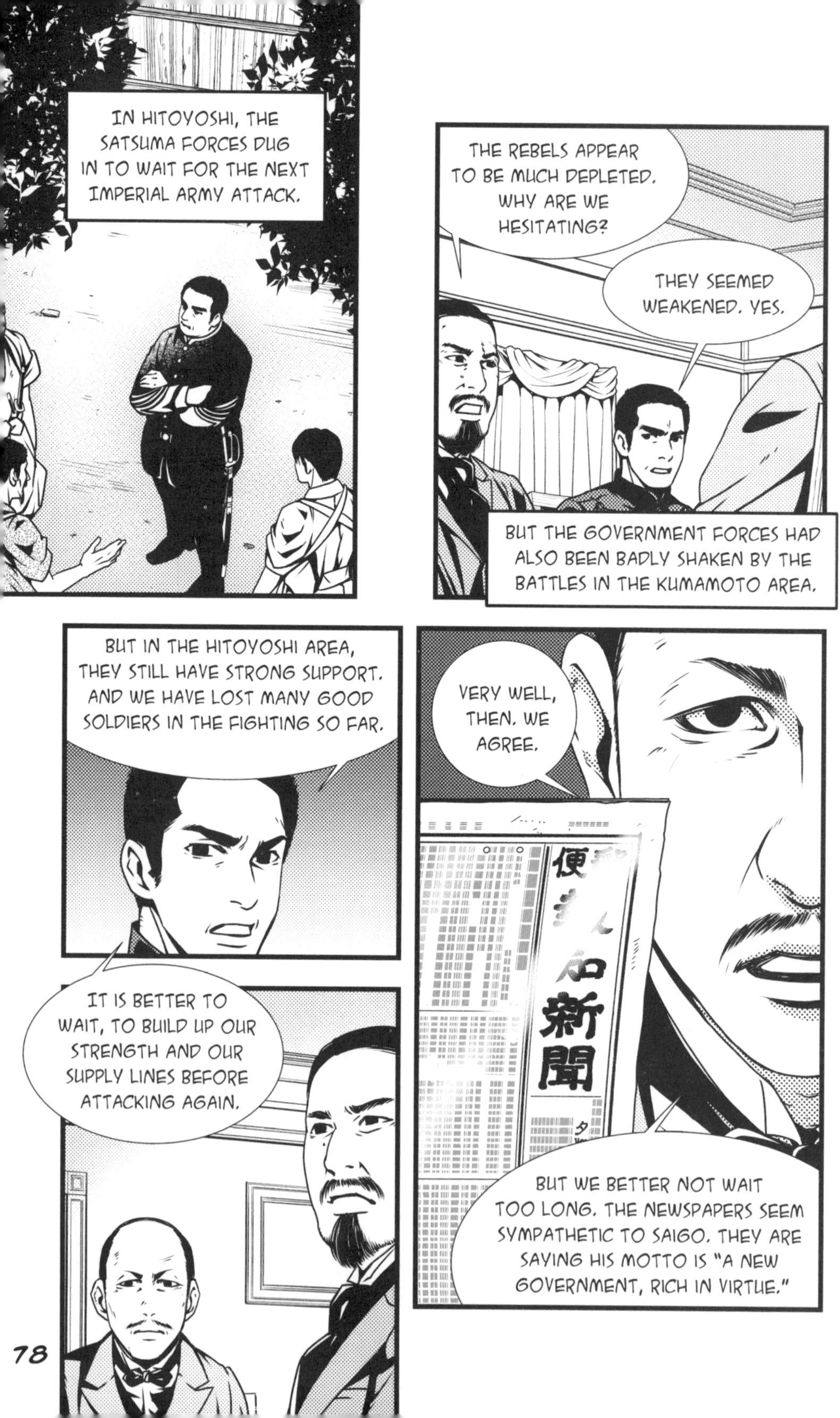
IN HITOYOSHI, THE SATSUMA FORCES DUG IN TO WAIT FOR THE NEXT IMPERIAL ARMY ATTACK.
THE REBELS APPEAR TO BE MUCH DEPLETED. WHY ARE WE HESITATING?
THEY SEEMED WEAKENED. YES.
BUT THE GOVERNMENT FORCES HAD ALSO BEEN BADLY SHAKEN BY THE BATTLES IN THE KUMAMOTO AREA.
BUT IN THE HITOYOSHI AREA, THEY STILL HAVE STRONG SUPPORT. AND WE HAVE LOST MANY GOOD SOLDIERS IN THE FIGHTING SO FAR.
IT IS BETTER TO WAIT, TO BUILD UP OUR STRENGTH AND OUR SUPPLY LINES BEFORE ATTACKING AGAIN.
VERY WELL, THEN. WE AGREE.
BUT WE BETTER NOT WAIT TOO LONG. THE NEWSPAPERS SEEM SYMPATHETIC TO SAIGO. THEY ARE SAYING HIS MOTTO IS "A NEW GOVERNMENT, RICH IN VIRTUE."

CHAPTER 4

THE EMPIRE CLOSES IN

THE IMPERIAL FORCES TOOK SEVERAL WEEKS OF REST AND PREPARATION.

THE REBELS TOOK REFUGE IN THE HILLS AND VALLEYS.

ONCE RECUPERATED, THE IMPERIAL FORCES WENT ON THE OFFENSIVE AGAIN. THE REBELS WENT FARTHER EAST, TO MIYAZAKI.

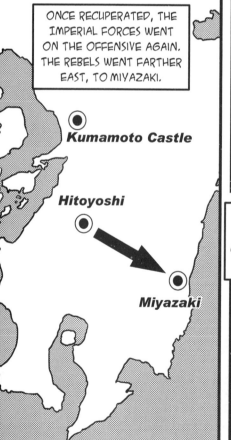

Kumamoto Castle

Hitoyoshi

Miyazaki

Hitoyoshi

AND WERE THEN PUSHED SOUTH TO MIYAKONOJO.

Miyazaki

Miyakonojo

BUT SAMURAI REBELS IN THE HILLS OF CENTRAL KYUSHU CONDUCTED GUERRILLA ATTACKS ON THE IMPERIAL FORCES.

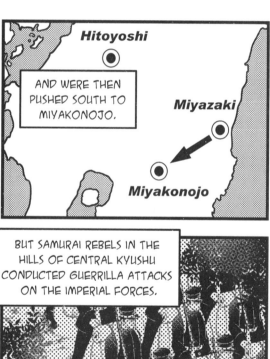

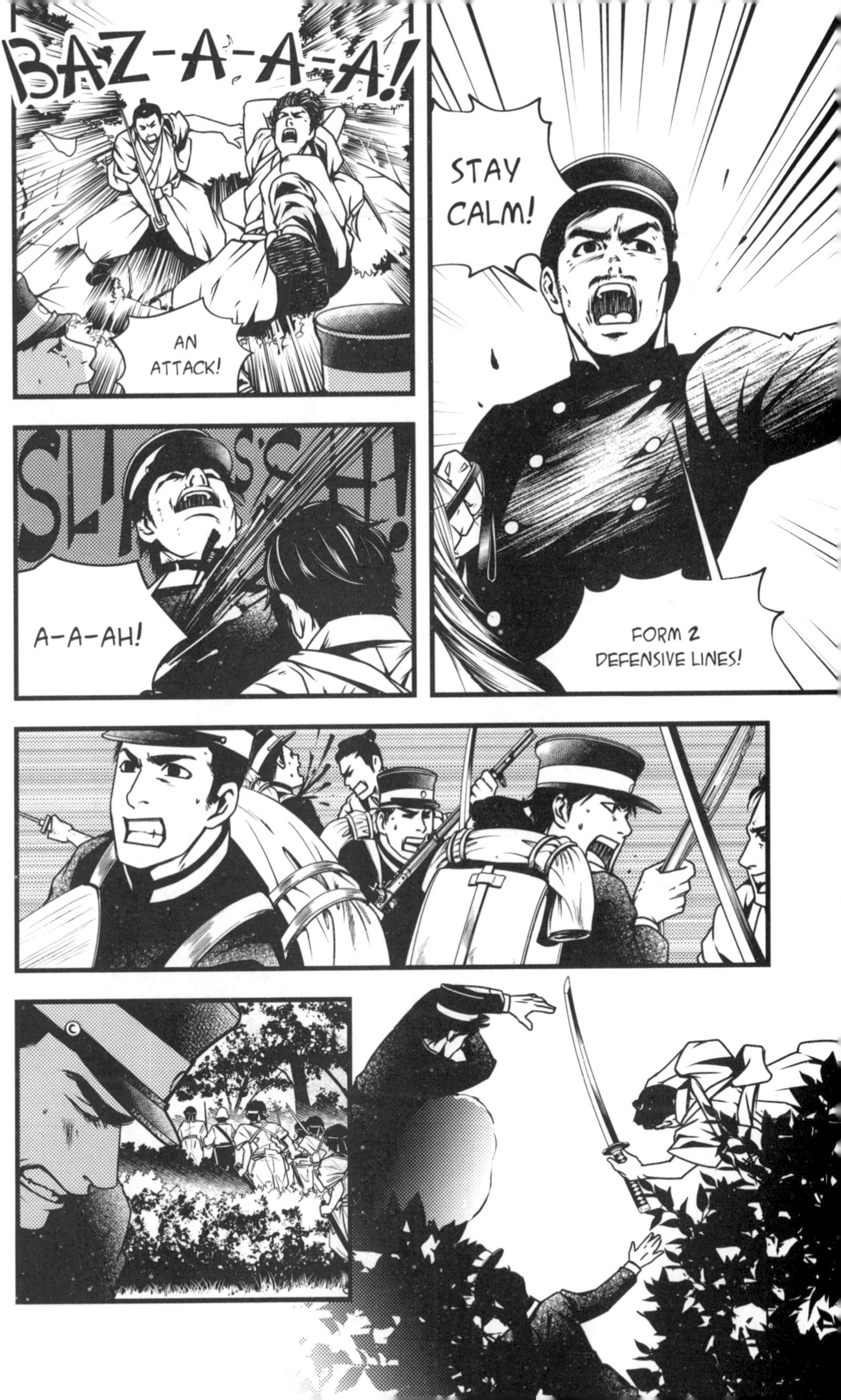
BAZ-A-A-A!
AN ATTACK!
STAY CALM!
A-A-AH!
FORM 2 DEFENSIVE LINES!

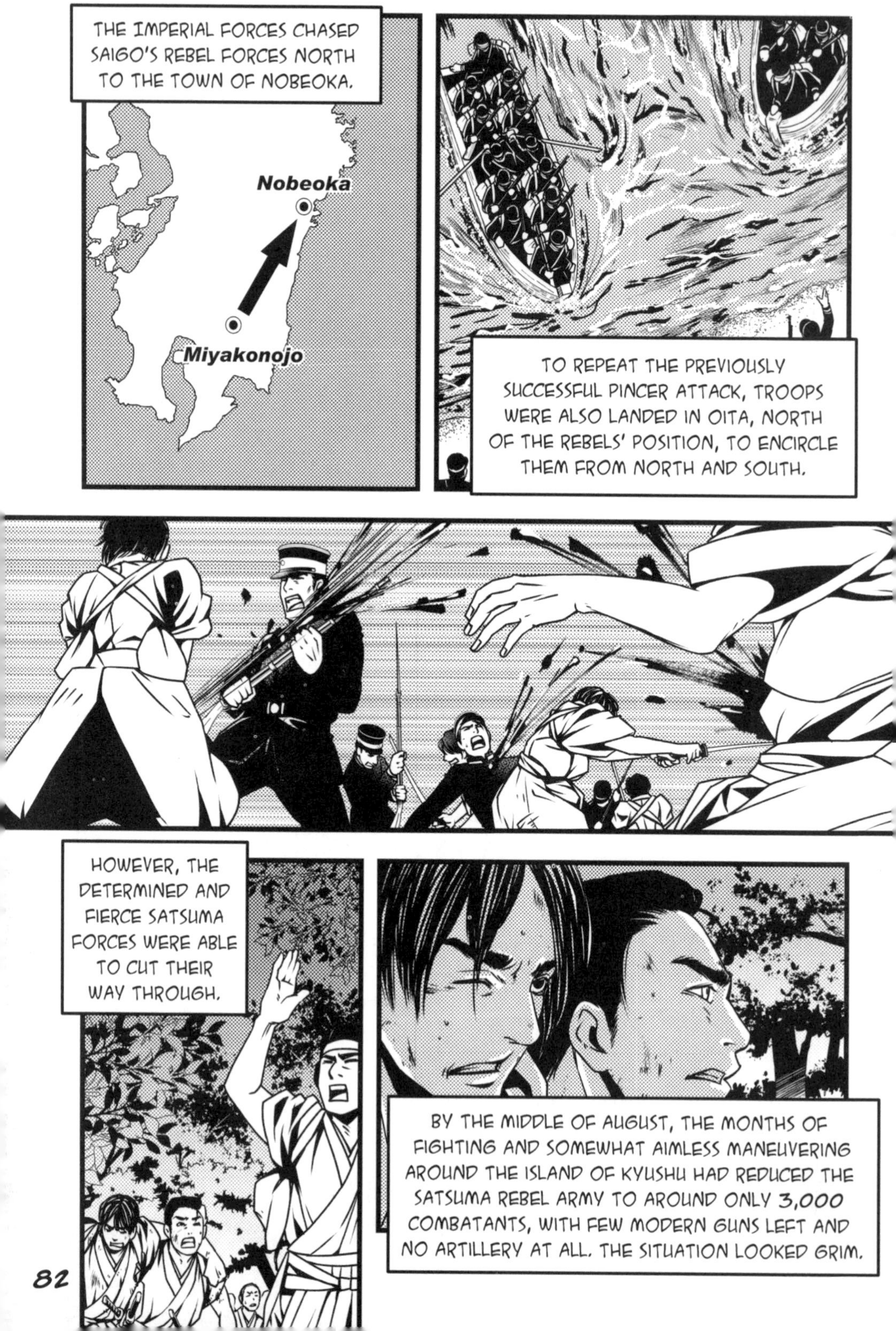
THE IMPERIAL FORCES CHASED SAIGO'S REBEL FORCES NORTH TO THE TOWN OF NOBEOKA.
Nobeoka
Miyakonojo
TO REPEAT THE PREVIOUSLY SUCCESSFUL PINCER ATTACK, TROOPS WERE ALSO LANDED IN OITA, NORTH OF THE REBELS' POSITION, TO ENCIRCLE THEM FROM NORTH AND SOUTH.
HOWEVER, THE DETERMINED AND FIERCE SATSUMA FORCES WERE ABLE TO CUT THEIR WAY THROUGH.
BY THE MIDDLE OF AUGUST, THE MONTHS OF FIGHTING AND SOMEWHAT AIMLESS MANEUVERING AROUND THE ISLAND OF KYUSHU HAD REDUCED THE SATSUMA REBEL ARMY TO AROUND ONLY 3,000 COMBATANTS, WITH FEW MODERN GUNS LEFT AND NO ARTILLERY AT ALL. THE SITUATION LOOKED GRIM.

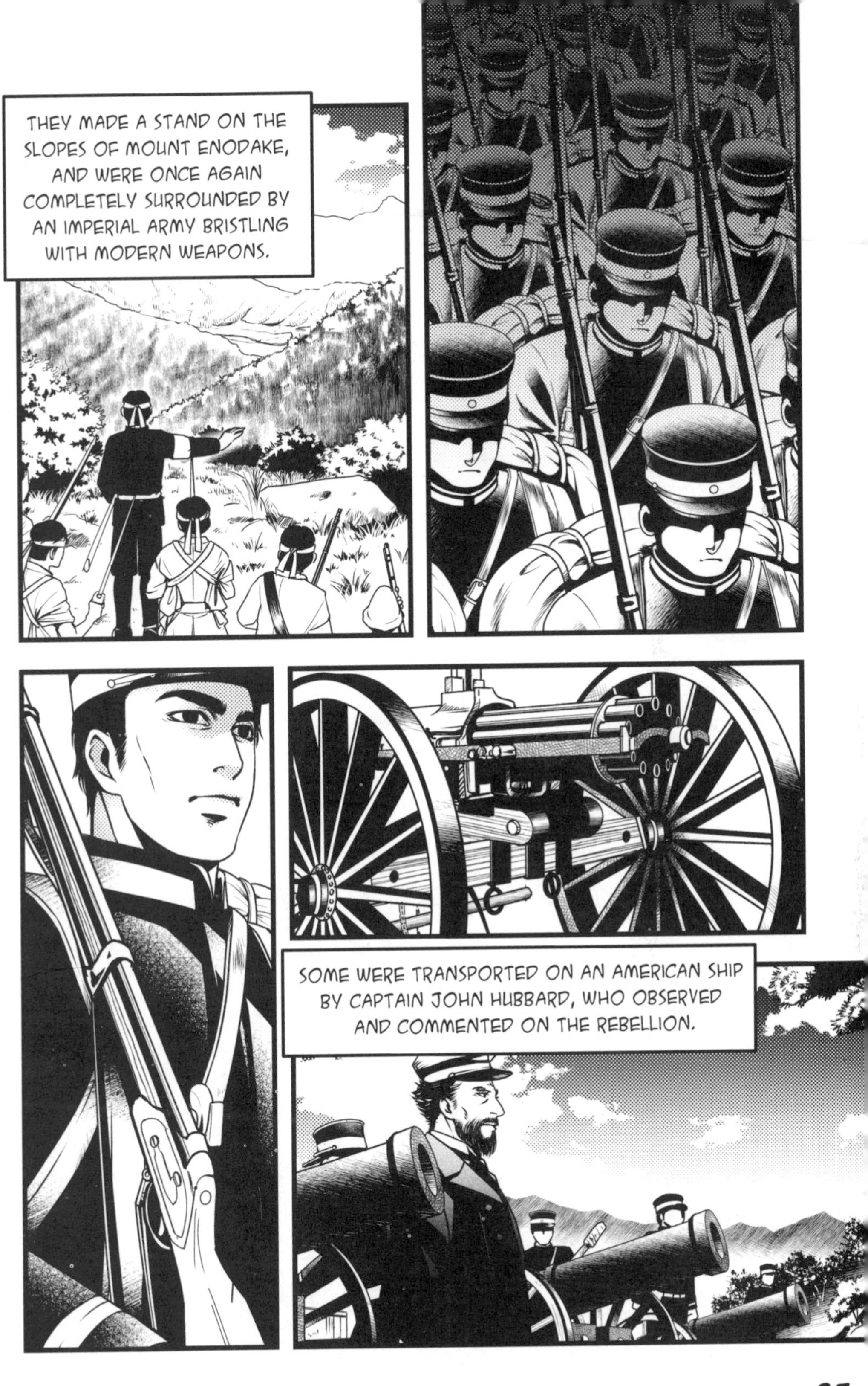
THEY MADE A STAND ON THE SLOPES OF MOUNT ENODAKE, AND WERE ONCE AGAIN COMPLETELY SURROUNDED BY AN IMPERIAL ARMY BRISTLING WITH MODERN WEAPONS.
SOME WERE TRANSPORTED ON AN AMERICAN SHIP BY CAPTAIN JOHN HUBBARD, WHO OBSERVED AND COMMENTED ON THE REBELLION.

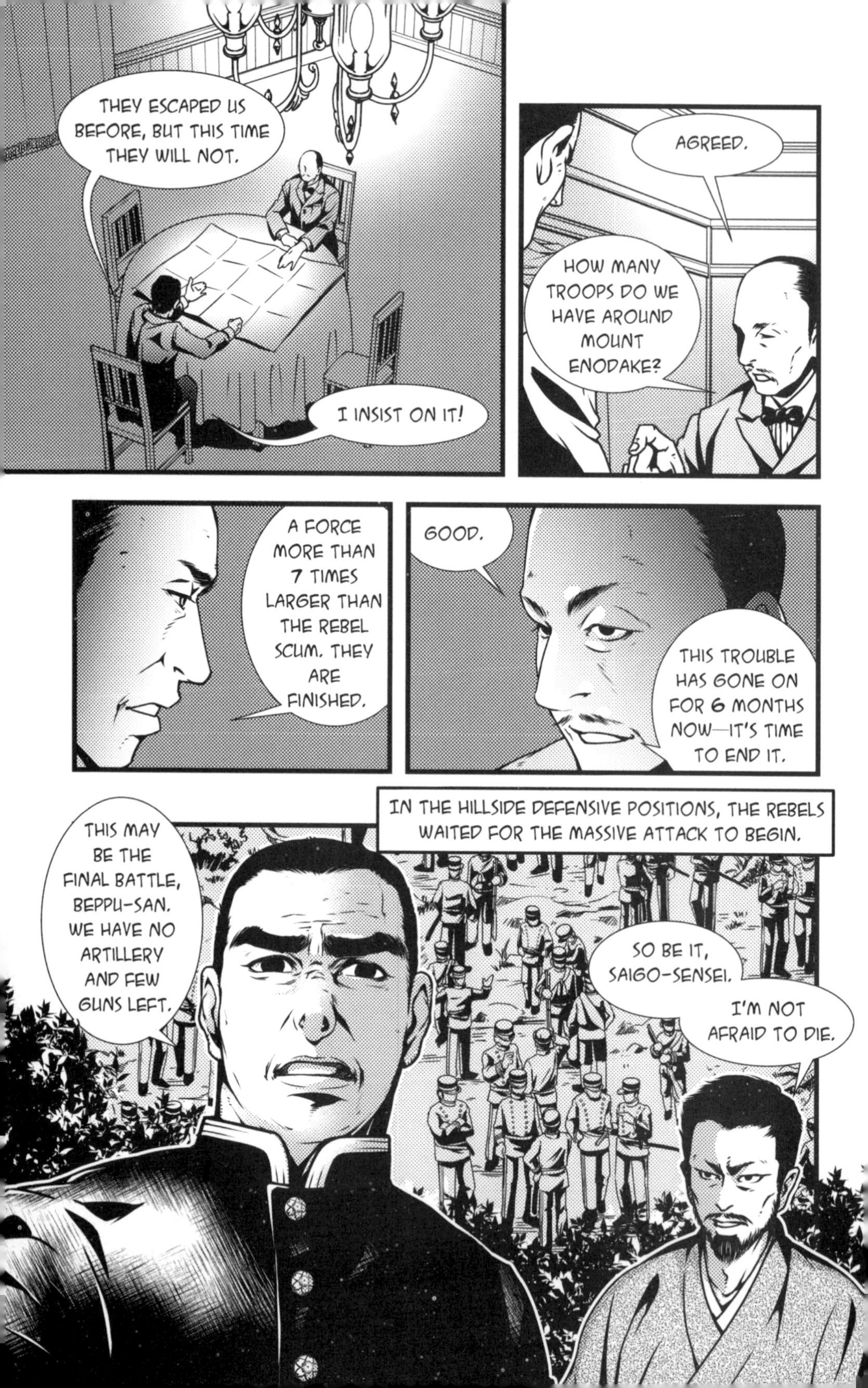
THEY ESCAPED US BEFORE, BUT THIS TIME THEY WILL NOT.
I INSIST ON IT!
AGREED.
HOW MANY TROOPS DO WE HAVE AROUND MOUNT ENODAKE?
A FORCE MORE THAN 7 TIMES LARGER THAN THE REBEL SCUM. THEY ARE FINISHED.
GOOD.
THIS TROUBLE HAS GONE ON FOR 6 MONTHS NOW—IT'S TIME TO END IT.
IN THE HILLSIDE DEFENSIVE POSITIONS, THE REBELS WAITED FOR THE MASSIVE ATTACK TO BEGIN.
THIS MAY BE THE FINAL BATTLE, BEPPU-SAN. WE HAVE NO ARTILLERY AND FEW GUNS LEFT.
SO BE IT, SAIGO-SENSEI.
I'M NOT AFRAID TO DIE.

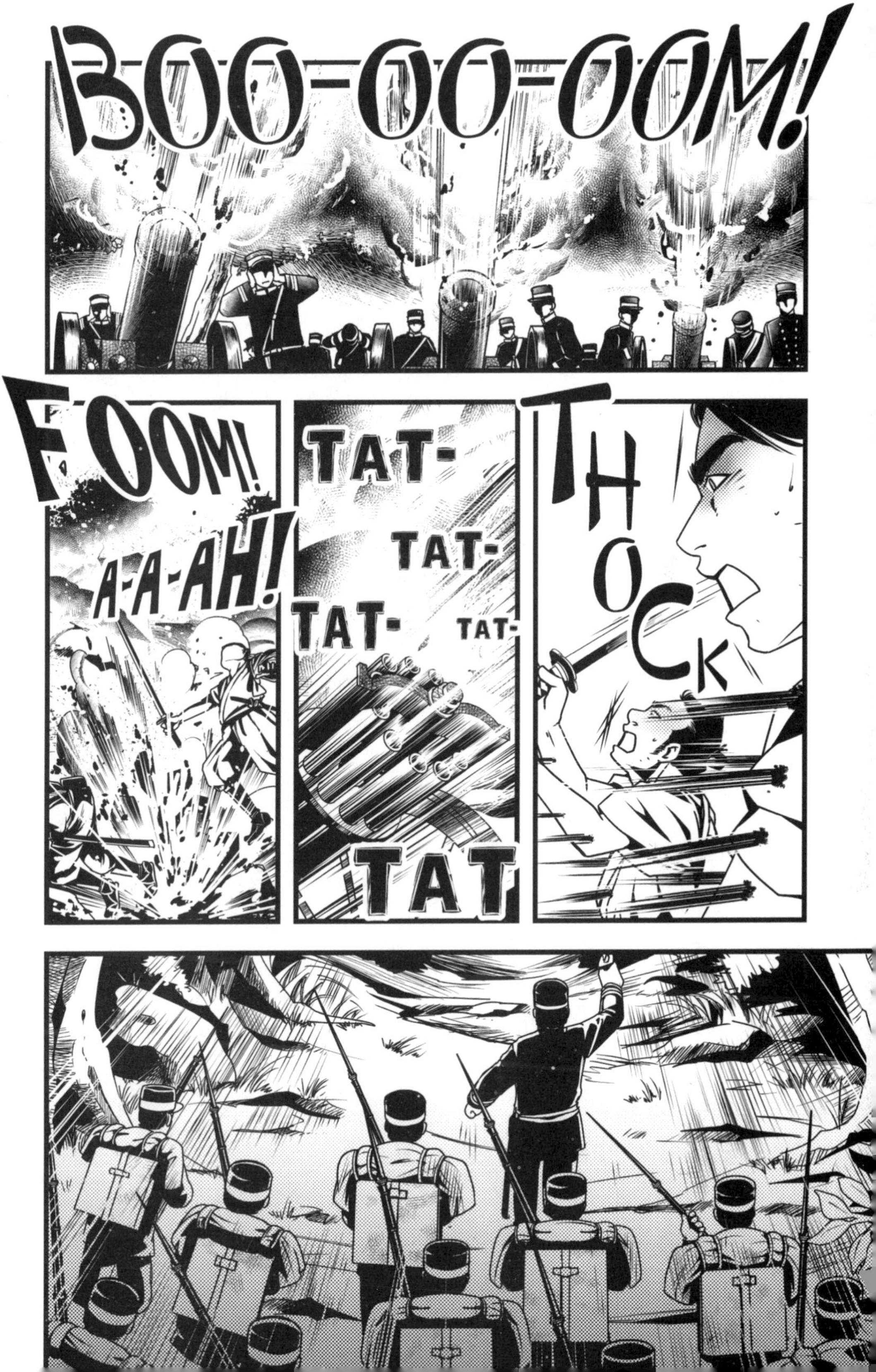
BOO-OO-OOM!
FOOM!
A-A-AH!
TAT-
TAT-
TAT-
TAT-
TAT
THOCK

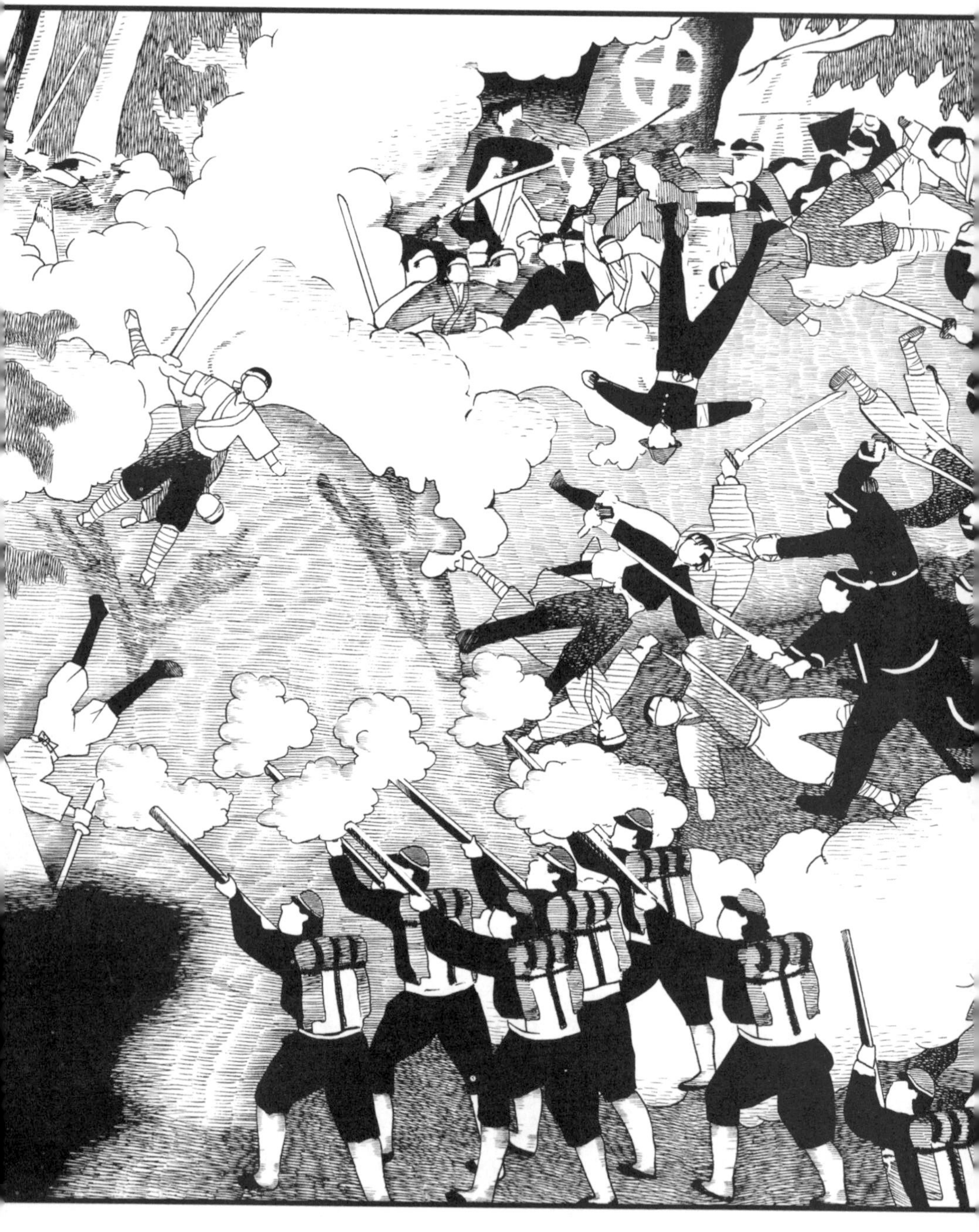

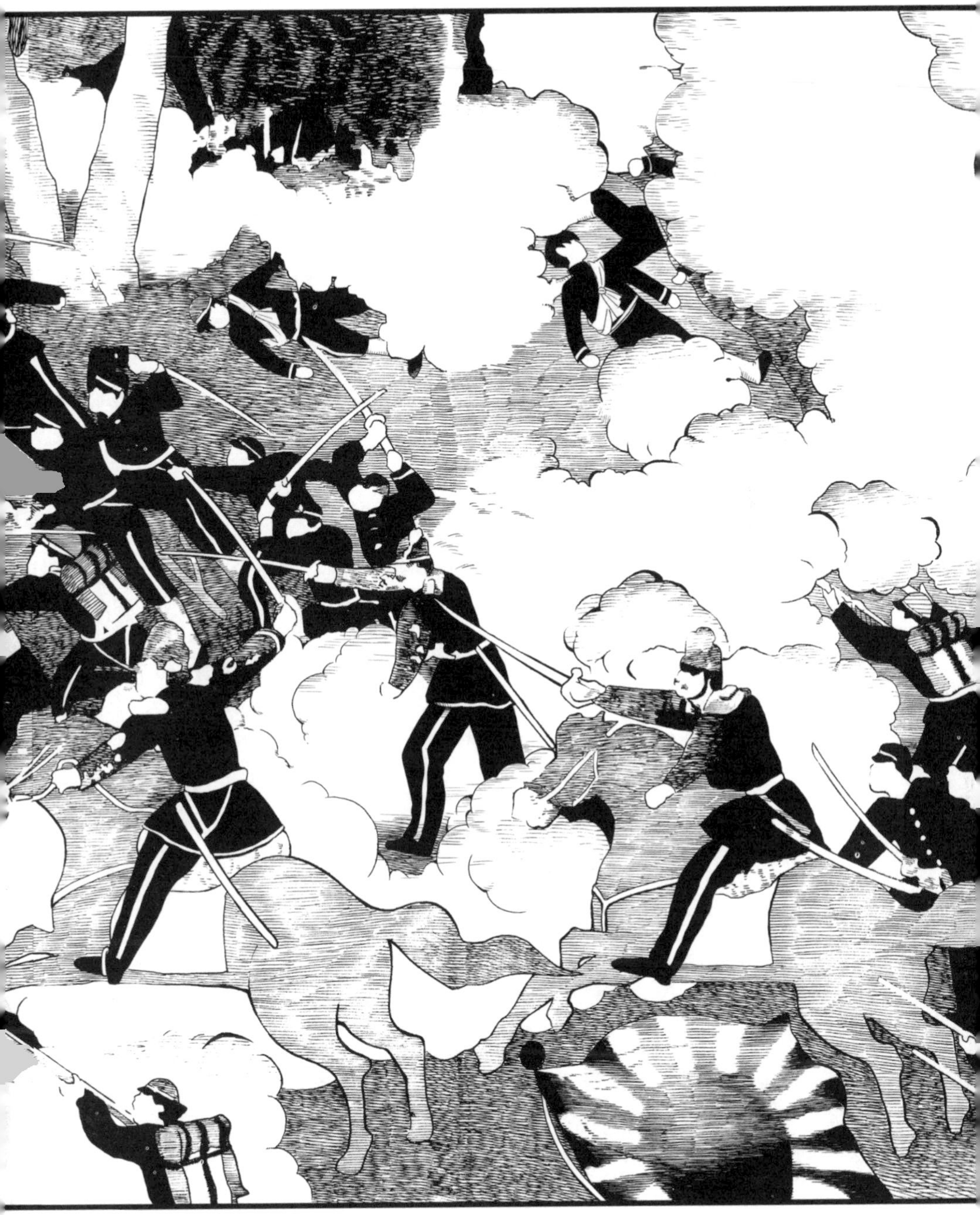

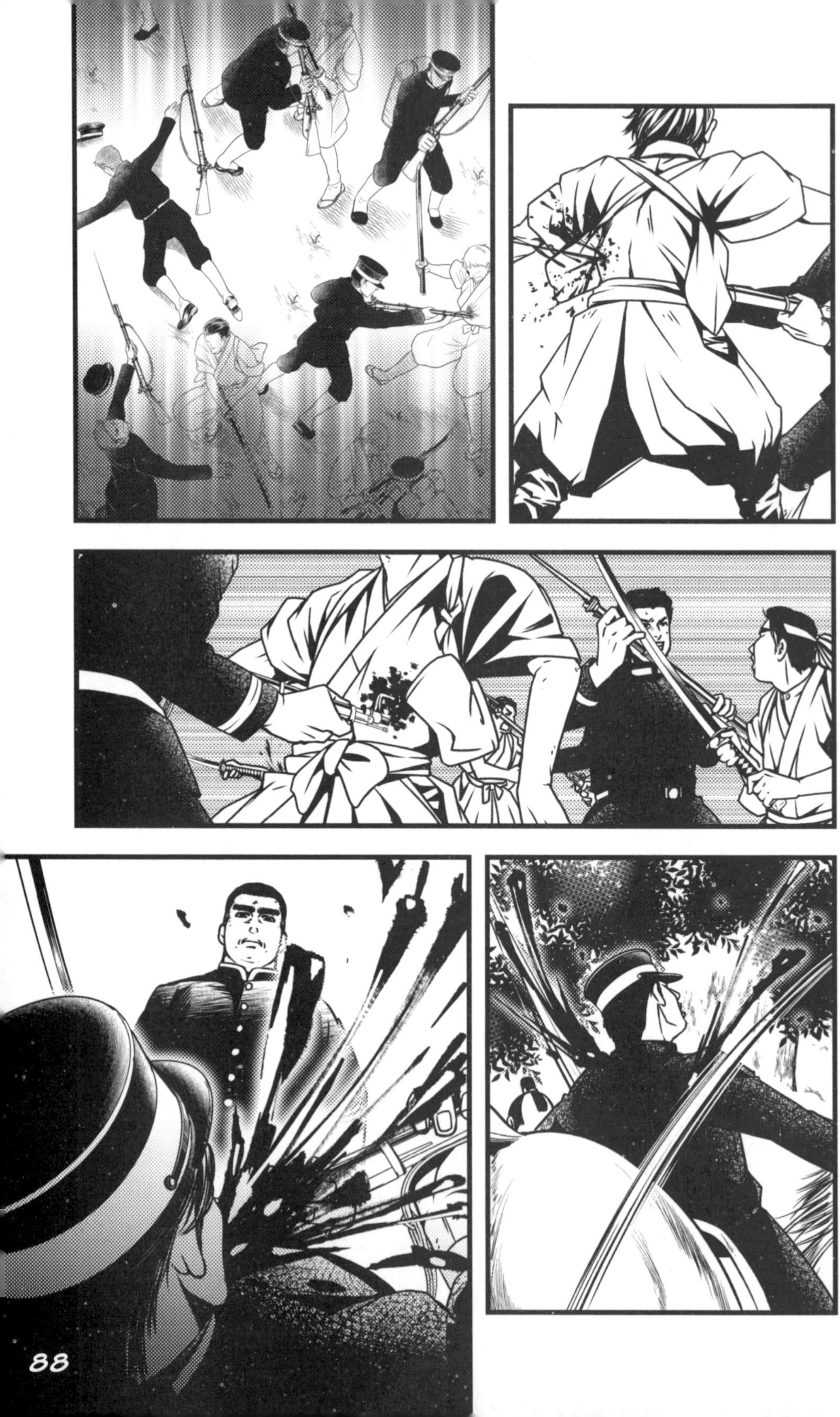

AFTER THE FEROCIOUS ONSLAUGHT, MOST OF THE REMAINING SATSUMA REBELS EITHER SURRENDERED ...

OR COMMITTED SEPPUKU.

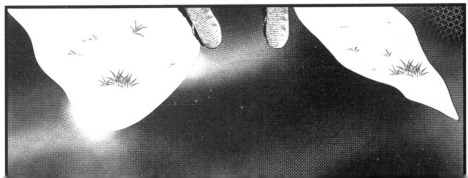

89

HOWEVER, SAIGO BURNED HIS PAPERS AND ARMY UNIFORM …

AND SLIPPED AWAY WITH AROUND 500 REMAINING STOIC REBELS.

DESPITE THE GOVERNMENT'S EFFORTS TO FIND THEM, THEY SLIPPED THROUGH AND GOT BACK TO KAGOSHIMA ON SEPTEMBER 1, ALMOST 7 MONTHS AFTER THEY HAD LEFT.

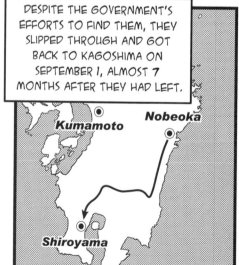

Kumamoto

Nobeoka

Shiroyama

THEY SEIZED THE HIGH POINT OF SHIROYAMA, NEAR THE CITY—AN OLD CASTLE THAT HAD ONCE BEEN THE RESIDENCE OF THE SHIMAZU LORDS OF THE AREA. A SYMBOLIC PLACE TO MAKE A FINAL STAND!

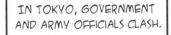

IN TOKYO, GOVERNMENT AND ARMY OFFICIALS CLASH.

DON'T YOU DARE BLAME THE ARMY!

I WON'T STAND FOR THAT.

THE ARMY SAID LAST TIME THAT IT WAS THE END FOR THE REBELS ...

YET THEY ESCAPED AGAIN!

WE TOLD YOU AT THE BEGINNING NOT TO UNDERESTIMATE SAIGO OR THE SATSUMA FIGHTERS.

INDEED, AND YOU WERE RIGHT.

BUT THIS REALLY HAS TO END NOW.

WE CANNOT ALLOW THE REBELS TO MOVE AROUND FROM PLACE TO PLACE ...

WITH OUR MEN CHASING AFTER THEM LIKE A CAT AFTER AN ELUSIVE BUTTERFLY.

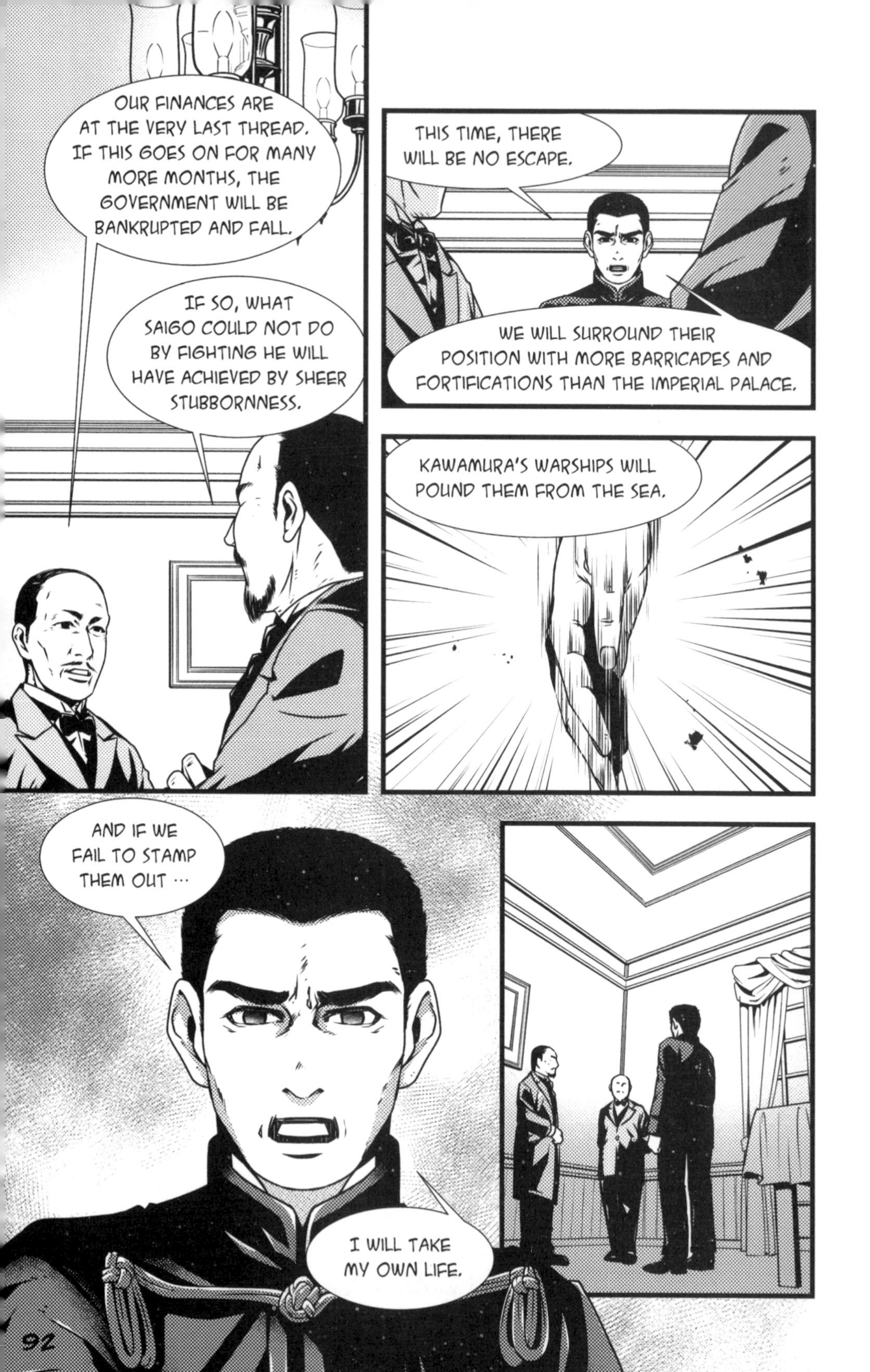
OUR FINANCES ARE AT THE VERY LAST THREAD. IF THIS GOES ON FOR MANY MORE MONTHS, THE GOVERNMENT WILL BE BANKRUPTED AND FALL.
IF SO, WHAT SAIGO COULD NOT DO BY FIGHTING HE WILL HAVE ACHIEVED BY SHEER STUBBORNNESS.
THIS TIME, THERE WILL BE NO ESCAPE.
WE WILL SURROUND THEIR POSITION WITH MORE BARRICADES AND FORTIFICATIONS THAN THE IMPERIAL PALACE.
KAWAMURA'S WARSHIPS WILL POUND THEM FROM THE SEA.
AND IF WE FAIL TO STAMP THEM OUT …
I WILL TAKE MY OWN LIFE.

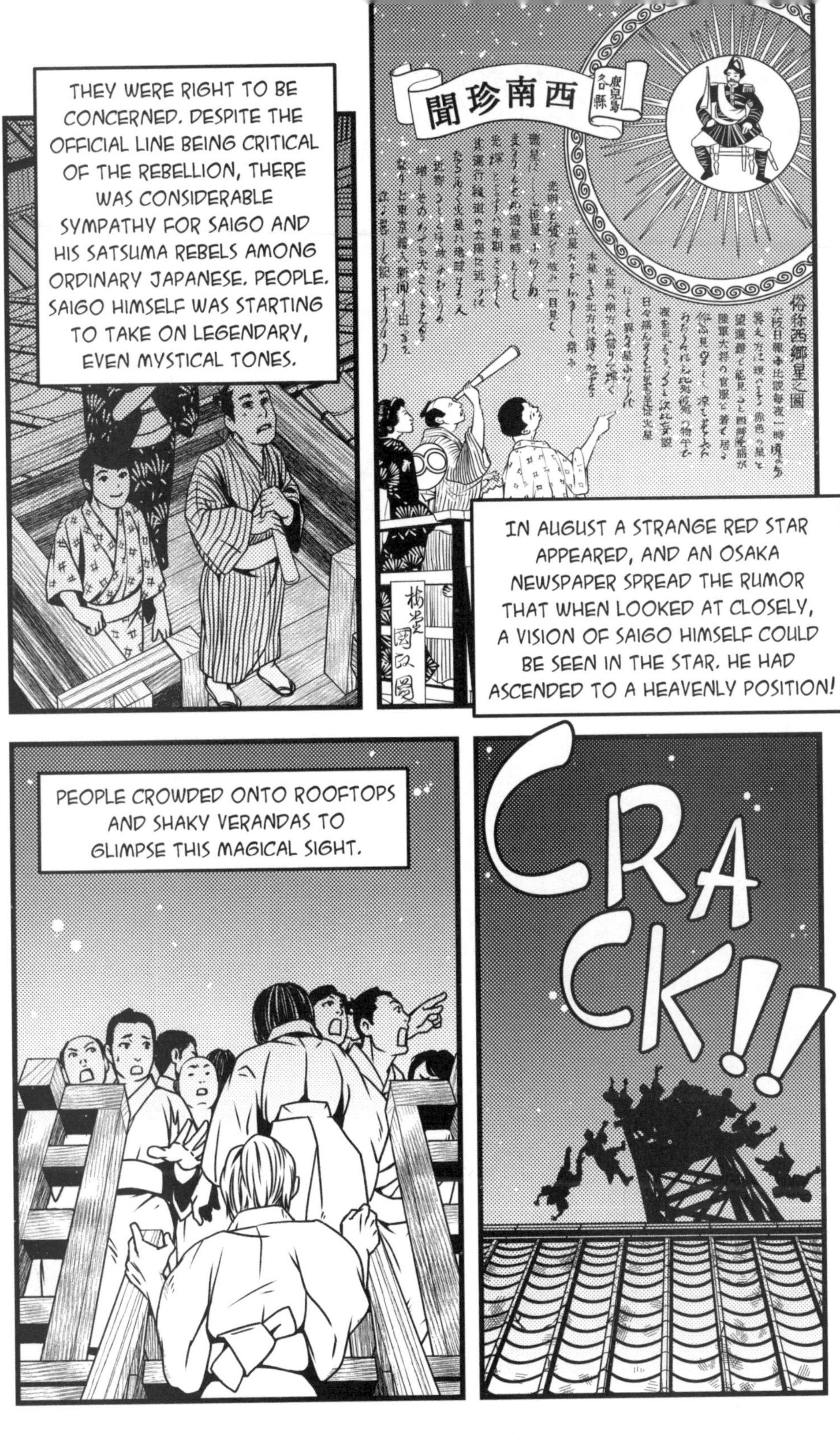

They were right to be concerned. Despite the official line being critical of the rebellion, there was considerable sympathy for Saigo and his Satsuma rebels among ordinary Japanese. People. Saigo himself was starting to take on legendary, even mystical tones.
西南珍聞
俗称西郷星之図
In August a strange red star appeared, and an Osaka newspaper spread the rumor that when looked at closely, a vision of Saigo himself could be seen in the star. He had ascended to a heavenly position!
People crowded onto rooftops and shaky verandas to glimpse this magical sight.
CRACK!!

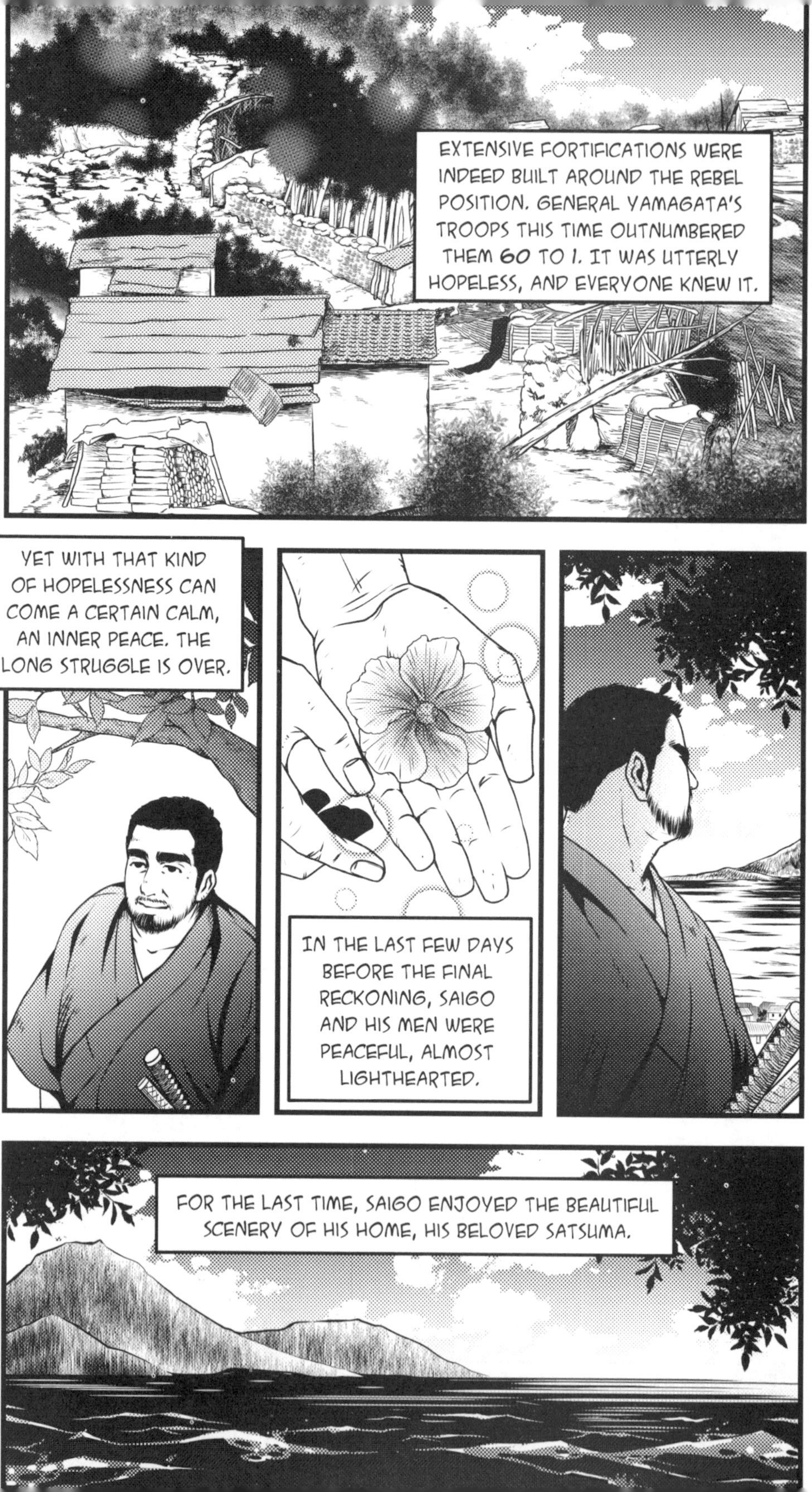
EXTENSIVE FORTIFICATIONS WERE INDEED BUILT AROUND THE REBEL POSITION. GENERAL YAMAGATA'S TROOPS THIS TIME OUTNUMBERED THEM 60 TO 1. IT WAS UTTERLY HOPELESS, AND EVERYONE KNEW IT.
YET WITH THAT KIND OF HOPELESSNESS CAN COME A CERTAIN CALM, AN INNER PEACE. THE LONG STRUGGLE IS OVER.
IN THE LAST FEW DAYS BEFORE THE FINAL RECKONING, SAIGO AND HIS MEN WERE PEACEFUL, ALMOST LIGHTHEARTED.
FOR THE LAST TIME, SAIGO ENJOYED THE BEAUTIFUL SCENERY OF HIS HOME, HIS BELOVED SATSUMA.

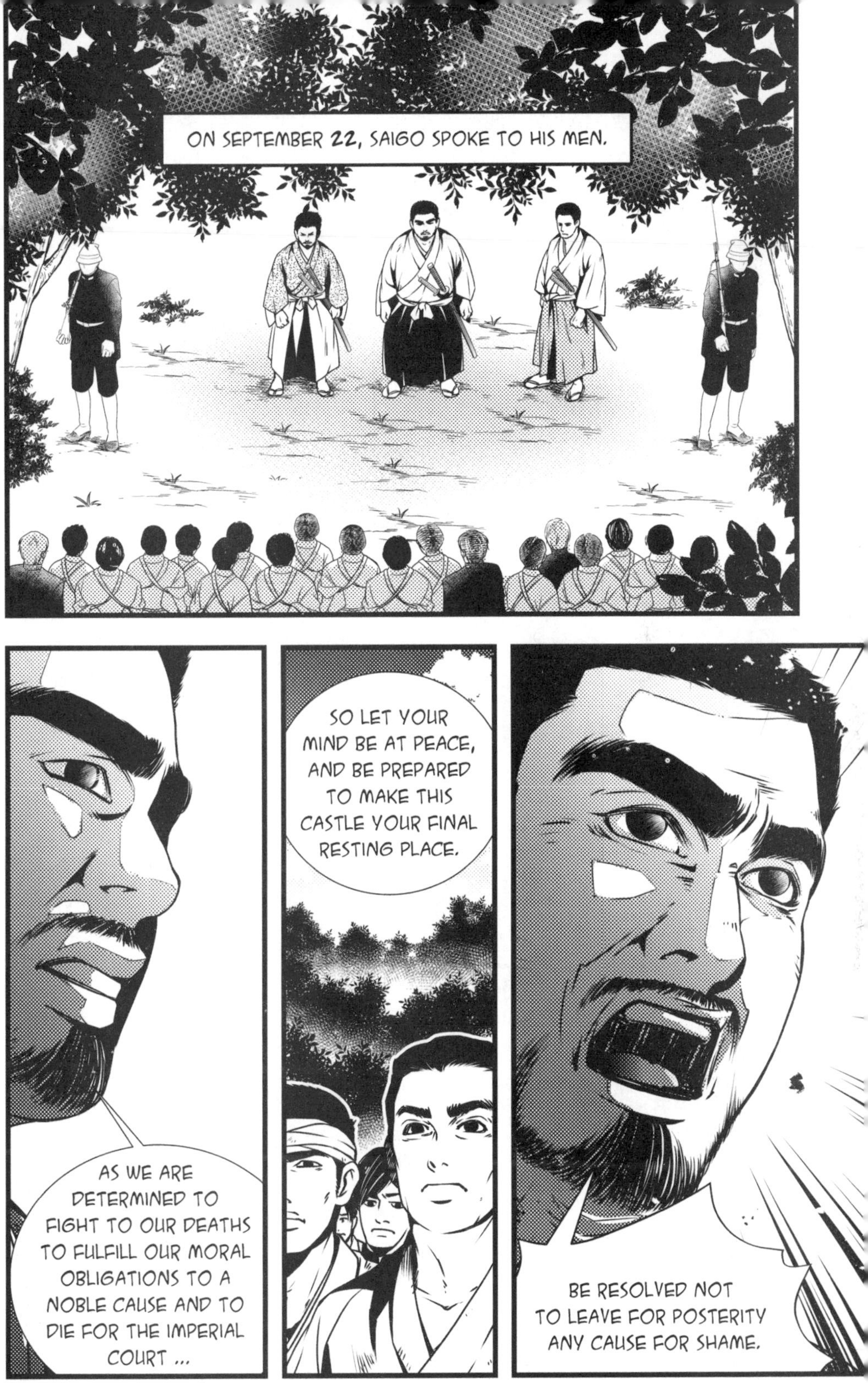
ON SEPTEMBER 22, SAIGO SPOKE TO HIS MEN.
AS WE ARE DETERMINED TO FIGHT TO OUR DEATHS TO FULFILL OUR MORAL OBLIGATIONS TO A NOBLE CAUSE AND TO DIE FOR THE IMPERIAL COURT ...
SO LET YOUR MIND BE AT PEACE, AND BE PREPARED TO MAKE THIS CASTLE YOUR FINAL RESTING PLACE.
BE RESOLVED NOT TO LEAVE FOR POSTERITY ANY CAUSE FOR SHAME.

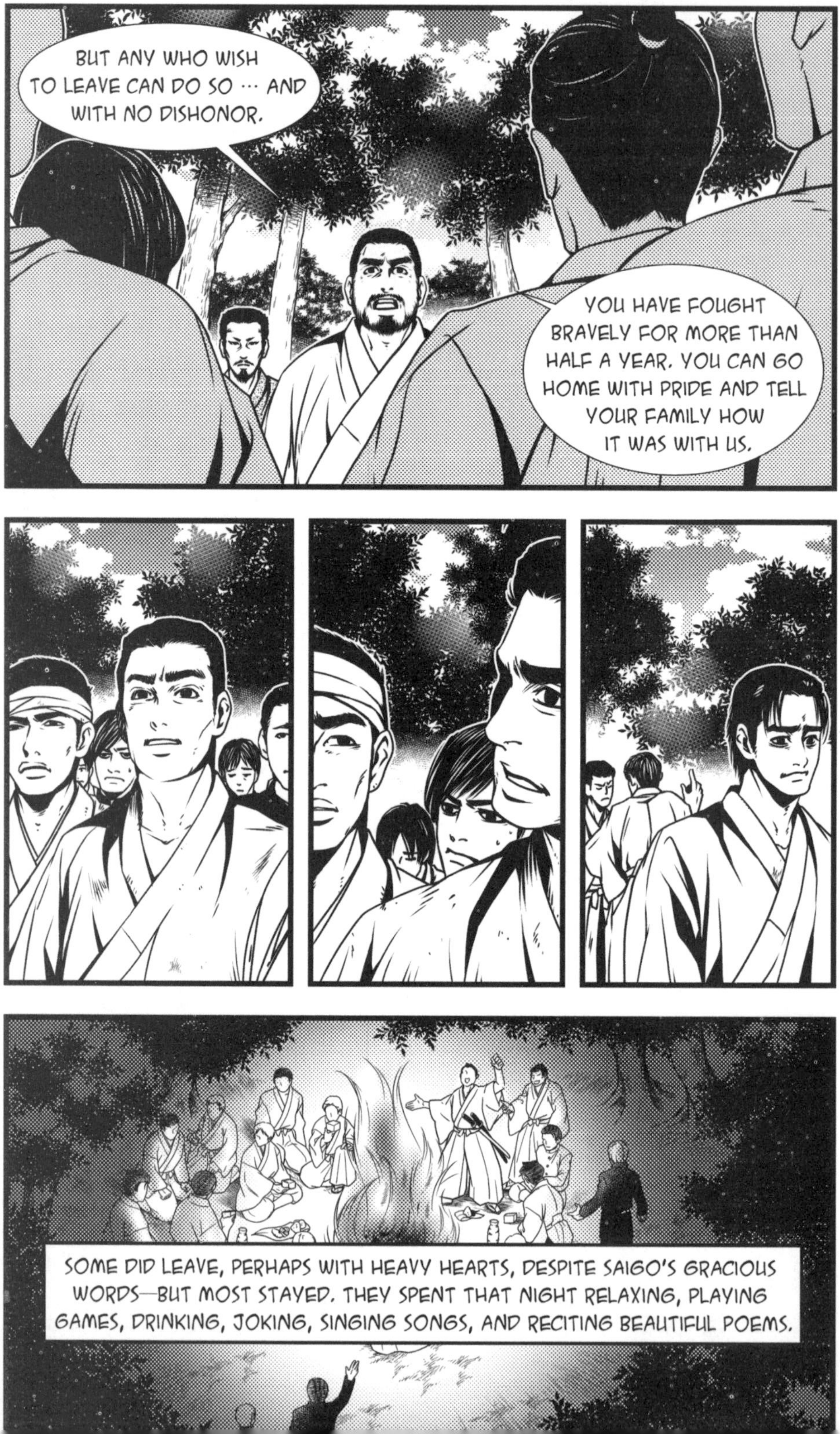

BUT ANY WHO WISH TO LEAVE CAN DO SO … AND WITH NO DISHONOR.
YOU HAVE FOUGHT BRAVELY FOR MORE THAN HALF A YEAR. YOU CAN GO HOME WITH PRIDE AND TELL YOUR FAMILY HOW IT WAS WITH US.
SOME DID LEAVE, PERHAPS WITH HEAVY HEARTS, DESPITE SAIGO'S GRACIOUS WORDS—BUT MOST STAYED. THEY SPENT THAT NIGHT RELAXING, PLAYING GAMES, DRINKING, JOKING, SINGING SONGS, AND RECITING BEAUTIFUL POEMS.

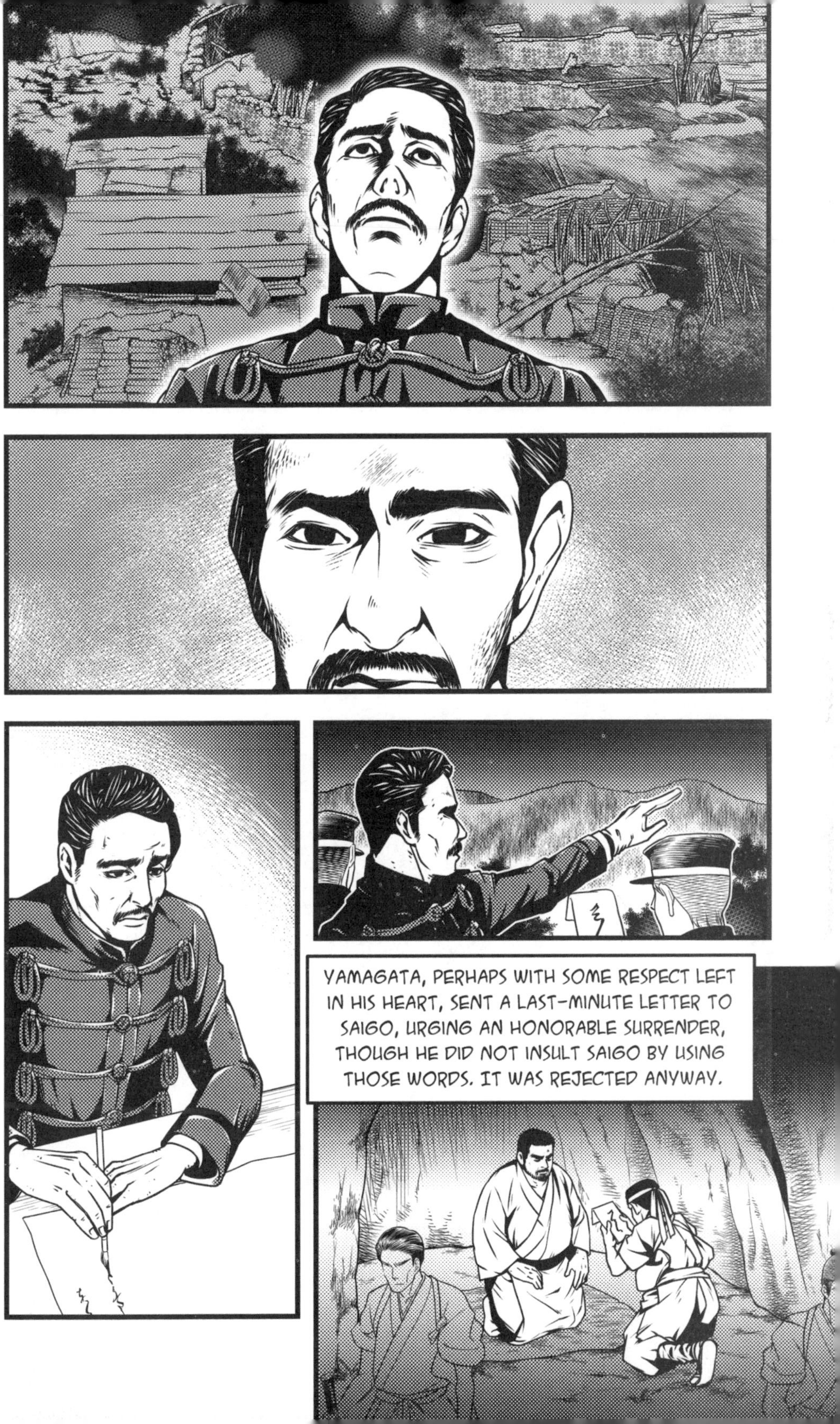
YAMAGATA, PERHAPS WITH SOME RESPECT LEFT IN HIS HEART, SENT A LAST-MINUTE LETTER TO SAIGO, URGING AN HONORABLE SURRENDER, THOUGH HE DID NOT INSULT SAIGO BY USING THOSE WORDS. IT WAS REJECTED ANYWAY.

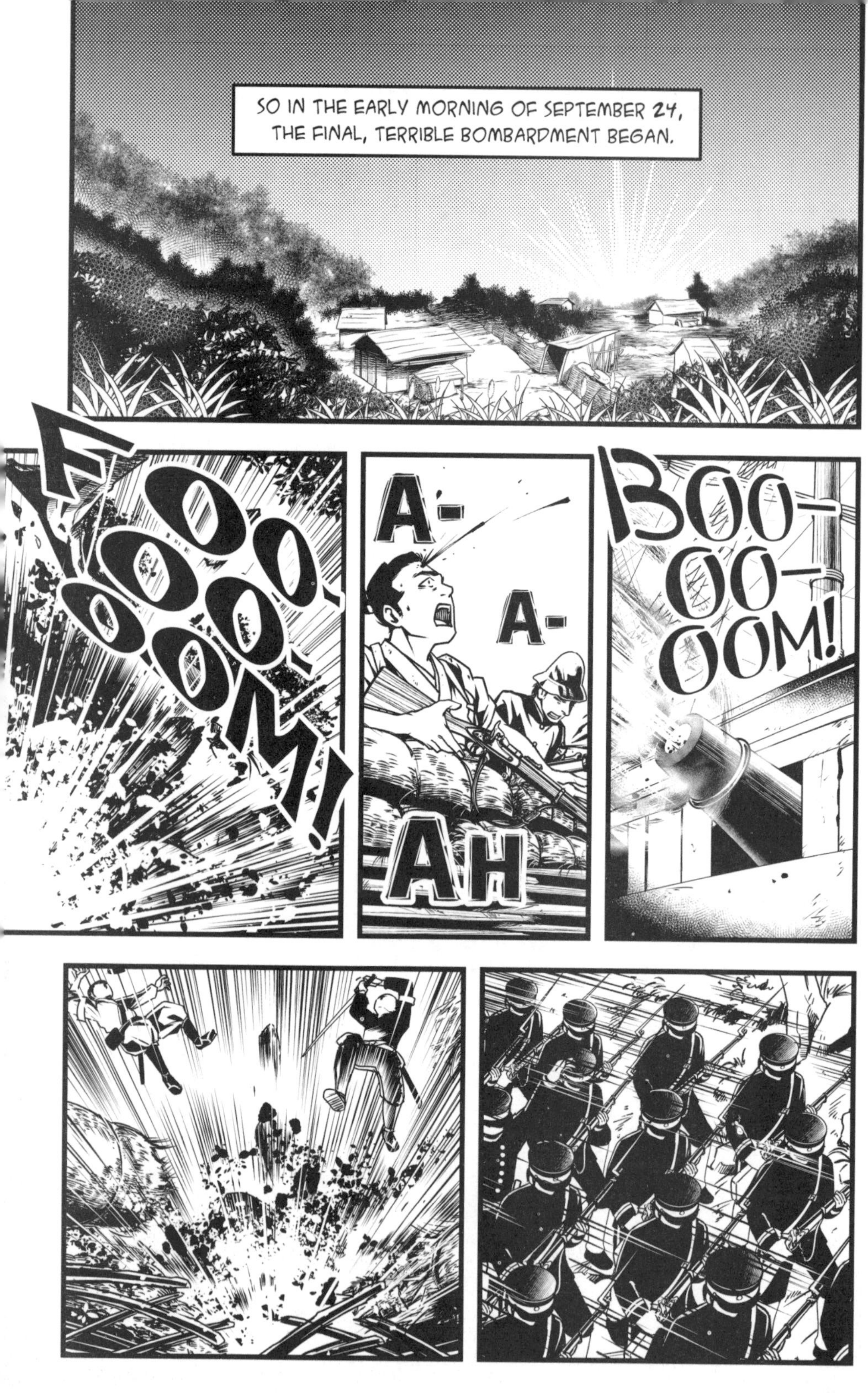
SO IN THE EARLY MORNING OF SEPTEMBER 24, THE FINAL, TERRIBLE BOMBARDMENT BEGAN.
FOOOOOOM!
A-
A-
AH
BOO-OO-OOM!

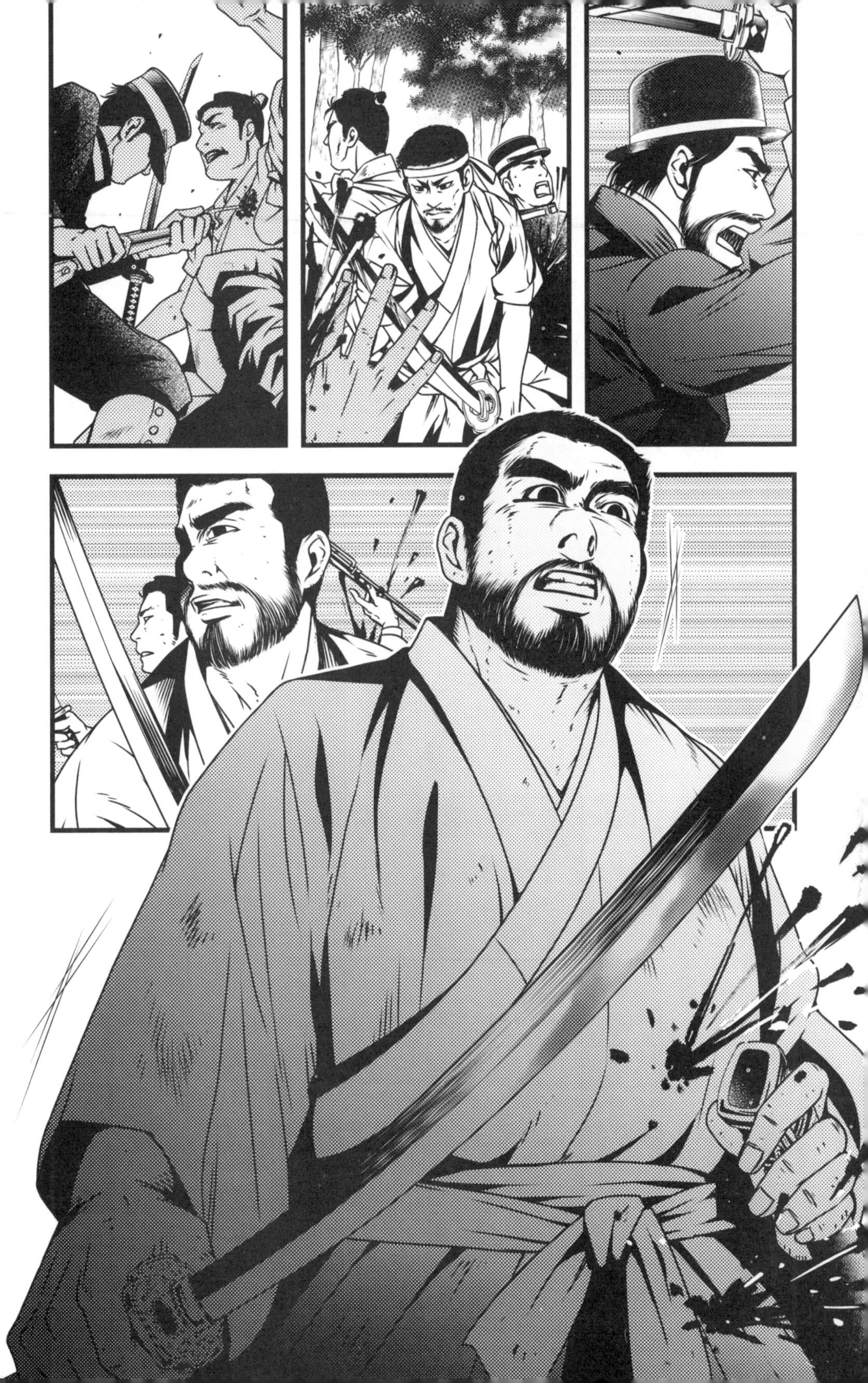

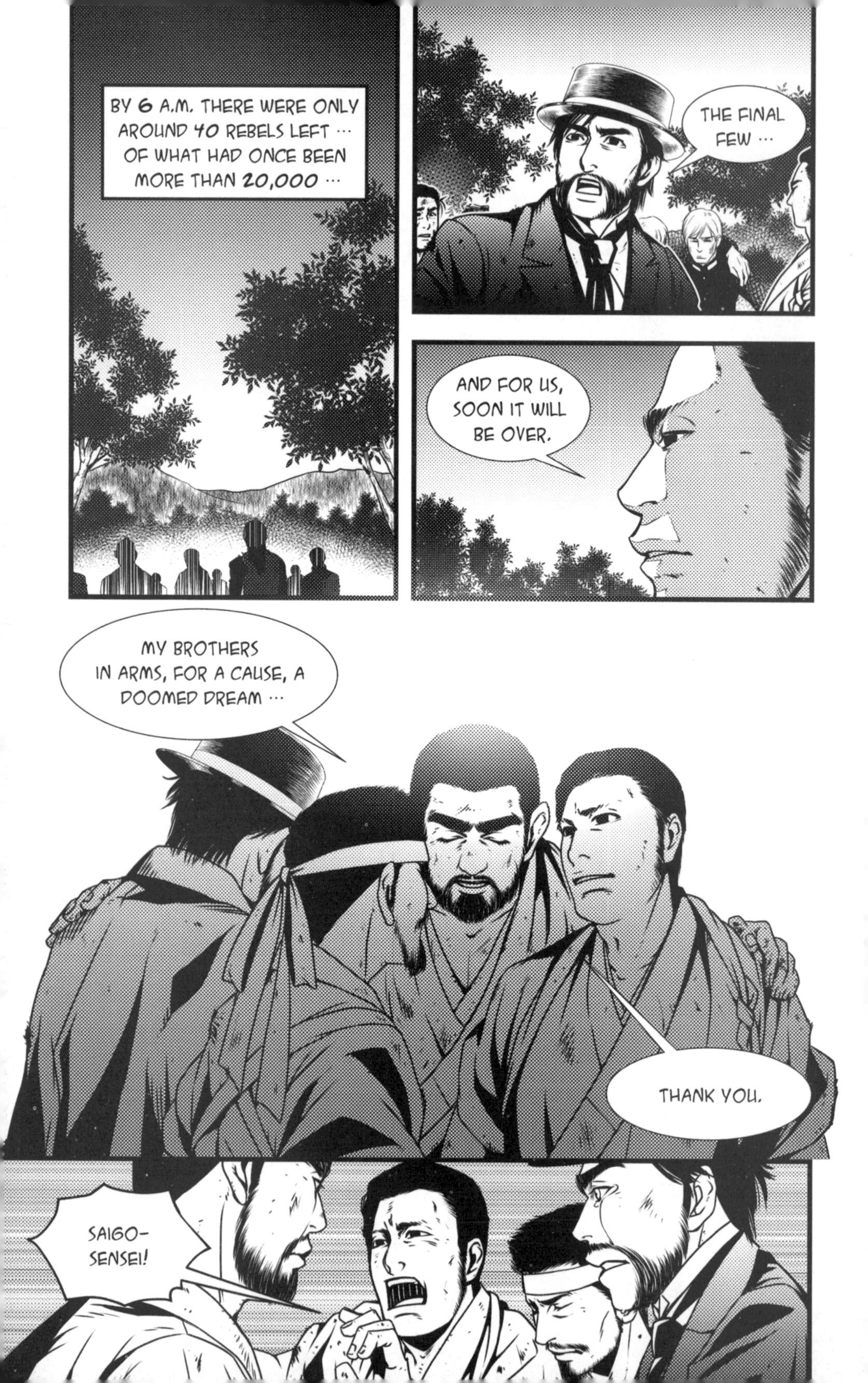
BY 6 A.M. THERE WERE ONLY AROUND 40 REBELS LEFT ... OF WHAT HAD ONCE BEEN MORE THAN 20,000 ...
THE FINAL FEW ...
AND FOR US, SOON IT WILL BE OVER.
MY BROTHERS IN ARMS, FOR A CAUSE, A DOOMED DREAM ...
THANK YOU.
SAIGO-SENSEI!

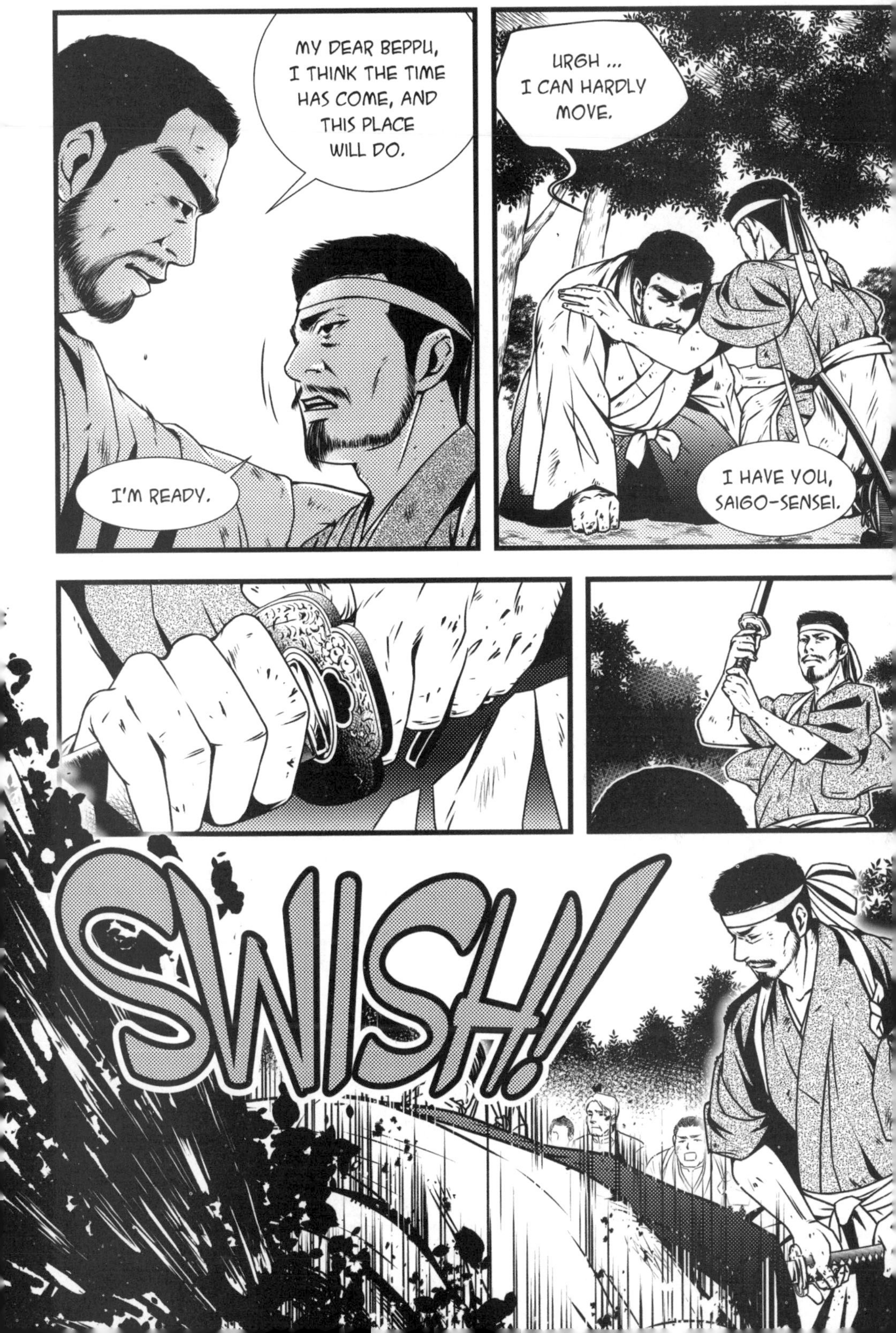
MY DEAR BEPPU, I THINK THE TIME HAS COME, AND THIS PLACE WILL DO.
I'M READY.
URGH ... I CAN HARDLY MOVE.
I HAVE YOU, SAIGO-SENSEI.
SWISH!

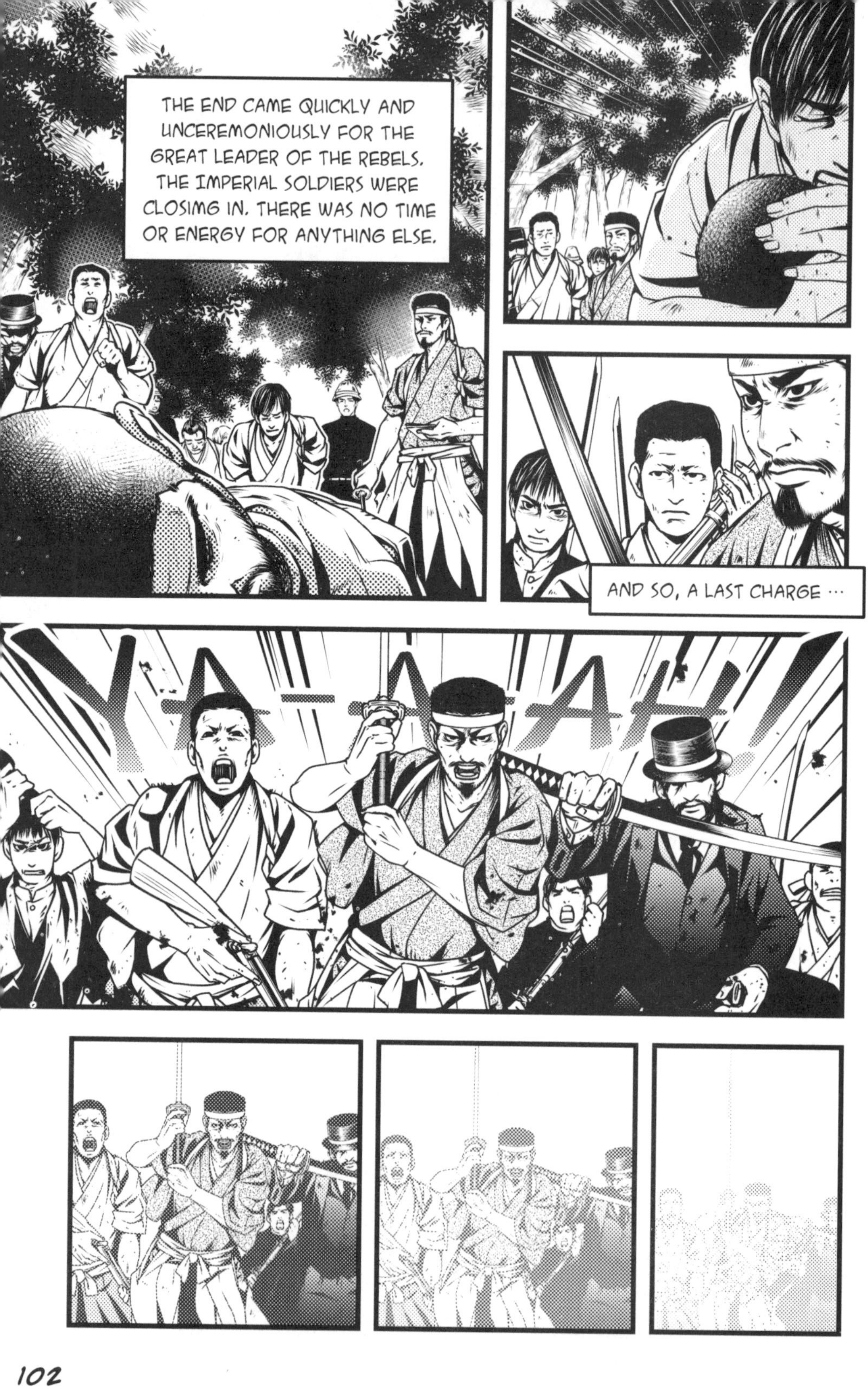
THE END CAME QUICKLY AND UNCEREMONIOUSLY FOR THE GREAT LEADER OF THE REBELS. THE IMPERIAL SOLDIERS WERE CLOSIMG IN. THERE WAS NO TIME OR ENERGY FOR ANYTHING ELSE.
AND SO, A LAST CHARGE …
YA-A-AH!!

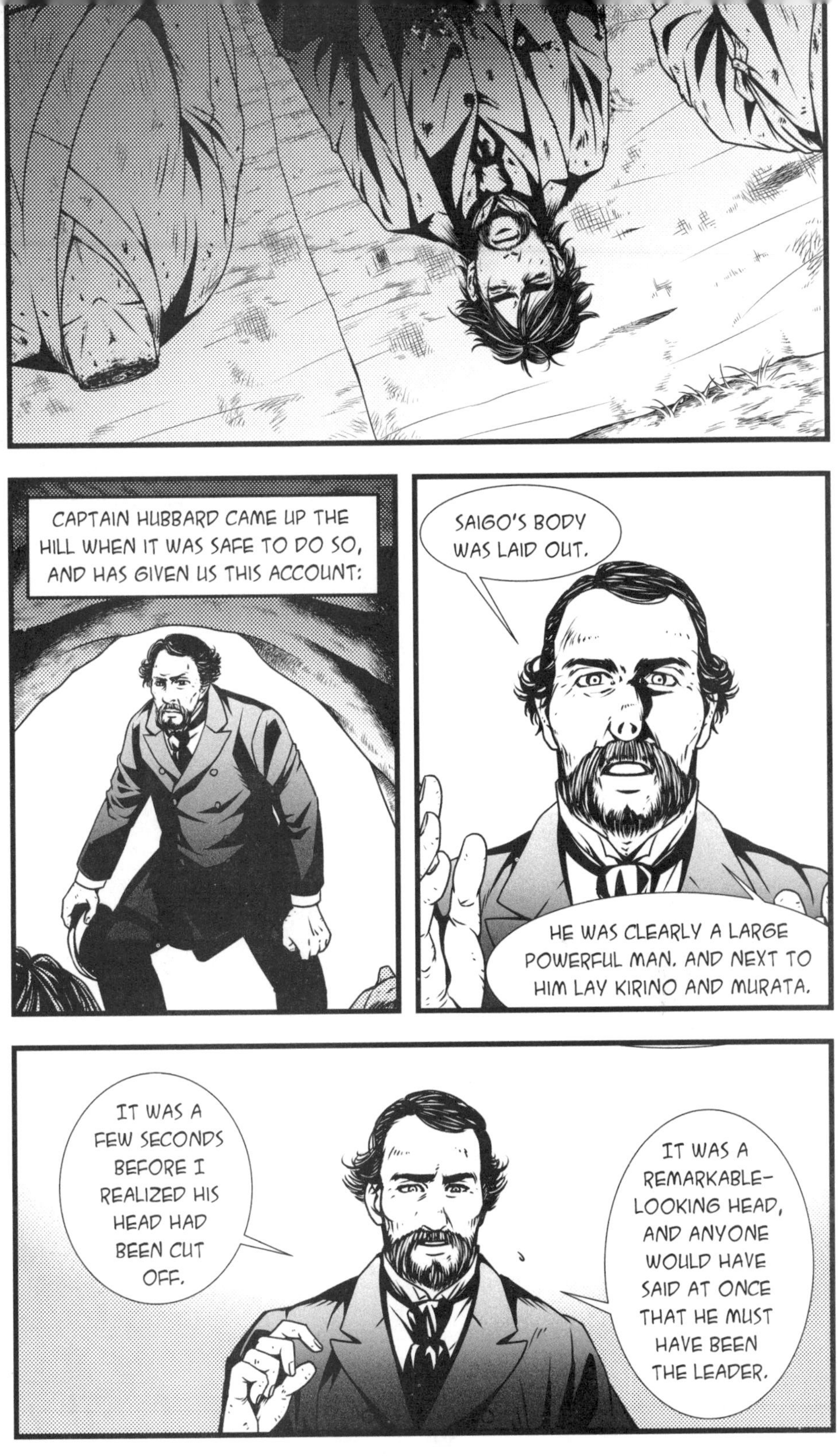
CAPTAIN HUBBARD CAME UP THE HILL WHEN IT WAS SAFE TO DO SO, AND HAS GIVEN US THIS ACCOUNT:
SAIGO'S BODY WAS LAID OUT.
HE WAS CLEARLY A LARGE POWERFUL MAN. AND NEXT TO HIM LAY KIRINO AND MURATA.
IT WAS A FEW SECONDS BEFORE I REALIZED HIS HEAD HAD BEEN CUT OFF.
IT WAS A REMARKABLE-LOOKING HEAD, AND ANYONE WOULD HAVE SAID AT ONCE THAT HE MUST HAVE BEEN THE LEADER.

BUT THIS FACTUAL, BARE ACCOUNT IS IN CONTRAST TO THE MYTHS THAT GREW UP. ACCORDING TO THESE STORIES, SAIGO'S HEAD WAS PRESENTED IN A GRAND RITUAL OF *KUBI JIKKEN* (AN INSPECTION OF HEADS) TO GENERAL YAMAGATA AND THE IMPERIAL PRINCE.

HERE IS THE HEAD OF A HERO!

ONCE A COMRADE. ONE OF THE 3 MOST POWERFUL MEN IN THE LAND.

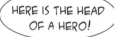

HOW CALM HIS EXPRESSION LOOKS.

WHAT A GLORIOUS DEATH!

WHATEVER THE TRUTH OF IT, WHATEVER REALLY HAPPENED, THIS MUCH IS CLEAR: SAIGO TAKAMORI WAS DEAD; THE SATSUMA REBELLION WAS OVER. THE REBELS LOST. THE OLD JAPAN LOST, AND THE NEW JAPAN WON ... THINGS MOVE ON ... FOREVER CHANGE.

THE END.

ABOUT THE AUTHOR AND ILLUSTRATOR

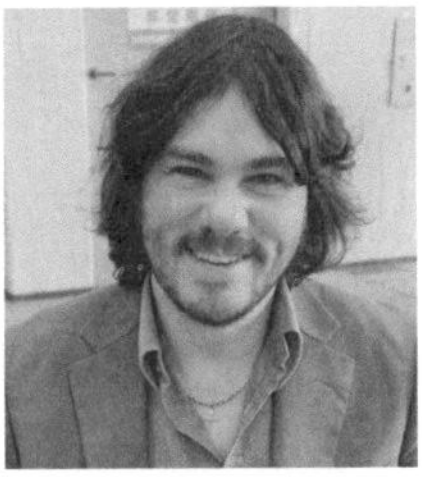

Photo by Asahi Shinbun

SEAN MICHAEL WILSON is a Scottish writer living in Japan. He has written more than twenty books, published by a variety of American, British, and Japanese publishers, and translated into ten languages. In 2016 his book of Lafcadio Hearn stories, *The Faceless Ghost* was nominated for the prestigious Eisner Book Awards and received a medal in the 2016 Independent Publisher Book Awards. In 2017, his book *Secrets of the Ninja* won an International Manga Award from the Japanese government. He is the first British person to receive this award.

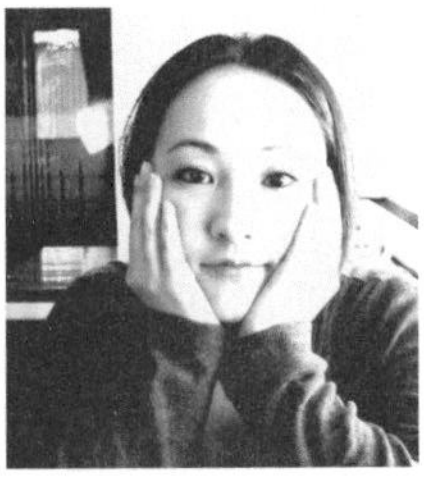

AKIKO SHIMOJIMA is a manga artist from Japan. A teacher of digital comic art at a school in Tokyo, she has contributed work to many publications in Japanese. In collaboration with Sean Michael Wilson she has had six books published in English, including *The 47 Ronin*, *Black Ships*, and the award-winning *Secrets of the Ninja*. Her influences include Trawar Asada, Naoki Urasawa, and Taiyou Matsumoto.